Mometrix
TEST PREPARATION

IB®

Psychology (SL and HL) Examination Secrets Study Guide

I0892283

DEAR FUTURE EXAM SUCCESS STORY

First of all, **THANK YOU** for purchasing Mometrix study materials!

Second, congratulations! You are one of the few determined test-takers who are committed to doing whatever it takes to excel on your exam. **You have come to the right place.** We developed these study materials with one goal in mind: to deliver you the information you need in a format that's concise and easy to use.

In addition to optimizing your guide for the content of the test, we've outlined our recommended steps for breaking down the preparation process into small, attainable goals so you can make sure you stay on track.

We've also analyzed the entire test-taking process, identifying the most common pitfalls and showing how you can overcome them and be ready for any curveball the test throws you.

Standardized testing is one of the biggest obstacles on your road to success, which only increases the importance of doing well in the high-pressure, high-stakes environment of test day. Your results on this test could have a significant impact on your future, and this guide provides the information and practical advice to help you achieve your full potential on test day.

Your success is our success

We would love to hear from you! If you would like to share the story of your exam success or if you have any questions or comments in regard to our products, please contact us at **800-673-8175** or **support@mometrix.com**.

Thanks again for your business and we wish you continued success!

Sincerely,
The Mometrix Test Preparation Team

Need more help? Check out our flashcards at:
http://MometrixFlashcards.com/IB

Written and edited by the Mometrix Exam Secrets Test Prep Team
Printed in the United States of America

TABLE OF CONTENTS

Introduction

Thank you for purchasing this resource! You have made the choice to prepare yourself for a test that could have a huge impact on your future, and this guide is designed to help you be fully ready for test day. Obviously, it's important to have a solid understanding of the test material, but you also need to be prepared for the unique environment and stressors of the test, so that you can perform to the best of your abilities.

For this purpose, the first section that appears in this guide is the **Secret Keys**. We've devoted countless hours to meticulously researching what works and what doesn't, and we've boiled down our findings to the five most impactful steps you can take to improve your performance on the test. We start at the beginning with study planning and move through the preparation process, all the way to the testing strategies that will help you get the most out of what you know when you're finally sitting in front of the test.

We recommend that you start preparing for your test as far in advance as possible. However, if you've bought this guide as a last-minute study resource and only have a few days before your test, we recommend that you skip over the first two Secret Keys since they address a long-term study plan.

If you struggle with **test anxiety**, we strongly encourage you to check out our recommendations for how you can overcome it. Test anxiety is a formidable foe, but it can be beaten, and we want to make sure you have the tools you need to defeat it.

Secret Key #1 – Plan Big, Study Small

There's a lot riding on your performance. If you want to ace this test, you're going to need to keep your skills sharp and the material fresh in your mind. You need a plan that lets you review everything you need to know while still fitting in your schedule. We'll break this strategy down into three categories.

Information Organization

Start with the information you already have: the official test outline. From this, you can make a complete list of all the concepts you need to cover before the test. Organize these concepts into groups that can be studied together, and create a list of any related vocabulary you need to learn so you can brush up on any difficult terms. You'll want to keep this vocabulary list handy once you actually start studying since you may need to add to it along the way.

Time Management

Once you have your set of study concepts, decide how to spread them out over the time you have left before the test. Break your study plan into small, clear goals so you have a manageable task for each day and know exactly what you're doing. Then just focus on one small step at a time. When you manage your time this way, you don't need to spend hours at a time studying. Studying a small block of content for a short period each day helps you retain information better and avoid stressing over how much you have left to do. You can relax knowing that you have a plan to cover everything in time. In order for this strategy to be effective though, you have to start studying early and stick to your schedule. Avoid the exhaustion and futility that comes from last-minute cramming!

Study Environment

The environment you study in has a big impact on your learning. Studying in a coffee shop, while probably more enjoyable, is not likely to be as fruitful as studying in a quiet room. It's important to keep distractions to a minimum. You're only planning to study for a short block of time, so make the most of it. Don't pause to check your phone or get up to find a snack. It's also important to **avoid multitasking**. Research has consistently shown that multitasking will make your studying dramatically less effective. Your study area should also be comfortable and well-lit so you don't have the distraction of straining your eyes or sitting on an uncomfortable chair.

The time of day you study is also important. You want to be rested and alert. Don't wait until just before bedtime. Study when you'll be most likely to comprehend and remember. Even better, if you know what time of day your test will be, set that time aside for study. That way your brain will be used to working on that subject at that specific time and you'll have a better chance of recalling information.

Finally, it can be helpful to team up with others who are studying for the same test. Your actual studying should be done in as isolated an environment as possible, but the work of organizing the information and setting up the study plan can be divided up. In between study sessions, you can discuss with your teammates the concepts that you're all studying and quiz each other on the details. Just be sure that your teammates are as serious about the test as you are. If you find that your study time is being replaced with social time, you might need to find a new team.

Secret Key #2 – Make Your Studying Count

You're devoting a lot of time and effort to preparing for this test, so you want to be absolutely certain it will pay off. This means doing more than just reading the content and hoping you can remember it on test day. It's important to make every minute of study count. There are two main areas you can focus on to make your studying count.

Retention

It doesn't matter how much time you study if you can't remember the material. You need to make sure you are retaining the concepts. To check your retention of the information you're learning, try recalling it at later times with minimal prompting. Try carrying around flashcards and glance at one or two from time to time or ask a friend who's also studying for the test to quiz you.

To enhance your retention, look for ways to put the information into practice so that you can apply it rather than simply recalling it. If you're using the information in practical ways, it will be much easier to remember. Similarly, it helps to solidify a concept in your mind if you're not only reading it to yourself but also explaining it to someone else. Ask a friend to let you teach them about a concept you're a little shaky on (or speak aloud to an imaginary audience if necessary). As you try to summarize, define, give examples, and answer your friend's questions, you'll understand the concepts better and they will stay with you longer. Finally, step back for a big picture view and ask yourself how each piece of information fits with the whole subject. When you link the different concepts together and see them working together as a whole, it's easier to remember the individual components.

Finally, practice showing your work on any multi-step problems, even if you're just studying. Writing out each step you take to solve a problem will help solidify the process in your mind, and you'll be more likely to remember it during the test.

Modality

Modality simply refers to the means or method by which you study. Choosing a study modality that fits your own individual learning style is crucial. No two people learn best in exactly the same way, so it's important to know your strengths and use them to your advantage.

For example, if you learn best by visualization, focus on visualizing a concept in your mind and draw an image or a diagram. Try color-coding your notes, illustrating them, or creating symbols that will trigger your mind to recall a learned concept. If you learn best by hearing or discussing information, find a study partner who learns the same way or read aloud to yourself. Think about how to put the information in your own words. Imagine that you are giving a lecture on the topic and record yourself so you can listen to it later.

For any learning style, flashcards can be helpful. Organize the information so you can take advantage of spare moments to review. Underline key words or phrases. Use different colors for different categories. Mnemonic devices (such as creating a short list in which every item starts with the same letter) can also help with retention. Find what works best for you and use it to store the information in your mind most effectively and easily.

Secret Key #3 – Practice the Right Way

Your success on test day depends not only on how many hours you put into preparing, but also on whether you prepared the right way. It's good to check along the way to see if your studying is paying off. One of the most effective ways to do this is by taking practice tests to evaluate your progress. Practice tests are useful because they show exactly where you need to improve. Every time you take a practice test, pay special attention to these three groups of questions:

- The questions you got wrong
- The questions you had to guess on, even if you guessed right
- The questions you found difficult or slow to work through

This will show you exactly what your weak areas are, and where you need to devote more study time. Ask yourself why each of these questions gave you trouble. Was it because you didn't understand the material? Was it because you didn't remember the vocabulary? Do you need more repetitions on this type of question to build speed and confidence? Dig into those questions and figure out how you can strengthen your weak areas as you go back to review the material.

Additionally, many practice tests have a section explaining the answer choices. It can be tempting to read the explanation and think that you now have a good understanding of the concept. However, an explanation likely only covers part of the question's broader context. Even if the explanation makes perfect sense, **go back and investigate** every concept related to the question until you're positive you have a thorough understanding.

As you go along, keep in mind that the practice test is just that: practice. Memorizing these questions and answers will not be very helpful on the actual test because it is unlikely to have any of the same exact questions. If you only know the right answers to the sample questions, you won't be prepared for the real thing. **Study the concepts** until you understand them fully, and then you'll be able to answer any question that shows up on the test.

It's important to wait on the practice tests until you're ready. If you take a test on your first day of study, you may be overwhelmed by the amount of material covered and how much you need to learn. Work up to it gradually.

On test day, you'll need to be prepared for answering questions, managing your time, and using the test-taking strategies you've learned. It's a lot to balance, like a mental marathon that will have a big impact on your future. Like training for a marathon, you'll need to start slowly and work your way up. When test day arrives, you'll be ready.

Start with the strategies you've read in the first two Secret Keys—plan your course and study in the way that works best for you. If you have time, consider using multiple study resources to get different approaches to the same concepts. It can be helpful to see difficult concepts from more than one angle. Then find a good source for practice tests. Many times, the test website will suggest potential study resources or provide sample tests.

Practice Test Strategy

If you're able to find at least three practice tests, we recommend this strategy:

Untimed and Open-Book Practice

Take the first test with no time constraints and with your notes and study guide handy. Take your time and focus on applying the strategies you've learned.

Timed and Open-Book Practice

Take the second practice test open-book as well, but set a timer and practice pacing yourself to finish in time.

Timed and Closed-Book Practice

Take any other practice tests as if it were test day. Set a timer and put away your study materials. Sit at a table or desk in a quiet room, imagine yourself at the testing center, and answer questions as quickly and accurately as possible.

Keep repeating timed and closed-book tests on a regular basis until you run out of practice tests or it's time for the actual test. Your mind will be ready for the schedule and stress of test day, and you'll be able to focus on recalling the material you've learned.

Secret Key #4 – Pace Yourself

Once you're fully prepared for the material on the test, your biggest challenge on test day will be managing your time. Just knowing that the clock is ticking can make you panic even if you have plenty of time left. Work on pacing yourself so you can build confidence against the time constraints of the exam. Pacing is a difficult skill to master, especially in a high-pressure environment, so **practice is vital**.

Set time expectations for your pace based on how much time is available. For example, if a section has 60 questions and the time limit is 30 minutes, you know you have to average 30 seconds or less per question in order to answer them all. Although 30 seconds is the hard limit, set 25 seconds per question as your goal, so you reserve extra time to spend on harder questions. When you budget extra time for the harder questions, you no longer have any reason to stress when those questions take longer to answer.

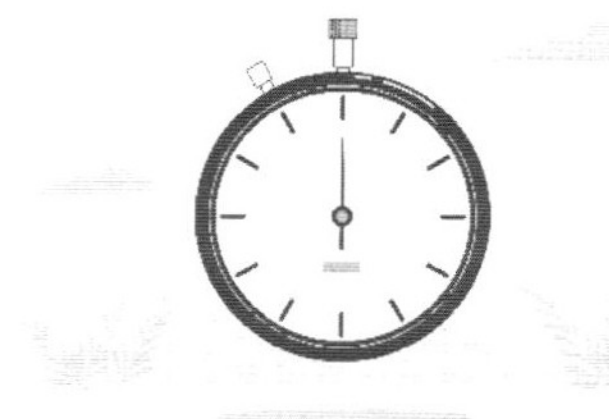

Don't let this time expectation distract you from working through the test at a calm, steady pace, but keep it in mind so you don't spend too much time on any one question. Recognize that taking extra time on one question you don't understand may keep you from answering two that you do understand later in the test. If your time limit for a question is up and you're still not sure of the answer, mark it and move on, and come back to it later if the time and the test format allow. If the testing format doesn't allow you to return to earlier questions, just make an educated guess; then put it out of your mind and move on.

On the easier questions, be careful not to rush. It may seem wise to hurry through them so you have more time for the challenging ones, but it's not worth missing one if you know the concept and just didn't take the time to read the question fully. Work efficiently but make sure you understand the question and have looked at all of the answer choices, since more than one may seem right at first.

Even if you're paying attention to the time, you may find yourself a little behind at some point. You should speed up to get back on track, but do so wisely. Don't panic; just take a few seconds less on each question until you're caught up. Don't guess without thinking, but do look through the answer choices and eliminate any you know are wrong. If you can get down to two choices, it is often worthwhile to guess from those. Once you've chosen an answer, move on and don't dwell on any that you skipped or had to hurry through. If a question was taking too long, chances are it was one of the harder ones, so you weren't as likely to get it right anyway.

On the other hand, if you find yourself getting ahead of schedule, it may be beneficial to slow down a little. The more quickly you work, the more likely you are to make a careless mistake that will affect your score. You've budgeted time for each question, so don't be afraid to spend that time. Practice an efficient but careful pace to get the most out of the time you have.

Secret Key #5 – Have a Plan for Guessing

When you're taking the test, you may find yourself stuck on a question. Some of the answer choices seem better than others, but you don't see the one answer choice that is obviously correct. What do you do?

The scenario described above is very common, yet most test takers have not effectively prepared for it. Developing and practicing a plan for guessing may be one of the single most effective uses of your time as you get ready for the exam.

In developing your plan for guessing, there are three questions to address:

- When should you start the guessing process?
- How should you narrow down the choices?
- Which answer should you choose?

When to Start the Guessing Process

Unless your plan for guessing is to select C every time (which, despite its merits, is not what we recommend), you need to leave yourself enough time to apply your answer elimination strategies. Since you have a limited amount of time for each question, that means that if you're going to give yourself the best shot at guessing correctly, you have to decide quickly whether or not you will guess.

Of course, the best-case scenario is that you don't have to guess at all, so first, see if you can answer the question based on your knowledge of the subject and basic reasoning skills. Focus on the key words in the question and try to jog your memory of related topics. Give yourself a chance to bring the knowledge to mind, but once you realize that you don't have (or you can't access) the knowledge you need to answer the question, it's time to start the guessing process.

It's almost always better to start the guessing process too early than too late. It only takes a few seconds to remember something and answer the question from knowledge. Carefully eliminating wrong answer choices takes longer. Plus, going through the process of eliminating answer choices can actually help jog your memory.

Summary: Start the guessing process as soon as you decide that you can't answer the question based on your knowledge.

How to Narrow Down the Choices

The next chapter in this book (**Test-Taking Strategies**) includes a wide range of strategies for how to approach questions and how to look for answer choices to eliminate. You will definitely want to read those carefully, practice them, and figure out which ones work best for you. Here though, we're going to address a mindset rather than a particular strategy.

Your odds of guessing an answer correctly depend on how many options you are choosing from.

Number of options left	5	4	3	2	1
Odds of guessing correctly	20%	25%	33%	50%	100%

You can see from this chart just how valuable it is to be able to eliminate incorrect answers and make an educated guess, but there are two things that many test takers do that cause them to miss out on the benefits of guessing:

- Accidentally eliminating the correct answer
- Selecting an answer based on an impression

We'll look at the first one here, and the second one in the next section.

To avoid accidentally eliminating the correct answer, we recommend a thought exercise called **the $5 challenge**. In this challenge, you only eliminate an answer choice from contention if you are willing to bet $5 on it being wrong. Why $5? Five dollars is a small but not insignificant amount of money. It's an amount you could afford to lose but wouldn't want to throw away. And while losing $5 once might not hurt too much, doing it twenty times will set you back $100. In the same way, each small decision you make—eliminating a choice here, guessing on a question there—won't by itself impact your score very much, but when you put them all together, they can make a big difference. By holding each answer choice elimination decision to a higher standard, you can reduce the risk of accidentally eliminating the correct answer.

The $5 challenge can also be applied in a positive sense: If you are willing to bet $5 that an answer choice *is* correct, go ahead and mark it as correct.

Summary: Only eliminate an answer choice if you are willing to bet $5 that it is wrong.

Which Answer to Choose

You're taking the test. You've run into a hard question and decided you'll have to guess. You've eliminated all the answer choices you're willing to bet $5 on. Now you have to pick an answer. Why do we even need to talk about this? Why can't you just pick whichever one you feel like when the time comes?

The answer to these questions is that if you don't come into the test with a plan, you'll rely on your impression to select an answer choice, and if you do that, you risk falling into a trap. The test writers know that everyone who takes their test will be guessing on some of the questions, so they intentionally write wrong answer choices to seem plausible. You still have to pick an answer though, and if the wrong answer choices are designed to look right, how can you ever be sure that you're not falling for their trap? The best solution we've found to this dilemma is to take the decision out of your hands entirely. Here is the process we recommend:

Once you've eliminated any choices that you are confident (willing to bet $5) are wrong, select the first remaining choice as your answer.

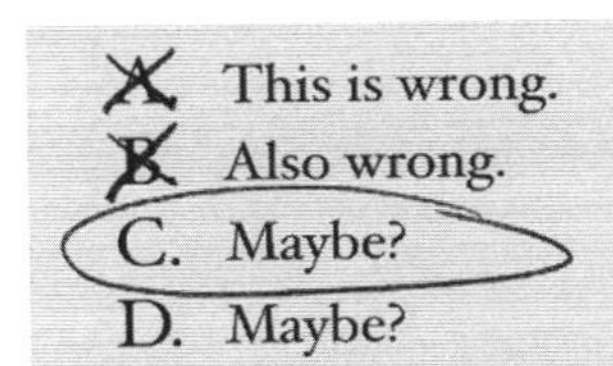

Whether you choose to select the first remaining choice, the second, or the last, the important thing is that you use some preselected standard. Using this approach guarantees that you will not be enticed into selecting an answer choice that looks right, because you are not basing your decision on how the answer choices look.

This is not meant to make you question your knowledge. Instead, it is to help you recognize the difference between your knowledge and your impressions. There's a huge difference between thinking an answer is right because of what you know, and thinking an answer is right because it looks or sounds like it should be right.

Summary: To ensure that your selection is appropriately random, make a predetermined selection from among all answer choices you have not eliminated.

Test-Taking Strategies

This section contains a list of test-taking strategies that you may find helpful as you work through the test. By taking what you know and applying logical thought, you can maximize your chances of answering any question correctly!

It is very important to realize that every question is different and every person is different: no single strategy will work on every question, and no single strategy will work for every person. That's why we've included all of them here, so you can try them out and determine which ones work best for different types of questions and which ones work best for you.

Question Strategies

✓ Read Carefully

Read the question and the answer choices carefully. Don't miss the question because you misread the terms. You have plenty of time to read each question thoroughly and make sure you understand what is being asked. Yet a happy medium must be attained, so don't waste too much time. You must read carefully and efficiently.

✓ Contextual Clues

Look for contextual clues. If the question includes a word you are not familiar with, look at the immediate context for some indication of what the word might mean. Contextual clues can often give you all the information you need to decipher the meaning of an unfamiliar word. Even if you can't determine the meaning, you may be able to narrow down the possibilities enough to make a solid guess at the answer to the question.

✓ Prefixes

If you're having trouble with a word in the question or answer choices, try dissecting it. Take advantage of every clue that the word might include. Prefixes can be a huge help. Usually, they allow you to determine a basic meaning. *Pre-* means before, *post-* means after, *pro-* is positive, *de-* is negative. From prefixes, you can get an idea of the general meaning of the word and try to put it into context.

✓ Hedge Words

Watch out for critical hedge words, such as *likely, may, can, often, almost, mostly, usually, generally, rarely,* and *sometimes.* Question writers insert these hedge phrases to cover every possibility. Often an answer choice will be wrong simply because it leaves no room for exception. Be on guard for answer choices that have definitive words such as *exactly* and *always.*

✓ Switchback Words

Stay alert for *switchbacks.* These are the words and phrases frequently used to alert you to shifts in thought. The most common switchback words are *but, although,* and *however.* Others include *nevertheless, on the other hand, even though, while, in spite of, despite,* and *regardless of.* Switchback words are important to catch because they can change the direction of the question or an answer choice.

✓ FACE VALUE

When in doubt, use common sense. Accept the situation in the problem at face value. Don't read too much into it. These problems will not require you to make wild assumptions. If you have to go beyond creativity and warp time or space in order to have an answer choice fit the question, then you should move on and consider the other answer choices. These are normal problems rooted in reality. The applicable relationship or explanation may not be readily apparent, but it is there for you to figure out. Use your common sense to interpret anything that isn't clear.

Answer Choice Strategies

✓ ANSWER SELECTION

The most thorough way to pick an answer choice is to identify and eliminate wrong answers until only one is left, then confirm it is the correct answer. Sometimes an answer choice may immediately seem right, but be careful. The test writers will usually put more than one reasonable answer choice on each question, so take a second to read all of them and make sure that the other choices are not equally obvious. As long as you have time left, it is better to read every answer choice than to pick the first one that looks right without checking the others.

✓ ANSWER CHOICE FAMILIES

An answer choice family consists of two (in rare cases, three) answer choices that are very similar in construction and cannot all be true at the same time. If you see two answer choices that are direct opposites or parallels, one of them is usually the correct answer. For instance, if one answer choice says that quantity x increases and another either says that quantity x decreases (opposite) or says that quantity y increases (parallel), then those answer choices would fall into the same family. An answer choice that doesn't match the construction of the answer choice family is more likely to be incorrect. Most questions will not have answer choice families, but when they do appear, you should be prepared to recognize them.

✓ ELIMINATE ANSWERS

Eliminate answer choices as soon as you realize they are wrong, but make sure you consider all possibilities. If you are eliminating answer choices and realize that the last one you are left with is also wrong, don't panic. Start over and consider each choice again. There may be something you missed the first time that you will realize on the second pass.

✓ AVOID FACT TRAPS

Don't be distracted by an answer choice that is factually true but doesn't answer the question. You are looking for the choice that answers the question. Stay focused on what the question is asking for so you don't accidentally pick an answer that is true but incorrect. Always go back to the question and make sure the answer choice you've selected actually answers the question and is not merely a true statement.

✓ EXTREME STATEMENTS

In general, you should avoid answers that put forth extreme actions as standard practice or proclaim controversial ideas as established fact. An answer choice that states the "process should be used in certain situations, if..." is much more likely to be correct than one that states the "process should be discontinued completely." The first is a calm rational statement and doesn't even make a definitive, uncompromising stance, using a hedge word *if* to provide wiggle room, whereas the second choice is far more extreme.

✓ Benchmark

As you read through the answer choices and you come across one that seems to answer the question well, mentally select that answer choice. This is not your final answer, but it's the one that will help you evaluate the other answer choices. The one that you selected is your benchmark or standard for judging each of the other answer choices. Every other answer choice must be compared to your benchmark. That choice is correct until proven otherwise by another answer choice beating it. If you find a better answer, then that one becomes your new benchmark. Once you've decided that no other choice answers the question as well as your benchmark, you have your final answer.

✓ Predict the Answer

Before you even start looking at the answer choices, it is often best to try to predict the answer. When you come up with the answer on your own, it is easier to avoid distractions and traps because you will know exactly what to look for. The right answer choice is unlikely to be word-for-word what you came up with, but it should be a close match. Even if you are confident that you have the right answer, you should still take the time to read each option before moving on.

General Strategies

✓ Tough Questions

If you are stumped on a problem or it appears too hard or too difficult, don't waste time. Move on! Remember though, if you can quickly check for obviously incorrect answer choices, your chances of guessing correctly are greatly improved. Before you completely give up, at least try to knock out a couple of possible answers. Eliminate what you can and then guess at the remaining answer choices before moving on.

✓ Check Your Work

Since you will probably not know every term listed and the answer to every question, it is important that you get credit for the ones that you do know. Don't miss any questions through careless mistakes. If at all possible, try to take a second to look back over your answer selection and make sure you've selected the correct answer choice and haven't made a costly careless mistake (such as marking an answer choice that you didn't mean to mark). This quick double check should more than pay for itself in caught mistakes for the time it costs.

✓ Pace Yourself

It's easy to be overwhelmed when you're looking at a page full of questions; your mind is confused and full of random thoughts, and the clock is ticking down faster than you would like. Calm down and maintain the pace that you have set for yourself. Especially as you get down to the last few minutes of the test, don't let the small numbers on the clock make you panic. As long as you are on track by monitoring your pace, you are guaranteed to have time for each question.

✓ Don't Rush

It is very easy to make errors when you are in a hurry. Maintaining a fast pace in answering questions is pointless if it makes you miss questions that you would have gotten right otherwise. Test writers like to include distracting information and wrong answers that seem right. Taking a little extra time to avoid careless mistakes can make all the difference in your test score. Find a pace that allows you to be confident in the answers that you select.

⊘ Keep Moving

Panicking will not help you pass the test, so do your best to stay calm and keep moving. Taking deep breaths and going through the answer elimination steps you practiced can help to break through a stress barrier and keep your pace.

Final Notes

The combination of a solid foundation of content knowledge and the confidence that comes from practicing your plan for applying that knowledge is the key to maximizing your performance on test day. As your foundation of content knowledge is built up and strengthened, you'll find that the strategies included in this chapter become more and more effective in helping you quickly sift through the distractions and traps of the test to isolate the correct answer.

Now that you're preparing to move forward into the test content chapters of this book, be sure to keep your goal in mind. As you read, think about how you will be able to apply this information on the test. If you've already seen sample questions for the test and you have an idea of the question format and style, try to come up with questions of your own that you can answer based on what you're reading. This will give you valuable practice applying your knowledge in the same ways you can expect to on test day.

Good luck and good studying!

Biological Psychology

Parts of the Neuron

- Dendrites extend away from the body of the neuron cell to receive messages from other neurons at synapses. They are somewhat treelike in structure, and not all neurons have them.
- Synapses allow the dendrites from a particular neuron to receive signals from and interact with other neurons.
- Axons send signals to other neurons, organs, or muscles and are tubelike in structure. Not all neurons have them.
- The soma is where the signals from the dendrites are linked and sent on. Along with the nucleus, the soma helps maintain the cell and keep it functional.
- Mitochondria are a support structure for the neuron that provide energy for it.
- The Golgi apparatus packages products created by the neuron and secretes them outside the cell wall.

Action Potential

A part of the process that happens during the firing of a neuron is called an action potential. During this process, part of the neural membrane opens and allows positively charged ions inside the cell and negatively charged ions out. Through this process, there is a quick increase in the positive charge of the nerve fiber. When this positive charge is high enough, the impulse is spread down the nerve fiber. The nerve carries this electric impulse down throughout itself through a series of these action potentials.

Types of Neurons

- Neuromodulators moderate circuits or regions of the brain by affecting a group of neurons and thus causing a modulation of that group. Some neuromodulators act as neurotransmitters.
- Neurotransmitters affect only one other neuron. This can be called a neuron-to-neuron exchange of information. They are chemicals used to relay, modulate, and amplify electric signals between a neuron and another cell. If a chemical meets all of the following conditions, it can be classified as a neurotransmitter:
    - Synthesized endogenously (within the presynaptic neuron)
    - Available in adequate quantity in the presynaptic neuron to cause an effect on the post synaptic neuron
    - Externally administered and mimics the endogenously released substance
    - Present biochemical mechanism for inactivation
- A ganglion is a group of neuromodulators. There are 32 pairs of ganglion throughout the human body to control all autonomic and somatic actions.
- Sensory neurons travel from the organs of the body to the brain to relay information related to the five senses.
- Motor neurons that travel from the brain back down to the organs of the body with the response based on the information the sensory neuron sent.
- Interneurons are located within the brain and serve as an internal communication system from one part of the brain to another.

Types of Neurotransmitters

- Acetylcholine works on muscle functioning, learning, and memory. It is present at all neuro synapses surrounding the skeletal muscles and is released when muscles contract.
- Dopamine is responsible for learning, attention, and emotion, as well as movement. It is necessary for the normal functioning of the brain, and too much or too little dopamine may result in physical and psychological problems. Too much dopamine (either naturally or due to drug use) can cause suspicious personality, paranoia, and withdrawal from social situations. A buildup of dopamine (such as from amphetamines or cocaine) can lead to drug-induced psychosis or schizophrenia. Too little dopamine can cause difficulty in movement and conditions such as Parkinson's.
- Serotonin strongly influences arousal, mood, sleep, and hunger. It is believed that too little of it has a role in causing depression. Too much can cause excessive nerve cell activity and a possibly deadly collection of symptoms referred to as serotonin syndrome.

Organization of the Nervous System

The nervous system is the communication network between the organs of the body and the brain. This system consists of nerve cells that send chemical impulses from organs to the brain to receive information on how to respond to stimuli. The two main subsystems of the nervous system include the central nervous system (CNS) and the peripheral nervous system (PNS). The central nervous system includes the spine and brain, and the peripheral nervous system includes all organs and areas of the body outside of the spine and brain.

The sympathetic nervous system works to initiate the appropriate functions for action. In other words, the sympathetic nervous system will arouse the body in times of stress. Conversely, the parasympathetic nervous system acts to conserve energy and will calm the body during times of rest.

The somatic nervous system is a part of the peripheral nervous system and controls all skeletal muscles. The autonomic nervous system is also part of the peripheral nervous system; however, this system controls the internal organs of the body and the glands. Additionally, the autonomic nervous system serves two functions; on the sympathetic side, arousal occurs, and on the parasympathetic side, an inhibition or a calming effect occurs.

Lobes of the Brain

The brain is divided into four main lobes: the frontal lobe, the parietal lobe, the occipital lobe, and the temporal lobes. The frontal lobe located in the front of the brain is responsible for short-term and working memory and information processing as well as decision-making, planning, and judgment. The parietal lobe is located slightly toward the back of the brain and the top of the head and is responsible for sensory input as well as spatial positioning of the body. The occipital lobe is located at the back of the head just above the brain stem. This lobe is responsible for visual input, processing, and output; specifically, nerves from the eyes enter directly into this lobe. Finally, the temporal lobes are located at the left and right sides of the brain. These lobes are responsible for all auditory input, processing, and output.

Motor Cortex and Sensory Cortex

The motor cortex is located near the back of the frontal lobes and is responsible for voluntary movement. Of note, the hemispheres of the brain control the opposite side of the body; therefore, the left side of the motor cortex will control the right side of the body and vice versa. The sensory cortex is located at the front of the parietal lobes and is responsible for the input and processing of touch and other sensations related to movement. Those body parts that are more sensitive are correlated to a larger area of the sensory cortex.

Audio Cortex, Visual Cortex, and Motor Cortex in Speech Processing

The audio cortex, also referred to as Wernicke's area, processes all audio information. This area is located in the temporal lobe of the brain and is involved in the understanding of information. Damage in this area of the brain results in a deficiency in being able to read a word from a page or explain the events depicted in a picture. Once processed through the audio cortex, information passes to the visual cortex, also called the angular gyrus located in the occipital lobe, where the person sees or visualizes the word. The angular gyrus is also essential to reading aloud, and damage to this area of the brain will affect this function. Finally, information is sent to be processed in the motor cortex, or Broca's area. Once information is processed, the individual will respond appropriately. Broca's area is key in speech; therefore, damage to this area will affect the individual's response to processed information.

Hemispheres of the Brain, Corpus Callosum, and Lateralization

The brain is divided into two hemispheres down the middle, and each hemisphere appears to specialize in certain functions. That each hemisphere has different functions is called the lateralization theory. The two sides communicate with each other through a band of fibers called the corpus callosum. The corpus callosum consists of a number of fibrous nerves that are gathered in a band and stretch from the left hemisphere to the right hemisphere. This band of fibers passes information from one side of the brain to the other, allowing the brain in the left and right sides of the body to coordinate and function as one. In cases of a split brain, the corpus callosum is severed, inhibiting the individual to coordinate left and right hemisphere processes. For example, when presented with the word *car* in the right visual field, an individual with a split brain will be able to draw the word, however, will not be able to read the word. This is because information in the right visual field is processed on the left side of the brain, which is responsible for verbal activities; conversely, the right side of the brain is responsible for visual and artistic activities, and therefore the individual can draw the picture.

Limbic System

The limbic system is a collection of structures in the brain that controls basic emotions (e.g., pleasure and fear) and drives (e.g., hunger and sex). The four main structures of the limbic system are the amygdala, the hippocampus (important in memory and learning), regions of the limbic cortex, and the septal area. The limbic system is connected to the hypothalamus, thalamus, and cerebral cortex. Functions associated with the limbic system include learning, behavior, sense of smell, emotions, long-term memory, and drives. The limbic system influences other systems, including the endocrine system and the autonomic nervous system, and is linked to the prefrontal cortex and the pleasure center of the brain.

Cerebellum, Thalamus, and Hypothalamus

The cerebellum is a part of the brain that appears to be a separate structure located at the bottom of the brain. It plays an important role in motor control and possibly in some cognitive functions such as attention and language or also in regulating fear or pleasure responses. The cerebellum does not set off the process of movement but is key to coordination and timing. The thalamus is located at the top of the brain stem and serves as the center for sensory information processing. The thalamus receives and processes information from every sense except smell. The hypothalamus is located below the thalamus, serves as the manager of the endocrine system, and monitors basic needs including hunger, thirst, and sleep.

Methods for Studying the Brain

- Positron emission tomography (PET) evaluates the metabolism of the brain to glean information about its physiology and anatomy as well as its biochemical properties. PET is able to discover biochemical changes before other tests (which rely on only studying anatomical changes). To conduct a PET scan on the brain, radionuclides are formed by attaching a radioactive atom to glucose as this is the substance the brain uses for its metabolism. The activity of the glucose can then be observed.
- Magnetic resonance imaging (MRI) provides a picture of the soft tissue of the brain via magnetic fields and the radio waves produced by the brain during a given task.
- Functional MRI (fMRI) reveals brain function by visualizing the blood flow over a series of MRI images while the individual performs tasks. Uses of fMRI include examining the brain's anatomy; brain mapping (i.e., to determine which part of the brain handles critical functions such as thought, speech, etc.); assessing the effects of trauma, stroke, or degenerative disease on brain function; monitoring brain tumors, and guiding planning for surgery or radiation therapy.
- Electroencephalogram (EEG) detects the brain's electrical activity using electrodes attached to the scalp. Brain cells are always active and communicate through electrical impulses. The EEG can measure these impulses and is one of the primary diagnostic tests for epilepsy. It also plays a role in diagnosing other brain disorders. During the EEG, different stimuli will be presented to the individual to activate different brain waves.

Adrenal Glands

The adrenal glands are located above the kidneys and generate a wide variety of hormones. They are made of several different layers that all affect the composition and function of the glands. Each adrenal gland consists of an outer cortex that surrounds a core of medulla. The adrenal cortex creates a type of steroid hormones called corticosteroids. These corticosteroids include mineralocorticoids (which help in blood pressure regulation and balance of electrolytes). Another type is glucocorticoids, like cortisol, that helps regulate glycogen, lipometabolism, and suppression of the immune system. The internal layer of the adrenal cortex generates androgens, which the gonads convert to fully functional sex hormones. The medulla produces epinephrine and norepinephrine, which work in the fight-or-flight response to increase the body's arousal in stressful situations.

Pituitary Gland

The pituitary gland is possibly the most important part of the endocrine system and is called the "master gland" as it controls several other of the hormone-producing glands, such as the thyroid and the adrenals. It sits behind the bridge of the nose, just below the base of the brain and is generally about the size of a pea. It has two parts, or lobes, the anterior pituitary and the posterior pituitary. The hormones that the pituitary gland produces control the functions of other endocrine glands. Several important hormones are produced by the anterior pituitary such as growth hormone, gonadotrophins (which are part of the puberty process), thyroid-stimulating hormone, prolactin, and adrenocorticotrophic hormone (ACTH). The posterior pituitary produces a hormone that balances fluid called anti-diuretic hormone (ADH).

Thyroid and Parathyroid Glands

The thyroid is located along the front of the windpipe, just below the Adam's apple and is a butterfly-shaped gland. It has two lobes connected by a bridge between them. The thyroid cannot be felt when it is its normal size. Thyroid hormones include thyroxine, or T4, and triiodothyronine, or T3. They are primarily responsible for metabolism regulation. Thyroid hormones also influence growth, development, and body temperature and are crucial for brain development in infancy and childhood.

The parathyroid glands are four small glands usually situated on the back of the thyroid. Along with calcitonin (which is produced by the thyroid) parathyroid hormone plays a key role in regulating the amount of calcium in the bones and blood.

PANCREAS

The pancreas is located in the abdominal cavity just behind the stomach and is a part of both the digestive and endocrine systems. It produces several hormones, which include insulin, glucagon, somatostatin, and pancreatic polypeptide.

TESTES

Otherwise known as gonads, the testes (testicles) produce sperm and maintain the health of the male reproductive system. Testes also secrete testosterone, a hormone that is critical to the development of male physical characteristics. It is necessary for the healthy development of male sex organs, growth of facial and body hair, vocal changes, increase in height and muscle mass, and growth of the Adam's apple. In adult males, testosterone maintains muscle strength, bone density, and libido.

OVARIES

The ovaries produce three major estrogens—estradiol, estrone, and estriol—that work together toward the healthy development of female sex characteristics during puberty and afterward to ensure fertility. These help in breast development; fat distribution in the legs, breasts, and hips; and development of reproductive organs. Other hormones produced by the ovaries are relaxin, which is released prior to giving birth, and inhibin, which communicates to the pituitary to inhibit follicle-stimulating hormone secretion. Close to the end of pregnancy, the pituitary gland is alerted by increased estrogen levels to release oxytocin, which causes uterine contractions to begin.

OTHER HORMONES

Melatonin is involved in the entrainment of circadian rhythms for physiological functions such as sleep. It is produced by the pineal gland in darkness, therefore typically at night. The pineal gland is found in the center of the brain, outside the blood-brain barrier.

Serotonin acts as a neurotransmitter and controls mood, appetite, and sleep cycles. It impacts some cognitive functions such as memory and learning. It is manufactured in the brain where its primary functions are performed, however, about 90% of the serotonin in the human body is in the digestive tract and blood platelets.

Dopamine helps regulate movement and emotional responses and also controls the heart rate. It also aids in perception, helping one to determine what is and isn't real. It is a neurotransmitter that helps manage the reward and pleasure centers in the brain. Low dopamine activity may be indicated in a person being more prone to addiction. Dopamine deficiency leads to Parkinson's disease. People known as risk takers, who tend to be sensation seekers, often have a certain type of dopamine receptor that others do not.

Growth hormone is produced by the pituitary gland and is the catalyst for growth in children and adolescents. It helps stimulate the growth and reproduction of cells in the body. Growth hormone also helps regulate body fluids, muscle growth, bone growth, metabolism of fat and sugar, and possibly heart function.

Leptin speeds up metabolism while concurrently slowing down the appetite.

Orexin increases alertness and energy levels and also increases appetite.

NATURE VERSUS NURTURE

Nature versus nurture is the idea that some of a person's traits result from genetic heritage and some result from environment. In this context, nature refers to any trait that an individual is born with or has acquired through genes. Nurture may be seen as the opposite of nature; it refers to any trait that an individual acquires from the environment. Nurture often refers specifically to the environment created by the parents of the child, but it can refer to any environmental condition that affects development. Historically, some philosophers have believed that the mind is a blank slate (*tabula rasa)* that requires experience and learning to develop. In contrast, other thinkers have purported that all of a person's characteristics are set at birth. Most psychologists today believe that the development of a human being is affected by both biology and experience.

EVOLUTIONARY PSYCHOLOGY

Evolutionary psychology is an approach that seeks to explain cognitive and psychological traits as the product of natural selection. Its focus is on how the processes of evolution have shaped the human mind and behavior. Examples of psychological adaptations that evolutionary psychology claims to explain are language acquisition, incest avoidance, intelligence, and so on. The roots of evolutionary psychology are in both cognitive psychology and evolutionary biology.

SENSORY ADAPTATION

Sensory adaptation is a phenomenon that occurs after a person is presented with a stimulus over a period of time, and his/her senses no longer perceive the stimulus but rather have become adapted to it. For example, when going from a dark room to a bright room our eyes receive intense sensory information from the light, which results in the desire to squint. However, after a short period of time, our eyes adapt to the light, no longer perceiving the light as threatening or too bright, and squinting is no longer needed. Sensory adaptation is necessary so that the information processing systems within our brains do not go into sensory overload. After a short period of time of adjustment, our attention can tune out some stimuli and focus on more important input.

FEATURE DETECTION AND PARALLEL PROCESSING

Feature detection refers to a process in which the nervous system can filter or sort complex stimuli so that one can extract significant characteristics that are more likely to belong to important objects. This process allows the brain to filter out more irrelevant or background stimuli. Parallel processing is the phenomenon in which the brain is able to concurrently process incoming stimuli of varying quality and importance.

PLACE THEORY

Place theory proposed by Hermann von Helmholtz states that an individual's ability to hear pitch is the result of sound waves stimulating different parts of the cochlea basilar membrane. This theory suggests it is not necessarily the sound or the pitch that the brain is processing but rather the place at which the stimulus hits the ear. This theory was supported through research that found that the cochlea vibrates in different places depending on the pitch of a sound. For example, the higher-frequency pitches vibrated the beginning of the cochlea membrane, whereas lower-frequency pitches vibrated the end of the cochlea membrane. It is important to note, however, that lower-frequency pitches do not always vibrate only the end of the cochlea membrane, and therefore this theory does not fully explain them.

Frequency Theory

Frequency theory suggests that an individual can perceive pitch based on the frequency of the pitch. When the sound waves of a pitch enter the ear, they have different effects, depending on their frequency, on the nerves surrounding the ear, creating different nerve impulses that travel to the brain. Based on these nerve impulses, the brain will perceive the pitch as high or low. Frequency theory provides a thorough explanation of how individuals perceive low-level pitches; however, it does not provide a comprehensive explanation for higher-pitched frequencies. Specifically, as neurons are unable to fire more than 1,000 times per second, this theory does not address pitch frequencies that require impulses above that rate, as some higher-pitched frequencies do.

Difference Threshold and Webster's Law

The difference threshold is the point at which an individual can detect differences in a stimulus at least 50% of the time. An example of a difference threshold would be when holding a weight of, for example, 100 ounces. To determine the difference threshold, small additions will be made, for example, 5 ounces at a time until the individual notices a difference in the weight. The difference threshold may depend on a number of factors, but the primary factor that will determine difference threshold is explained by Webster's law. Webster's law states that the proportion of two different stimuli must be equal to determine an adequate difference threshold. For example, whereas holding 100 ounces and adding 5 ounces at a time will result in one difference threshold, holding 1,000 ounces and adding 5 ounces at a time will result in a different difference threshold. However, the difference thresholds between the two cases will be equal if 50 ounces is added at a time to the 1,000 ounces being held.

Absolute Threshold

Absolute threshold refers to the amount or intensity that is required of a stimulus for an individual to perceive it at least 50% of the time. The absolute threshold will vary depending on age, experience, and environment. For example, older individuals may have a higher absolute threshold for hearing than younger individuals due to hearing loss associated with aging. Another example is the variance an absolute threshold may have depending on the environment that the individual is in. For example, if an individual is in complete darkness his/her absolute threshold for hearing may be lower than when the individual is in the light because a sense of hearing will be heightened in the absence of a sense of light.

Visual Sensory System

The visual sensory system allows humans to understand their environment through detecting and interpreting light. The eye receives light rays and changes them into a form that the brain can understand, that is, electrical and chemical signals. This is a process known as phototransduction. The brain decodes these chemical and electrical signals and forms images from them. There are three basic layers, known as tunics, in the human eye. The outermost layer is the fibrous tunic and is made up of the sclera and the cornea. The middle layer is the vascular tunic and includes the iris and pupil. This layer provides oxygen to the rest of the eye and also removes waste through the many blood vessels it contains. The innermost layer is the nervous tunic, which includes the retina. This layer is receptive to light and connects to the brain via the optic nerve. The retina is the part of the eye that converts light into neural signals. It contains photoreceptor cells, which both sense and respond to light. The two types of photoreceptor cells are rods and cones. Rods work with low levels of light; they do not detect color. Cones need much more light, are much less numerous than rods, and detect color, sharpness, and detail.

Auditory Sensory System

The auditory system allows the brain to distinguish sounds and extract meaning from them. As in the visual system, the auditory system utilizes transduction but, in this case, to convert sound waves (vs. light waves in the visual system) into electrical impulses that the brain can decode. The outer ear includes the parts of the ear that are visible to the naked eye, called the pinna, as well as the auditory canal. The pinna help reflect sound into the auditory canal, which amplifies the sound. The eardrum, also known as the tympanic membrane, is at the end of the auditory canal. The middle ear includes everything from the inside of the eardrum to the outside of the oval window of the inner ear. The three tiny bones of the middle ear, or ossicles, are the malleus (hammer), incus (anvil), and stapes (stirrup). The ossicles transmit sound vibrations in air from the eardrum to sound vibrations in the fluid of the cochlea. The cochlea and the vestibular system form the inner ear. When the stapes vibrates on the oval window (the beginning of the inner ear), it causes movement in the fluid of the inner ear. The cochlea takes these fluid sound waves and converts them into nerve impulses, which can be understood by the brain. The vestibular system (see what follows for more detail), also in the inner ear, is made of semicircular canals and uses the same fluid and hair cells that the cochlea uses for sound but to manage balance and motion.

Olfactory System

The olfactory system, or the sense of smell, transmits information about the chemical composition of substances to the brain. Through olfaction, people are able to perceive substances in the environment. These substances can be airborne, in which case they are detected by the main olfactory system, or in liquid form, in which case the accessory olfactory system deals with them. The sense of smell aids in the discovery and recognition of hazardous substances as well as more pleasant substances, such as food or pheromones. It is also closely connected to memory due to its close neural connections with parts of the brain concerned with emotions and memory. This means that often a scent or fragrance can stimulate memories. Olfaction also greatly contributes to the sense of taste, or the gustatory system. Older adults often experience a loss of the sense of smell, often due to accumulated damage caused by viruses and other minor trauma.

Gustation

Gustation, or the sense of taste, works in similar ways to the olfactory system. Through chemoreception, the brain is able to interpret chemical compounds as flavors. There are five main types of taste sensation: sweet, salty, bitter, sour, and savory (also referred to as umami). Taste buds on the tongue include gustatory cells, which are also called taste receptor cells. Taste receptors are found around the papillae on the surface of the tongue, cheek, upper esophagus, epiglottis, and soft palate. Despite a myth that there are certain zones of the tongue devoted to each of the different types of taste, any taste on the tongue can detect any of the five types of taste. Around age 50, human beings experience a loss of tongue papillae and a reduction in production of saliva. This leads to a decrease in the sense of taste.

Somatosensory System

The sense of touch is otherwise known as the somatosensory system. There are sensory receptor cells throughout the entire body that help the individual to detect sensations and changes on the surface of the body or within it. Different stimuli activate the sensory receptor cells. These stimuli include temperature, pain, vibrations, texture, and movement. The somatosensory system also helps the individual understand where his/her body is in space and how it is moving, which is related to the vestibular and proprioception systems.

Vestibular and Proprioception Systems

Like the other senses, the vestibular system gathers information about the outside world and communicates it to the brain. The vestibular system manages balance and motion through the fluid and hair cells in the inner ear. It helps the individual to know which way is up or down and in which direction a person's body is moving. The vestibular system helps the brain compensate for eye and body movement so that it can understand what the person is seeing without all input being hopelessly blurred and confusing.

In contrast to the other sensory systems, proprioception does not gather information from the outside world to communicate it to the brain. Instead, it gathers information about the body itself from receptors in the muscles, tendons, joints, and fascia. Movement is often necessary to trigger these receptors. This is similar to the vestibular system, which also requires movement. The vestibular and proprioception systems cannot easily be separated as many movements and activities involve both systems.

Perceptual Set

The phrase *perceptual set* describes the inclination to view objects or situations from a specific frame of reference. Perceptual sets generally lead one to form reasonably accurate conclusions, which are heavily influenced by expectations and prior knowledge. Perceptual sets are often guided by schemas, mental frameworks, and concepts. One example is that of faces. Human beings have a strong schema for faces, which makes it easier to recognize human faces in the environment. This can also mean that when a person sees an ambiguous image, he/she is more likely to see it as a face than as another kind of object.

Figure Ground

Figure ground organization is the ability to identify a figure from the background. This is an important factor in recognizing objects visually. The three types of figure ground situations are those in which the figure and the ground compete, those in which the figure should be the ground and the ground should be the figure, and those in which the figure and the ground create an optical illusion.

Depth Perception

Depth perception allows human beings to perceive the world visually in three dimensions and also allows humans to perceive the distance of an object. Sources of information from the environment or within the body that help one perceive how far away an object is are called depth cues. Depth cues can fall into two categories: binocular, which requires use of both eyes, and monocular, which requires the use of only one eye. Monocular cues include size, texture, overlap, shading, height, and clarity. Binocular cues include convergence and retinal disparity. Convergence describes the phenomenon in which the closer an object is, the more inward one's eyes need to turn to focus. Retinal disparity refers to the fact that each eye sees a slightly different image and extracts distance information from each of them.

Constancy

Perceptual constancy can also be referred to as object constancy or constancy phenomenon and describes the tendency to see familiar objects as having a standard shape, size, or color, regardless of changes in the perspective angle, distance, or lighting. This makes people able to identify objects under various conditions; for example, snow is understood to be white whether in the low illumination of moonlight or in bright sunlight.

Selective Attention

Selective attention is the individual's ability to process only necessary information while additional and unnecessary information or stimuli is blocked out. This is important as individuals are presented with millions of pieces of information per second that they could not possibly process. One common example of selective attention is the cocktail party effect. This effect occurs when individuals are having a conversation in a crowded, noisy room. They are able to tune out the other conversations and focus on their single conversation because of selective attention. Although humans do have this ability, in situations where attention is necessary, engaging in other tasks may result in a focus of attention moving from one activity to the other. For example, while driving and talking on a cell phone, an individual's attention may shift to the conversation and tune out the road.

Selective Inattention

Selective inattention is the phenomenon that humans are inattentive to the majority of incoming stimuli. For example, when presented with a series of pictures with only a slight change, the majority of individuals will not notice the change. This can also be referred to as change blindness, which suggests that unless paying attention to a possible change in the setting or environment, the individual will not notice a difference. Inattentional blindness occurs when the individual does not notice objects unless paying specific attention to them. For example, if instructed to look for a dog in a picture, then asked if a cat was in the picture, the individual will likely not notice the cat because they were not attending to this object.

Consciousness

The awareness that people have of themselves and their environment is referred to as consciousness. William James posited that consciousness is a steady stream of thoughts, emotions, and perceptions. There are two main aspects to consciousness: monitor and control. The ability to perceive one's surroundings, identify potential problems, and make decisions is monitoring. Control describes the ability to organize thoughts and use behaviors to complete tasks.

Pre-consciousness

In the field of psychoanalysis, pre-consciousness describes thoughts that are not repressed but are unconscious at a particular moment. They are available for recall and can easily become conscious thoughts. Priming is one of the most common forms of preconscious processing. Priming describes an effect of implicit memory in which one is exposed to a stimulus, which in turn influences a response to a second stimulus. Perceptual, semantic, or conceptual stimuli can lead to priming. An example of priming is giving a person a list of words to read that includes the word *cabinet* and later asking the person to name a word that starts with *cab-*. The person will be more likely to answer with *cabinet* than if he/she were not primed. Other types of preconscious processing are the tip-of-the-tongue phenomenon and blindsight.

Altered States

An altered state of consciousness describes a mental state brought on by psychological, physiological, or pharmacological causes and deviates from the normal waking conscious state. They may be caused either intentionally or accidentally. Accidental altered states are generally considered pathological and include traumatic experiences, epilepsy, infections, oxygen deficiency, fasting, sleep deprivation, or psychosis. Intentional altered states are often recreational and are generally caused by pharmacological substances, such as MDMA (ecstasy), opiates, cocaine, or alcohol. Some altered states of consciousness can be caused by a combination of factors, for example a person with a psychiatric disorder who consumes psycho-active substances.

Stages of Sleep

Most individuals experience five stages of sleep, 1 through 4 and rapid eye movement (REM). Stages 1 through 4 are differentiated by the brain waves that are most active during that stage and include: beta, alpha, theta, and delta. Also associated with these four states of sleep are differences in muscle activity, temperature, and blood pressure. Beta waves are high-frequency waves (18–24 cycles/second) and are most prevalent while awake. Alpha waves are slower (8–12 cycles/second) and occur during states of relaxation. Theta waves occur every 4 to 7 cycles/second and indicate the transition from alpha, relaxation, to sleep (Stage 1). Stage 2 sleep occurs when the body falls into a deeper sleep and the body and brain continue to slow. Stages 3 and 4 are indicated by deep sleep and delta waves. The final stage of sleep is referred to as REM sleep. It is during the REM period that dreaming occurs.

During REM sleep, breathing speeds up and becomes more irregular and shallow, limb muscles are temporarily paralyzed, and eyes jerk rapidly. Brain waves increase to levels like those when a person is awake. Blood pressure rises, heart rate increases, and the body loses some temperature regulation ability. Most people go through three to five REM intervals every night. Infants spend nearly half of their sleep time in REM sleep, whereas adults spend about half their sleep time in Stage 2, 20% in REM, and the rest divided between the other stages. As adults age, they will spend progressively less time in REM sleep.

Activation-Synthesis Theory

The activation-synthesis model states that brain activation during REM sleep results in synthesis of dream creation. It suggests that dreams are caused by the physiological processes of the brain when circuits in the brain stem are activated during REM sleep. Once they are activated, parts of the limbic system that deal with emotions, sensations, and memories become active. The brain then synthesizes and interprets all of this activity and seeks to create meaning from these signals, which results in dreaming. This model was developed by researchers J. Allan Hobson and Robert McCarley. Hobson has five dream characteristics, which are as follows: illogical content, intense emotions, acceptance of strange content, strange sensory experiences, and difficulty remembering content.

Dreams in Psychoanalytic Theory

Freud saw dreams as highly instructive and believed that they perform important functions for the unconscious mind and serve as valuable clues to how it operates. According to Freud, the manifest content of a dream is what the dreamer remembers, and the symbolic meaning is the latent content. Through a process called dream work, one can come to translate the underlying wish in the latent content.

Sleep Theories

There are theories that attempt to explain why we sleep. The adaptive or evolutionary theory proposes that being inactive at night helped keep our ancestors out of harm's way at times they would be more vulnerable. The energy conservation theory puts forward that sleep's primary function is to reduce the demand for energy expenditure, particularly at times that searching for food is less efficient. Another explanation can be referred to as the restorative theory and suggests that sleep is necessary for the body to repair and rejuvenate itself. Recent empirical evidence appears to support this theory as animals that are entirely deprived of sleep die in a matter of weeks. Specific restorative functions that sleep provides include muscle growth, tissue repair, protein synthesis, and growth hormone release. The brain plasticity theory purports that sleep is necessary for organization and growth of brain structures. Evidence of this theory can be seen in the negative effect that sleep deprivation has on people's ability to learn and perform tasks.

PSYCHOACTIVE DRUGS

A psychoactive drug can be any chemical substance that changes brain function and causes alterations in mood, perception, or consciousness. The main categories of psychoactive drugs are narcotics, depressants, stimulants, and hallucinogens. Other drugs that have psychoactive effects but do not fit into these categories are cannabis (marijuana) and steroids.

A person who uses a drug repeatedly may develop a tolerance to the drug. Sometimes larger and larger doses are needed to produce the same effect when a substance is used over a long period of time. Dependence describes factors that make it difficult for a person to stop using a drug. Dependence factors include craving and withdrawal. Dependence may be either psychological or physical. Addiction describes a chronic brain disease that causes compulsive substance use in spite of harmful consequences.

Drugs that cause psychological dependence typically produce one or more of the following effects: reduced tension/anxiety, elation/euphoria, feeling of a temporary escape from reality, altered perceptions, or feelings of increased mental or physical ability. Psychological dependence can lead to the user continuing to use the drug despite knowing it may be physically harmful or interferes with important parts of life, such as family or work.

If a drug causes physical dependence, stopping the use of that drug will result in unpleasant or even painful physical symptoms. These symptoms occur due to the body's adaptation to the continuous presence of the substance. Withdrawal describes the physical problems and emotions that a person experiences if he/she is dependent on a substance and then suddenly stops or greatly reduces intake of it. Withdrawal symptoms range from the mild to the life-threatening. A person in withdrawal may experience nausea, shakiness, sweating, extreme confusion, jumpiness, or hallucinations (auditory, visual, or tactile). Delirium tremens (DTs) can include all the aforementioned symptoms plus seizures. If untreated, delirium tremens can lead to death.

NARCOTICS

Narcotics are drugs that are used medicinally to relieve pain. They cause relaxation with an immediate rush, or high, and have a high potential for abuse. Their effects include restlessness, nausea, euphoria, drowsiness, respiratory depression, and constricted pupils. Examples of narcotics include morphine, heroin, oxycodone, and fentanyl.

DEPRESSANTS

Depressants are used medicinally to relieve anxiety, irritability, or tension. They produce a state of intoxication that is similar to the effect of alcohol and have a high potential for abuse and tolerance development. Depressants have a synergistic effect with alcohol, and this combination is risky. They cause sensory alteration, lessened anxiety, and intoxication. In small amounts they can cause muscle relaxation and calmness, whereas larger amounts can cause slurred speech, impaired judgment, and loss of motor coordination. Large doses of depressants can cause respiratory depression, coma, and even death. Examples of depressants include barbiturates, benzodiazepines, narcotics, and alcohol. Some consider marijuana a depressant.

STIMULANTS

Stimulants increase alertness and relieve fatigue. Users can feel stronger, more decisive, and euphoric. Some use stimulants to counteract the "down" feeling of depressants or alcohol. Stimulants cause an increase in heart rate and respiratory rate and an elevation in blood pressure. Their effects include dilated pupils and a decreased appetite. High doses of stimulants can cause a rapid or irregular heartbeat, a loss of coordination, perspiration, collapse, blurred vision, dizziness, and feelings of restlessness, anxiety, and delusions. Examples of stimulants include cocaine, amphetamines, and methamphetamine.

Hallucinogens, Marijuana, and Alcohol

Hallucinogens can cause hallucinations, illusions, dizziness, and confusion, along with rapidly changing moods. Large doses can cause convulsions, heart/lung failure, coma, and aneurism. There can sometimes be delayed effects, often called flashbacks, which can occur long after the use of the drug. Chronic use of hallucinogens can cause depression, violent behavior, anxiety, and a distorted perception of time. Examples of hallucinogens include LSD and ecstasy.

Marijuana is derived from cannabis, which is a hemp plant. Effects of marijuana include euphoria soon followed by relaxation, loss of coordination, and increased perception of the senses. Marijuana can impair memory, concentration, and knowledge retention and can cause irritation to the lungs and respiratory system.

Alcohol is the most available and widely used psychoactive substance. Its misuse can represent a difficult diagnostic problem as it is legal to obtain and use. Progression of alcoholism dependence often occurs over an extended period of time. This is unlike some other substances whose progression can be quite rapid. Because of this slow progression, dependence on alcohol can be denied and hidden for long periods of time.

Cognitive Psychology

Basic Principles of Learning

Principles of learning, also known as laws of learning, provide additional understanding about what makes people learn most effectively. The first three laws of learning were developed by Edward Thorndike in the early 20th century. They are readiness, exercise, and effect. Five additional principles have joined the first three laws since that time: primacy, recency, intensity, freedom, and requirement.

The principle of readiness includes motivation and concentration. People learn best when they are ready to learn, physically, mentally, and emotionally. Having a strong purpose, a clear objective, and a specific reason for learning something ensures that an individual will make more progress. Also, key to learning is having sufficient rest, health, and physical ability. Learning is an active process and requires that basic needs be met before an individual is capable of learning.

The principle of exercise has to do with repetition, drill, and practice. Students learn best and better retain information with meaningful practice and repetition. Meaningful practice includes positive feedback. The human mind does not usually retain and apply new concepts after a single exposure. Learning continues every time practice occurs. Practice includes recall, review, summary, manual drill, and physical applications, which all serve to create learning habits.

The principle of effect has to do with the emotional reaction that the learner has. It is directly related to motivation. This principle contends that learning is strengthened with pleasant or satisfying feelings, and it is weakened with unpleasant feelings. Positive reinforcement helps motivate learners, and punishment may weaken motivation. Positive feelings accompany feelings of success and of making progress. Believing the task is too difficult may hamper motivation.

The principle of primacy means that the things learned first can create such a strong impression in the mind that they are difficult to erase. Teachers should be careful that that what is taught is right the first time, as unlearning an incorrect first impression is more difficult than learning it correctly the first time. Additionally, a subject matter is best taught in a logical order, step by step, which aids students' learning overall.

The principle of recency asserts that one best remembers the things most recently learned. Alternatively, facts are more difficult to remember the further removed in time the learner is from them. Information that one acquires last is often remembered best, and having important points repeated at the end of a lesson can help cement them in the learner's mind.

The principle of intensity teaches us that the more intense the material taught, the more likely the learner will retain it. Boring learning experiences are not retained as well as dramatic or exciting lessons. Intensity also asserts that a learner will learn more from genuine things than from substitutes or by performing tasks rather than reading about them or seeing them performed. Realism cannot always be achieved in the classroom, but the following can make lessons more intense for the learner: demonstrations, skits, role-playing, examples, analogies, personal experience, and fuller use of the senses (hearing, sight, touch, taste, smell, balance, rhythm, and depth perception).

The principle of freedom asserts that things learned freely and without coercion are better learned. Coercion and compulsion impede learning. Students benefit from freedoms of personal responsibility (freedom of choice, freedom of action, and freedom to bear the results of action) as learning is an active process. Without freedom, students may have little or no interest in learning.

Finally, the law of requirement teaches us that the learner must have something to obtain or do something. The starting point may be an ability, skill, instrument, or anything else that may assist in learning, but a starting point (or root) is necessary.

Classical Conditioning

Through classical conditioning a person can learn a new response or behavior by making associations between previously unrelated things. This type of learning was discovered by Ivan Pavlov, who was a physiologist experimenting with the hunger response of dogs. Pavlov noticed that the dogs he was working with salivated when in the presence of food. The dogs displayed an unconditioned response (salivating) when exposed to the food (the unconditioned stimulus). The unconditioned response is unlearned and occurs naturally (or unconditionally) in response to the unconditioned stimulus. Later, Pavlov paired the food with the sound of a bell. After some time, the dogs would salivate at the sound of the bell, even when it was not paired with food. The bell sound is the conditioned stimulus, and the dog's salivating at its sound is the conditioned response. The conditioned stimulus did not affect the dogs before it was paired with the unconditioned stimulus; after pairing, the dogs display the conditioned response, which is learned and not naturally occurring.

There are three phases to the process outlined here. First is the stage known as before conditioning. This would be the phase when the dogs salivated when exposed to the food. The second stage is during conditioning. This describes the time when the dogs were exposed to the food and bell together. Finally, the last phase is after conditioning. At this time the dogs salivate to the bell alone, without the food.

Fundamental Elements of Classical Conditioning

There are several key phenomena in classical conditioning that behavioral psychologists have described. Some of these are part of attaining the new (conditioned) response, and some have to do with this learned response fading away.

Acquisition describes the learning phase, when the conditioned response is first produced and then increasingly strengthened. For the example used here, a researcher could say that the subject (dog) has acquired the response when it salivates in response to the bell alone. Once the subject has acquired the response, it can be reinforced and strengthened to ensure the subject has learned the response effectively.

Extinction occurs when the learned response (i.e., the conditioned response) either disappears completely or is reduced in strength and/or frequency. Extinction can happen when the conditioned stimulus stops occurring together with the unconditioned stimulus. For Pavlov's dogs, this might occur if they continued to hear the bell without also receiving food. Eventually, the bell would stop causing the salivation response. Without the conditioned response (i.e., salivation) being reinforced at least some of the time with the unconditioned stimulus (i.e., food), the connection between the two weakens or breaks completely.

When a learned response (conditioned response) reappears even after extinction, this is known as spontaneous recovery. If the researchers stop presenting the subject with the conditioned stimulus (i.e., the sound of the bell), they may find that the bell later has no effect or a much decreased effect on the subject. After this has happened, if the conditioned stimulus (bell) is presented and the conditioned response (salivating) occurs, the subject has spontaneously recovered the previously conditioned/learned response. The conditioned stimulus and unconditioned stimulus must be re-associated, or the recovery will not last and extinction will again take place.

When a subject exhibits similar responses to other stimuli that it does to the conditioned stimulus, this is known as stimulus generalization. Examples include dogs that salivate not only to the sound of the bell but also to other similar sounds or a small child who was conditioned to fear a white rat also fearing other fuzzy white objects like stuffed toys.

The ability to differentiate between a conditioned stimulus and other stimuli is stimulus discrimination. Using the examples in the previous paragraph, stimulus discrimination would be seen in the dogs that only salivate to the sound of the bell and not to any other sounds that have not been paired with an unconditioned stimulus, or the child would not fear all fuzzy white objects but only the white rat that was paired with the unconditioned stimulus.

Operant Conditioning

Like classical conditioning, operant conditioning involves behavioral learning affected by outside stimuli. However, classical conditioning involves involuntary reflexes or automatic behaviors (i.e., salivation), and operant conditioning deals with voluntary behaviors. Through operant conditioning, a person makes a connection between a certain behavior and a consequence, either positive or negative.

B. F. Skinner did not believe that classical conditioning was able to adequately explain the complexity of human behavior. Skinner based much of his work on Edward Thorndike's law of effect, which is that behavior that results in satisfying consequences is more likely to be repeated, but behavior that results in unsatisfying or unpleasant consequences is less likely to be repeated. Unlike Thorndike, Skinner was uninterested in studying states of mind or feelings (like satisfaction) and instead developed his framework on things that can be observed, that is, behavior and its consequences.

Skinner added a new concept to the law of effect. Reinforcement is the key to behaviors being strengthened or weakened, according to Skinner. When a behavior is reinforced, it will be repeated, or strengthened; behaviors that are not reinforced will be weakened or even stopped completely. Skinner referred to the responses, or consequences, of behaviors as operants. Operants are categorized as follows:

> *Neutral*—those that do not strengthen nor weaken a behavior
>
> *Reinforcers*—those that raise the chances that a behavior will strengthened (repeated), which can be either positive or negative
>
> *Punishers*—those that lower the chances that a behavior will be strengthened (repeated), which can be positive or negative

Positive reinforcement gives an outcome or consequence that a subject finds pleasant or rewarding. For example, Skinner placed rats in special boxes. If they pressed a certain lever, they would immediately get food.

Negative reinforcement removes an outcome or consequence that a subject does not like. For example, the rat in one of Skinner's boxes could have a loud and unpleasant buzzer going off. The buzzer stops if the rat presses a certain lever.

Positive punishment occurs when an unpleasant stimulus follows a certain behavior; for example, a rat in one of Skinner's boxes could be given a shock when he pushed the "wrong" lever.

Negative punishment involves taking away something positive from the subject, following a certain behavior. For example, a child may have his/her television viewing time taken away if he/she misbehaves.

In positive reinforcement or punishment, something is given to the subject. In negative reinforcement or punishment, something is taken away from the subject. Reinforcement is meant to be pleasant, this is, giving something positive or taking away something negative. Punishment is meant to be unpleasant, that is, giving something negative or taking away something positive. Punishment is often less effective than reinforcement. Often the punished behavior is simply repressed for a time and returns after the punishment no longer occurs.

Schedules of Reinforcement

Behaviorists have learned that not only does the type of reinforcement matter, but when and how often it is delivered matters greatly to how likely it is that a behavior will strengthen or weaken. There are different patterns in which reinforcement can be given. These patterns can be called schedules. Schedules can affect the response rate (i.e., how quickly the subject does the behavior or how hard the subject works) and also the extinction rate (how quickly the subject stops doing the behavior in the absence of reinforcement). Different types of schedules include the following:

> *Continuous reinforcement*—every time a behavior occurs, the subject receives reinforcement. For example, you give your dog a treat every time he/she brings you the ball. With this schedule, the response rate is slow, while the extinction rate is fast.
>
> *Fixed interval schedule*—after a fixed amount of time since the previous reinforcement, new reinforcement is given as soon as a new correct response is made. For example, you give your dog a treat when he/she brings you the ball after 5 minutes have passed since the last treat. Both response rate and extinction rate are medium for this schedule.
>
> *Variable interval schedule*—as long as at least one correct response is made, reinforcement comes after a variable (or unpredictable) amount of time goes by. For example, you give your dog a treat when he/she brings you the ball after varying amounts of time have passed since the last treat. In this schedule the response rate is fast, while extinction rate is slow.
>
> Fixed ratio schedule—reinforcement is given after a certain number of correct responses. For example, you give your dog a treat after he/she brings you the ball five times. Response rate is fast, while extinction rate is medium in this schedule.
>
> Variable ratio schedule—reinforcement is given after an unpredictable number of correct responses. For example, you give your dog a treat at random times after he/she brings you the ball. In this schedule response rate is fast, while extinction rate is slow.

Researchers have found that the variable ratio schedule has the best outcomes for consistent responses and low extinction, although the variable interval schedule also produces a strong outcome. The key appears to be the variable or randomness factor.

Shaping

Skinner developed the process of shaping, a type of behavior modification through operant conditioning. Through shaping, both humans and animals can learn new behaviors, behaviors that do not come naturally to them. An example of shaping is the way that Skinner taught the rats he was working with to press the lever in the Skinner box. Pressing a lever is not something that a rat will do instinctively, so Skinner started by reinforcing behaviors that led the rats closer to the target behavior. This idea of reinforcing behaviors that come closer to the target behavior is referred to as successive approximation. Skinner would first reward the rats when they stepped closer to the lever. Once they did that, he would reward them only for new behaviors, such as stepping even closer, standing on hind legs, and eventually touching the lever. Skinner would not continue to reward previously rewarded behaviors to focus the rats on new behaviors that came closer to the target. Shaping can be used to housetrain dogs, to teach children to do chores, or even to help someone overcome a phobia.

Cognition and Culture in Learning

Situated cognition, or situated learning, is the theory that a person's knowledge is rooted in the context, culture, and activity in which it was learned. As people learn while interacting with each other and through language and shared ideas, learning is social and not isolated. Learning occurs as people discuss, share knowledge, and solve problems together. A form of socio-cultural learning is cognitive apprenticeship in which an expert shares important skills, interactions, and experiences with a novice learner. This theory has helped researchers better understand how people learn as it focuses on what people learn in their everyday lives, which are authentic contexts for a variety of skills. The theory also helps educators understand how to build on knowledge and skills that their students may already possess.

Albert Bandura asserted that the world (environment) and a person's behavior cause or influence each other. He called this reciprocal determinism. This contrasts with behaviorism's assertion that one's environment causes one's behavior. See the previous section on Albert Bandura and his social learning theory for more on this topic.

Environmental and Cultural Influences on Learning

Some factors that influence the process of learning include relationships, stress, and physical health. The more positive the relationship between student and teacher, whether in a formal or informal setting, the better the student will learn and make connections between old and new knowledge. A certain level of stress can be beneficial to learning as adrenaline can stimulate the brain. Chronically stressful environments have a negative influence on learners. Students who live in chronically stressful environments tend to have lower levels of immunity, aptitude, concentration, and comprehension skills. Physical health factors that influence learning include being sufficiently rested, having sufficient physical activity during one's day, and nutrition.

Culture can also influence learning style. People from some cultures prefer verbal instructions, whereas those from other cultures may prefer visual or written instructions. Still others learn best by observing and then doing.

Some cultures emphasize hierarchy. In these cultures, teachers are often seen as the experts, and students are expected to respect them and expect that they will give them the information they need. In such cultures debate and discussion can be seen as a lack of respect for the teacher. Other cultures are more egalitarian, and teachers serve as facilitators and expect debate and discussion from their students.

Another cultural distinction is between individualism and communitarianism. Western countries, and by extension their educational systems, are generally individualistic. Students are expected to be as independent as possible, and teachers provide only essential information and guidance for them to get started on their assignments. In most Western contexts, students are expected to work independently and not collaborate with other students, which can be seen as copying others' work or ideas. Other cultures, for example, most Asian cultures along with others, are more community oriented. In communitarian cultures, group collaboration is the norm, and teachers may be more accessible and supportive than those found in more individualistic contexts.

There are two main models to explain cultural differences in learning and work settings. The first is Geert Hofstede's cultural dimensions, which he identified to help distinguish one culture from another. He later collaborated with Michael Bond and Michael Minkov to round out the list. Hofstede's dimensions include the following:

- Power distance index (high vs. low)
- Individualism versus collectivism
- Masculinity versus femininity
- Uncertainty avoidance index (high vs. low)
- Pragmatic versus normative
- Indulgence versus restraint

Trompenaars's model of national cultural difference was developed by Fons Trompenaars and Charles Hampden-Turner. It includes five orientations that deal with the ways in which people deal with each other: one that deals with time and one that deals with the environment. Their seven dimensions include the following:

- Universalism versus particularism
- Individualism versus communitarianism
- Specific versus diffuse
- Neutral versus emotional
- Achievement versus ascription
- Sequential time versus synchronous time
- Internal direction versus outer direction

Memory Encoding

Information that enters a person's memory system from sensory input must be changed into a form that the system can cope with to store it. The three primary ways that information can be changed or encoded include the following:

- Visual
- Acoustic
- Semantic (meaning)

There is evidence to suggest that the principal coding system in short-term memory (STM) is acoustic coding. People often try to hold a long list of new information, such as a list of numbers or names, by verbally rehearsing them. The principal encoding system in long-term memory (LTM) is likely semantic coding (i.e., by meaning). Information in LTM can be coded both acoustically and visually. STM is also referred to as working memory.

Effortful processing describes learning or storing/encoding information that requires attention and effort. This is used when one requires practice and rehearsal to remember something. When any type of technique is utilized to better remember information, one is engaged in effortful processing.

Automatic processing describes a situation in which an activity can be completed successfully without any thought. Often this is something that has been completed many times before and can also be referred to as muscle memory.

Memory Storage

The term *memory storage* describes where information is stored, the duration of the storage, the capacity for storage, and what kind of information is being stored. The way that information is stored affects the way it is retrieved, and there is a considerable amount of research about the differences between short-term memory (STM) and long-term memory (LTM).

A normal adult has between five and nine slots for items in STM. The amount of information can be expanded greatly depending on how much information one can "chunk" together in each of the slots. This contrasts with the capacity of LTM, which is believed to be unlimited. Information in STM is stored for a brief period of time, between 0 and 30 seconds, whereas LTM can last an entire lifetime.

For memories to pass from STM to LTM memory, they must go through stabilization, which allows the memory to become resistant to interference from competing stimuli or disrupting factors. Stabilization requires the passage of time and leads to consolidation, or short-term memories finding a permanent place in LTM. Physiologically establishing long-term memories involves physical changes in the structure of neurons in the brain. This is known as long-term potentiation. At the most basic level, when something is learned, circuits of neurons in the brain called neural networks are created, altered, or strengthened. These neural networks are made up of neurons that communicate through special junctions called synapses. With repeated use, the strength of these circuits of neurons is reinforced. This reinforcement facilitates the passage of nerve impulses and may involve connections to the visual cortex, the auditory cortex, or other associative regions of the cortex.

Short-term memories are sustained by neural networks in the frontal, prefrontal, and parietal lobes of the brain. Long-term memories are supported and maintained by more stable and permanent changes in neural networks spread widely throughout the brain. The hippocampus serves as a type of temporary transit point for long-term memories, although it is not itself used to store information. The hippocampus is essential to the process of consolidation of information from STM to LTM. Additionally, it is believed to be involved in modifying neural connections for 3 months or more after the initial learning of the information.

Memory Retrieval

Memory retrieval refers to accessing the information that is in storage. When one is unable to remember something, the issue may be that he/she is unable to retrieve it. In retrieval, the differences between STM and LTM are clear. In STM items are stored and retrieved sequentially, whereas in LTM items are stored and retrieved by association. Organization, such as sequencing, can help aid retrieval.

Forgetting in LTM can be explained by interference. The theory of interference proposes that information that is similar in format sometimes gets in the way of the information that one is attempting to recall. The two types of interference are retroactive and proactive. Retroactive interference describes a situation in which more recent information gets in the way of trying to recall older information. Proactive interference is the reverse; old information prevents the recall of new information.

The so-called tip-of-the-tongue phenomenon describes difficulty retrieving information from LTM. Usually this is a commonplace or well-known piece of information such as someone's name, and may feel just out of reach. A retrieval cue can be helpful in retrieving this type of information. A retrieval cue is a type of stimulus to help one remember the information one is trying to retrieve. This can include information about where one was when he/she learned the information; what other people were there; what the topics of conversation were; what tastes, sounds, or smells were present; or even what mood someone was in.

Context dependency in memory has to do with the phenomenon of the added ease of memory retrieval when the context (i.e., circumstances around the memory) is the same for both the original encoding and the retrieval. Research has shown improvement in recall of specific information when these two contexts match. An example of this is seen when someone returns to a childhood home and is able to more readily remember events that occurred. A practical use for this phenomenon is to physically reenact an event to remember some details, such as retracing one's steps after misplacing an item.

At times, a person will add in details to a memory that did not actually occur. This is referred to as constructive memory. Constructive memory describes using knowledge to organize new information and fill in gaps. Human memory is not an unvarnished duplicate of the past but rather relies on constructive processes. These sometimes have a tendency to have errors and distortions.

Sensory Memory

Sensory memory describes the ability to retain the impression of sensory information for a brief time after the original stimuli have ended. It is the shortest-term element of memory and allows a person to remember great sensory detail about a complex stimulus just after its presentation. Sensory memory is an automatic response and is thought to be outside of cognitive control. No manipulation of the incoming information occurs in sensory memory as it is transferred quickly to working memory. During this transfer, the amount of information is greatly reduced due to the lack of capacity of working memory to handle all the input from our sensory organs.

It is thought that there is a subtype of sensory memory for each of the five major senses: touch, taste, sight, hearing, and smell. Only three of these types have been studied extensively: those of echoic memory (auditory), iconic memory (visual), and haptic memory (touch).

Iconic memory, named for the mental representations of visual stimuli (icons), has a duration of about 100 milliseconds and fades quickly. Echoic memory (auditory system) can hold information for a bit longer, about 3 to 4 seconds. Haptic memory holds memories of sensations all over the body before these either vanish or are transported into STM and seems to last about 2 seconds.

Implicit and Explicit Memory

Implicit memory, or non-declarative memory, is a long-term memory function and includes motor skills, cognition, and learning. Implicit memory is also known as procedural memory. In contrast, explicit memory, or declarative memory, deals with how one knows something and includes general knowledge and events that an individual has personally experienced.

Mnemonic Devices

Mnemonic devices are tools or techniques that one can use to remember something better. They are shortcuts that help a person associate the facts or information one wants to remember with an image, a sentence, or a word. These techniques are common and date back to ancient Greek times. Much of the time, one may be using a mnemonic device without even knowing it. Mnemonic devices are a way of memorizing information so that it stays in the brain longer and can be more easily recalled.

The following are types of mnemonic devices:

- *Music mnemonics*—use of songs or jingles, such as singing the ABCs
- *Name mnemonics*—combining the first letter of each word into a new word, such as ROY G BIV for the colors of the rainbow
- *Expression or word mnemonics*—combining the first letter of each word to form a phrase or sentence—Kings Play Chess On Funny Green Squares for the classifications of living organisms (Kingdom, Phylum, etc.)
- *Model mnemonics*—using a model, such as a pyramid or chart
- *Ode mnemonics*—using a poem or doggerel, such as "Thirty days hath September, April, June, and November"
- *Note organization mnemonics*—such as notecards, outlines, or the Cornell system (main ideas or questions to the left of a vertical line with details or answers to the right)
- *Image mnemonics*—constructed in the form of a picture, often the sillier the better, such as a picture of a sick bat for the depressant drugs (i.e., barbiturates, alcohol, or tranquilizers)
- *Connection mnemonics*—new knowledge connected to previously learned knowledge. For example, it's easy to remember the direction of longitude and latitude because longitude has an N it in, which stands for north, so longitude must run north-south. As latitude has no N, it must run east-west.
- *Spelling mnemonics*—for example, the princi<u>pal</u> at school is your <u>pal</u>, and a princip<u>le</u> is a ru<u>le</u>
- *Method of loci*—also called the memory palace. This method takes a place and assigns items to memorize with all the objects in the place. An example is using one's own home, and the rooms and furniture become the objects of information. Another example is the route one takes to work, with the landmarks standing for the information to be memorized.

Elaborative Rehearsal and Levels of Processing

Elaborative rehearsal is another memory technique; it entails contemplating the meaning of the term or idea to be remembered rather than simply repeating it to oneself over and over. It can be used to relate two concepts to one another to give them meaning or relating new knowledge to older knowledge.

The levels of processing model concentrates on the depth of processing involved in memory. This model predicts that the deeper the information is processed, the longer the memory will last. Depth refers to the meaningfulness taken from the exercise rather than how much the material is analyzed. This model comes from the basic idea that memory is what happens as a result of processing information. According to this approach, there are three ways to process information: structural processing and phonemic processing, which both are called shallow processing, or semantic processing, which is referred to as deep processing.

Structural processing is based on appearance and occurs when one encodes the physical qualities of something, such as the typeface of a word or how the letters look. Phonemic processing occurs when one encodes the sound of ideas or information. As both of these (structural and phonemic processing) are shallow processing, they involve only maintenance of information and lead to fairly short retention of the material.

Semantic processing is also considered deep processing and happens when one encodes the meaning of a word and relates it to similar words with similar meaning. Deep processing involves elaborate rehearsal and a more meaningful analysis of information. This leads to better recall.

Concepts and Prototypes

A concept is a mental grouping of similar items; it is used to better remember and understand what things are, their meaning, and what categories or groups they are part of. Concepts can be used for generalizing information, making associations and discriminations, speeding up memory, and guiding actions and behaviors.

A prototype is the best example or central member of a category. Prototypes can be used to enhance memory and recall as one can compare newer, similar items to the prototype to categorize, identify, or store the new item.

Schema

A schema is a way of organizing information about the world, a framework for understanding complex ideas. For example, a child may have a schema for dog—hair-covered animal with four legs and a tail. When he/she first sees a horse, he/she may erroneously call it a dog because it fits with the schema (i.e., hair covered with four legs and a tail). When he/she is corrected and learns that this is a different animal, he/she will then have a schema for horse, which is a bigger animal than a dog that also has hooves.

People have many types of schemata to help understand the world. Some may help one know how to behave in unfamiliar social situations; others may help one understand what new objects are. Schemata have been called the building blocks of a mental model for the world and how it works. People learn new information much more quickly when they can fit it into an existing schema—this is called assimilation. When new information does not fit into an existing schema, the person must either change the existing schema or create a new one—called accommodation. Many times, it is difficult for people, especially adults, to make these changes, and they instead ignore new information or distort it in their minds so that it fits with their worldview. An example of this is prejudice or stereotypes. These can be difficult to change, and people often ignore or create alternate explanations for compelling information that is contrary to their existing schemata.

Mental Set and Functional Fixedness

A mental set is a framework for thinking about a problem, shaped by habit or desire. A mental set can make it easy to solve a type of problem, but if one attaches to the wrong mental set, problem-solving and creativity is inhibited. Another way to think about mental sets is as subconscious tendencies to approach a problem in a particular way. Past experiences and habits shape them. An inappropriate mental set can obstruct the solution of otherwise straightforward problems. An example of this is the question, "When a US plane carrying Canadian passengers crashes in international waters, where should the survivors be buried?" The wording implies that this is a problem of international law (a mental set), when the fact is that survivors would not need to be buried.

One form of mental set is functional fixedness, which is a cognitive bias that limits a person to use an object or tool only in the way it is traditionally used. One example of this is someone who needs a weight but fails to use an available hammer because his/her mental set is to think of the hammer as for a specific purpose only and nothing else. Functional fixedness has been called a mental block against using an item in a new way to solve a problem.

Algorithms

An algorithm is a defined set of step-by-step procedures that will provide the correct answer to a particular problem. Often thought of as a purely mathematical term, one can follow the same type of process to guarantee finding the correct answer when problem-solving or decision-making. Step-by step approaches can be useful when each decision must be made following the same process and when accuracy is essential. A possible downside to using an algorithm to solve a problem is that the process tends to be time-consuming and may not work when decisions need to be made quickly. With algorithms, accuracy is increased and potential mistakes are minimized, but decisions cannot be made swiftly.

HEURISTICS

A heuristic is a mental shortcut that allows a person to make judgments and solve problems quickly. Heuristics are usually informed by one's past experiences and allow a person to act without delay. However, heuristics don't always guarantee a correct solution. Mistakes may occur, but heuristics allow for speedy decisions when time is of the essence. An example of a heuristic in everyday life is in deciding the best route to get from point A to point B. It would be most efficient to use a route that one knows has worked well in the past. An algorithm approach to this problem would entail mapping out every possible route to determine which one would be fastest, but this would be a time-consuming process. Heuristics can be helpful, but they can also lead to cognitive biases. They can speed up the decision-making process, but they can also introduce errors. Simply because something worked in the past does not mean it will work again. Relying on heuristics can make it difficult to see alternative solutions or come up with new ideas. They can also contribute to stereotypes and prejudice. As these mental shortcuts can be used to classify and categorize people, one can often overlook more relevant information.

Types of heuristics include the availability heuristic, the anchoring heuristic, and the representativeness heuristic

AVAILABILITY HEURISTIC

This strategy involves making decisions simply based on how easy it is to bring something to mind. One may remember most quickly a number of examples relevant to the decision or problem. As these are most readily available in the memory, one is likely to judge them as being more common or frequently occurring than they actually are. An example is thinking of recent plane crashes and thus believing that it is safer to travel by car. Simply because the examples of air disasters came to mind so easily, the availability heuristic leads one to think that plane crashes are more common than they actually are.

REPRESENTATIVENESS HEURISTIC

This strategy involves making a decision by comparing one's present situation to the more representative mental prototype. For example, if trying to determine another person's trustworthiness, one might compare aspects of the individual in question to other mental examples one holds. A sweet older man may remind a person of his/her grandfather, and he/she might assume the person is kind and trustworthy. If you meet someone who is into aromatherapy, yoga, and spiritual healing, you might assume that person is a holistic healer or yoga teacher rather than a scientist or teacher.

ANCHORING HEURISTIC

Also called focalism, this can be thought of as the first impression heuristic. This heuristic describes the tendency to rely too heavily on the first piece of information (which serves as the anchor) when making decisions. This gives the anchoring piece of information a great deal of influence over future assessments.

Confirmation Bias

Confirmation bias is the tendency to interpret new evidence as confirmation of one's existing beliefs or theories. It involves favoring information that confirms previously held beliefs and discounting information that does not support them. It impacts how people gather, interpret, and recall information. When a person supports or opposes a particular issue, he/she may seek only information that supports his/her beliefs and also interprets news stories in a way that upholds his/her ideas.

Hindsight Bias

Hindsight bias is also known as creeping determinism or the knew-it-all-along effect. It is the inclination, after an event has occurred, to see the event as having been predictable, despite there having been little or no objective basis for this prediction. Hindsight bias can cause memory distortion and can also lead to extreme methodological problems when trying to understand and interpret results of experimental studies. There are three levels of hindsight bias that "stack" on each other and compound the issue. The first level is memory distortion, such as misremembering an earlier opinion or judgment (i.e., "I said it would happen"). The second level is inevitability and centers on our belief that the event was inevitable (i.e., "It had to happen"). The third level is foreseeability and involves the belief that we personally could have foreseen the event (i.e., "I knew it would happen").

Sociocultural and Relational Psychology

Theories of Personality

There are four major approaches to personality theories: trait, psychoanalytic, humanistic, and social-cognitive.

Psychoanalytic Approach to Personality

The psychoanalytic perspective of personality was created by Sigmund Freud and emphasizes the unconscious mind and the importance of early childhood experiences. Freud asserted that dreams, free association, and slips of the tongue could reveal things hidden in the unconscious. Other theorists who follow the psychoanalytic perspective agreed with Freud about the importance of the unconscious but disagreed with other parts of his theories. These Neo-Freudian theorists include Erik Erikson, Carl Jung, Alfred Adler, and Karen Horney. Erikson emphasized how personality is shaped over the course of the entire life span, the social elements of personality development, and the identity crisis. Jung concentrated on ideas like psychological types, the collective unconscious, and archetypes. Adler asserted that the desire to achieve superiority is the core motive behind personality and that this stems from primal and universal feelings of inferiority. Horney's work emphasized the societal and cultural factors that play roles in personality including the significance of the parent-child relationship. She focused on the need to overcome a sense of isolation and basic anxiety.

The Humanistic Perspective on Personality

This approach emphasizes psychological growth, personal awareness, and free will. Its outlook on human nature is more positive than some other approaches. It focuses on how each individual can achieve his/her potential. Two major humanistic theorists are Carl Rogers and Abraham Maslow. Rogers focused on the importance of free will and psychological growth and believed in the goodness of people. Rogers asserted that the driving force behind human behavior is the actualizing tendency. Maslow theorized that people are motivated by a hierarchy of needs, with the most basic needs being those necessary for life (food, water, and shelter). Maslow asserted that as people move up in the hierarchy as the more basic needs are met, they can then focus on things such as love, belonging, and even self-actualization.

Trait Perspective of Personality

The trait perspective centers on identifying, measuring, and describing the specific traits that make up human personality. Researchers believe they can better comprehend the differences among individuals through understanding these traits. Major theorists of the trait perspective include Hans Eysenck Raymond Cattell, Robert McCrae, and Paul Costa. Eysenck asserted that there are three dimensions of personality: extraversion-introversion, emotional stability-neuroticism, and psychoticism. Cattell recognized 16 personality traits that he asserted could be used to understand and measure individual differences in personality. McCrae and Costa identified five key dimensions of personality in their big five theory. These dimensions are extraversion, neuroticism, openness to experience, conscientiousness, and agreeableness.

Social Cognitive Perspective on Personality

The social cognitive perspective emphasizes the importance of self-efficacy, cognitive processes, observational learning, and situational influences. The primary theorist is Albert Bandura, who promoted the importance of learning through observation or social learning. Bandura's theory highlighted the role of conscious thoughts, including our own beliefs in our abilities, or self-efficacy.

Personality Assessment Tools

Personality assessment tools, also called personality tests by the layperson, can be used both to help diagnose psychological problems as well as assess people applying for jobs or colleges or who are involved with the court system. These tools generally fall into two different categories: self-report assessments and projective assessments. Self-report assessments have the participant choose from set options. These can be true/false, a Likert scale (rating from strongly agree to strongly disagree), or multiple choice. Projective assessments require the participant to produce a response to an ambiguous prompt, such as a picture or an incomplete sentence. Projective assessments require much more input from the evaluator and often rely on the evaluator's interpretation of the participant's responses.

The Minnesota Multiphasic Personality Inventory (MMPI) is perhaps the most widely utilized assessment that assesses multiple dimensions of personality. A self-report assessment, it uses true/false questions and takes 1 to 2 hours to complete. The MMPI was originally developed to measure psychopathology. The first MMPI was published in 1942. The MMPI-2 is the updated version that came out in 1989; there is also a shorter version, the MMPI-2-RF, which takes about half the time to complete. It is now used widely in not only therapeutic assessment but also in screening candidates for jobs and for college and career counseling. The domains that the MMPI assesses are hypochondriasis, depression, hysteria, psychopathy, masculinity versus femininity, paranoia, psychasthenia, schizophrenia, hypomania, and social introversion. The MMPI can also be used to assess the big five personality traits (i.e., aggressiveness, psychoticism, disconstraint, neuroticism, and introversion).

An example of a projective assessment is the Rorschach Inkblot Test, created by 1921 by Hermann Rorschach. The participant is shown images of inkblots and is asked what they see in them. The evaluator can then interpret the participant's response and determine what unconscious feelings or thoughts the participant has revealed. The participant is taken through the inkblots twice and is asked to give a detailed response to explain his/her first impression of each one. The Rorschach test has been found to be useful to measure anxiety, psychosis, and depression. Evaluators for the Rorschach test must have proper training and experience to correctly interpret test results. The scoring system that has been developed for the Rorschach test is the Exner scoring system and is used to code the participant's responses for the following characteristics:

- Form
- Movement
- Chromatic color
- Achromatic color
- Shading-texture
- Shading-dimension
- Shading-diffuse
- Form dimension
- Pairs and reflections

A similar test is the Thematic Apperception Test (TAT), developed by Henry Murray and Christiana Morgan in the 1930s. The participant taking the TAT is shown eight to 12 pictures and is asked to tell a story about each one. The pictures are ambiguous and can be interpreted many ways. The evaluator gleans insight into the participant through the stories that the participant tells. The participant reveals interests, hopes, fears, and goals in the stories. Both the Rorschach and the TAT tests rely on the professional judgment of the evaluators, but the TAT test does not have a formal scoring system like the Exner system of the Rorschach.

Attribution

Attribution in social psychology is how individuals attach meaning to others' behavior or their own. It is the process through which a person explains the causes of behavior and events. One way to categorize the types of attribution is internal versus external. In internal attribution, or personal attribution, the cause of the behavior in question is credited to the person's characteristics such as personality, efforts, ability, mood, attitudes, or disposition. For external, or situational attributions, the cause of the behavior in question is credited to the situation in which the behavior was seen (e.g., task, other people, or luck). In other words, external attribution proposes that the individual produces the behavior because of the surrounding environment or social situation, whereas internal attribution proposes that a person's behavior is due to his/her own characteristics. These two attribution types cause different perceptions of the person engaging in a behavior.

When people seek to find rationale for behaviors, they are likely to become ensnared with biases and errors. Some examples of such attributional biases follow.

Fundamental Attribution Error and Self-Serving Bias

The fundamental attribution error is most noticeable when people explain and assume others' behavior. It is the habit to explain a person's behavior based on internal factors (such as character or intention) and disregard external factors (such as situational influences). It is more common for a person to exaggerate the influence of internal factors on others' behavior and ignore the situational context. In contrast, when evaluating one's own behavior, it is more common for a person to exaggerate situational factors when there is a negative outcome and dispositional factors when there is a positive outcome. This is also known as self-serving bias.

Dispositional Attribution

Dispositional attribution describes a person's tendency to attribute people's behavior to internal factors, such as personality, character, and ability. For example, when encountering a rude worker, a customer may decide that the worker is simply a bad person, not taking into account all the events and factors that may have led to the worker being rude in that moment. Dispositional attribution is attributing the worker's behavior to his/her personality instead of considering situational factors that may have contributed.

Cultural Bias

Cultural bias occurs when someone makes an assumption about the actions of another based on his/her own cultural beliefs and practices. People from individualist cultures, such as those of Anglo-Saxon European descent, generally value individuals' personal goals and independence, whereas those from collectivist cultures emphasize membership in families, tribes, nations, and other groups over individuality. Collectivist cultures value conformity and interdependence more than independence. The type of culture a person comes from (individualist or collectivist) affects how one makes attributions. People from individualist cultures are more likely to make fundamental attribution errors (attributing someone's behavior on internal factors), whereas collectivist cultures tend to attribute a person's behavior more to external factors. Also, those from individualist cultures utilize self-serving bias more than collectivist cultures. This is the tendency to attribute success to internal factors and failure to external factors. The reverse is typical of those from collectivist cultures. Called the self-effacing bias, a person is more likely to attribute success to externalities and failure on internalities (the individual).

Just-World Hypothesis

The just-world hypothesis is an example of defensive attribution, which refers to a set of beliefs an individual holds to defend his/herself from concerns that he or she will be the cause or victim of some misfortune. In the just-world hypothesis, good things happen to good people, and bad things happen to bad people. This perspective helps people avoid feeling vulnerable to situations over which they have no control. It can lead to victim blaming, even in catastrophic situations. For example, after a car accident, others may conclude that a person was at fault, even when little information is available. This allows them to believe it is something that they will not "allow" to happen to them.

Actor/Observer Difference

Individuals are more likely to attribute the behavior of other people to their dispositional factors and their own behavior to situational factors. The same behavior can be attributed differently depending on the person's role—as actor or observer. When individuals observe other people (especially those they do not know well), they are more likely to focus on the person, whereas when the same individuals are actors, they tend to focus on situational factors. An example is scoring poorly on a test. An individual is more likely to attribute his/her own poor score to situational factors (e.g., lack of sleep, illness, or teacher asking about material not covered in class) but is more likely to attribute others' poor scores to internal factors (laziness or inattentiveness).

Cognitive Dissonance

Cognitive dissonance is the psychological stress or mental discomfort a person experiences when he/she simultaneously holds contradictory beliefs, values, or ideas. Cognitive dissonance occurs when a person performs an action that contradicts his/her personal beliefs, values, and ideals or when he/she is confronted with new information that contradicts these same beliefs, values, and ideals. The level of dissonance experienced depends on factors including how highly a belief is valued and how much the beliefs/behaviors are inconsistent. More personal beliefs and the importance of the beliefs tend to result in greater dissonance. The greater that the dissonance is, the more pressure the individual will feel to relieve the feelings of discomfort. The three key ways to reduce cognitive dissonance are as follows:

- Focus on more supportive beliefs that outweigh the dissonant belief or behavior. For example, a person who works sitting at a desk all day learns that sitting for long periods of time is linked to a shortened life span. He/she may seek out other information that disputes this link.
- Reduce the importance of a conflicting belief. In the same example as described, the person may justify his/her behavior (prolonged sitting) by believing that other healthy behaviors make up for his/her sedentary lifestyle.
- Change the conflicting belief so that it is consistent with other beliefs or behaviors. This can be the most difficult strategy, particularly in the case of deeply held values.

Attitude

Attitude means a set of beliefs, behaviors, and emotions toward something or someone. Attitudes are enduring (although change is possible) and are often the result of upbringing or experience. They have a powerful influence over one's behavior. An attitude is a learned tendency to evaluate things in a certain way. The components that make up attitudes include the affective, the behavioral, and the cognitive. They can be explicit or implicit—conscious or unconscious—but they all affect our beliefs and behavior.

Attitudes can change through the same influences that lead to their formation. Classical conditioning, operant conditioning, and observational learning can all form or change one's attitudes. Cognitive dissonance (see pervious section) can also lead to change in attitude. People make changes to reduce the discomfort coming from incompatible beliefs. People can also be persuaded to change their attitudes both through message and messengers. Messages can appeal to one's logic or emotions. The characteristics of the person bringing the message can also lead to a shift in attitude, although this tends to be more temporary.

Stereotypes, Prejudice, and Discrimination

Prejudice is an unjustified or incorrect attitude toward an individual based solely on the individual's membership of a group (e.g., race, sex, national origin, religion, etc.). Discrimination involves actions that occur when this attitude is acted upon. An example of discrimination is different standards (consciously or unconsciously) for male and female students. Stereotypes are fixed, overgeneralized beliefs about a group or class of people. Stereotypes are a way that people simplify the world; they reduce the amount of processing (thinking) necessary when meeting a new person. Stereotyping leads one to infer a whole range of abilities and characteristics that one assumes all members of a certain group have.

Group Dynamics

The study of how different groups interact with each other and how individuals behave in groups is called group dynamics. Group dynamics looks at the processes of groups, including membership, influence, conflict, communication, leadership, and teamwork. In addition, group dynamics also examines how groups change over time and how individual people change within groups. Group dynamics are essential to understanding social prejudice and discrimination. The three primary components that affect how well a group works together are personal factors, leadership factors, and environmental factors.

Groupthink

Irving Janis formulated the groupthink model in the early 1970s. Groupthink occurs in groups of people and is a phenomenon in which the need for conformity in the group leads to dysfunctional or irrational decision-making. According to Janis, the eight symptoms of groupthink are the following:

- Illusions of invulnerability leads to overly optimistic risk taking.
- Unquestioned beliefs result in ignoring of consequences and possible moral problems.
- Rationalizing keeps members from re-evaluating their beliefs and can cause them to ignore warning signs.
- Stereotyping leads to ignoring or demonizing those who oppose or challenge the group's ideas.
- Self-censorship causes members who have doubts to hide their fears or misgivings.
- Mindguards are members or leaders who hide problematic information from the group.
- Illusions of unanimity are the belief that everyone is in agreement.
- Direct pressure to conform leads to those who question the group to being seen as disloyal.

Conformity

Conformity describes the tendency that people have to match their speech and actions to that of those around them. People can conform due to either overt social pressure or to unconscious influence of the group. There are many factors that influence the likelihood of conformity including size of the group, how clear or ambiguous the situation is, whether a person comes from an individualistic culture or a collectivist culture, how difficult a task is, how important a task is, and individual personality differences. As people grow older, they are less likely to conform, although we see conformity at all ages.

Sometimes people outwardly conform to the group but privately disagree. This is called compliance and is motivated by a desire for approval by the group. Identification describes a situation in which a person conforms to someone he/she respects and admires. Identification reflects a deeper conformity than compliance. The deepest form of conformity is internalization. Internalization occurs when the individual takes on the group's beliefs as his/her own; there is no difference between the public performance of the norm and the individual's private thoughts.

There are different types of conformity. A desire to fit in with the group and avoid rejection leads to normative conformity. This may lead to a weaker conformity (i.e., compliance) with the individual privately opposing the views of the group. Informational conformity stems from an individual's lack of knowledge and desire for guidance from the group. Informational conformity often leads to internalization, which is a stronger form of conformity.

Deindividuation

Deindividuation is the loss of self-awareness in groups. It occurs when a person loses his/her sense of individual identity. An example can be seen when a person who normally refrains from aggression displays aggressive behavior in an aggressive crowd. People in crowds can feel anonymous and have lessened awareness of individuality. This can reduce their sense of guilt and fear of punishment. This increases with the size of the crowd. Another example is that warriors who disguise their appearance (e.g., through face paint) tend to be more aggressive. Aggression in crowds can be reduced when there are obvious CCTV cameras at crowded events (such as sporting events). Deindividuation can also lead to pro-social behavior, for example, in religious gatherings. Not all people are negatively (or positively) affected by crowds as deindividuation does not affect everyone the same way.

Diffusion of Responsibility

Researchers have found that individuals are less inclined to act or intervene when they are with a large group. If someone has a medical issue on a sidewalk and obviously needs help, those around will be less likely to help if there is a large crowd of people there versus if there are just one or two. This may seem counterintuitive, but due to the presence of so many others, no single person feels compelled to respond—the feeling of responsibility has been diffused among all of the people in the crowd. Diffusion of responsibility causes the bystander effect described previously (the greater number of people present, the less likely anyone will help someone who needs it).

When bystanders actually know the person in distress, they are more likely to help. Bystanders are less likely to help in an ambiguous situation—if they are unsure about what is happening, if the person really needs help, or what should be done. If the distressed person makes eye contact with someone in the crowd and asks for help, that individual will be more likely to help.

Persuasion

Persuasion is a process through which one tries to convince others, without coercion, to change the way they think or behave. Persuasion takes place through straightforward methods and also through manipulation and deceit. Techniques can appeal to either one's logic or emotions. Robert Cialdini describes six different types of persuasion, which he calls weapons of influence. These "weapons" are as follows:

- *Reciprocity*—wanting to return a favor that has been done for you
- *Commitment/consistency*—the idea that people are more likely to follow through when they have committed to something
- *Social proof*—seeing others do something leading one to being willing to do it him/herself

- *Authority*—people trusting those they see as being knowledgeable and trustworthy
- *Liking*—people being more likely to be persuaded by someone they like
- *Scarcity*—limited availability making things more desirable

Methods of persuasion include the following:

- *Foot in the door*—people often feel obligated to comply with bigger requests if they first comply with a small request. The smaller request serves as an opening to the persuader.
- *Door in the face*—this is the opposite of the foot-in-the-door technique. The persuader makes a large request that is denied. The persuader then makes a much smaller request that is now more likely to be granted.
- *Ingratiation*—the persuader tries to acquire the approval of the other person, which makes them more likely to grant a request. Flattery is a form of ingratiation, as are opinion conformity (revising one's opinion to match the other person's) and self-presentation (presenting oneself in a pleasing way).
- *Low ball*—this is changing the price at the last moment from a lower price to a higher one. One may be more likely to go along with the change if it seems an agreement was already reached.
- *Norm of reciprocity*—if the persuader has already done something for the other person, he/she is more likely to comply with the persuader's request.

Obedience

Obedience occurs when one complies with a direct order or request, as opposed to conformity, which occurs through social pressure. The individual giving the order to be obeyed generally has some authority or a higher social status. Conformity relates to one's relationship to peers and the desire for social acceptance.

In the 1950s psychologist Stanley Milgram set up experiments to determine how obedient to authority most people are. Milgram was inspired by the trial of the Nazi Adolf Eichmann, who claimed he was only following orders and felt no guilt for his actions as he was only doing what his superiors requested. Milgram wanted to find out how far most people would go under the pressure to obey. Milgram placed participants in a room and instructed them to deliver electrical shocks to another person in another room. The person receiving the shocks was a part of the experiment and did not receive shocks but acted out the responses to the imaginary shocks. Milgram found that 65% of participants were willing to give the highest level of shocks when instructed to by the experimenter.

Following Milgram's experiments, psychologist Philip Zimbardo staged an experiment in the 1970s to study prisoners and prison life. He set up a "prison" and assigned participants in the study to play the roles of either prisoners or prison guards. Zimbardo himself acted as prison warden. The study was meant to last 2 weeks, but Zimbardo discontinued it after only 6 days. The participants had become so involved in their roles, and the guards were using authoritarian techniques to gain the prisoners' obedience. Some guards subjected prisoners to psychological abuse, harassment, and even physical torture. The results of the Stanford Prison experiment demonstrate how easily individuals are influenced by the roles they are asked to play and the situations they are put in.

Interpersonal Relationships

Interpersonal attraction refers to how much people are drawn to one another, either for romantic relationships or friendships. There are multiple factors affecting interpersonal attraction. One is simply proximity, or how physically close one person is to another. It is more likely that a person will form relationships with others who are nearby (i.e., same state, same city, or same part of town) than with those who are farther away. This idea is called the proximity principle. Propinquity is another factor that affects attraction; it refers to how often or how frequently one comes into physical contact with another person (or thing or idea). This frequency leads to increased familiarity with the other, which in turn leads to being more likely to like the other person, thing, or idea. This concept, that the more someone is exposed to something, the more they are attracted to it, is referred to as the mere exposure effect.

Another factor to attraction is similarity. People tend to be attracted more to others who are similar to them in some way. This may be in family background, level of physical attractiveness, political orientation, personal style, values, or manner of communication. People tend to view those like themselves more favorably and those who are different from them more negatively.

Motivation

Motivation is the reason behind a person's actions; it is why someone does what he/she does. Motivation can be either intrinsic or extrinsic. Intrinsic motivation comes from within the person and is focused on a person's interest or enjoyment of the activity and not on rewards or outer pressures. Extrinsic motivation is stimulated by other people or consequences outside of the individual person. A commonplace example of extrinsic motivation is the promise of a reward or the threat of a punishment. Rewards can be an effective way to motivate someone who does not have intrinsic motivation for the task at hand; however, overuse of rewards can lead to even less intrinsic motivation in a process called overjustification. (Research shows that some rewards are more likely to produce this effect than others.) Likewise, threat of punishment can often lead to increased interest in the forbidden activity or object. Because of these challenges with extrinsic motivation, many teachers and leaders wish to increase intrinsic motivation rather than focusing on extrinsic rewards and punishments. Ways to increase intrinsic motivation include an element of challenge in the task, having some control over what activities or tasks one engages in, curiosity about the activity or task, cooperation and competition, and having others recognize one's accomplishments.

Drive Reduction Theory

Clark Hull asserted that all motivation stems from the biological need to maintain homeostasis. Homeostasis is equilibrium: neither too hot nor too cold, neither too hungry nor too full. To maintain homeostasis, the body acts and responds in ways to balance itself. Hull called the tensions that come from an imbalance in homeostasis drives. According to Hull, drives serve as motivation for behavior. A person will seek to reduce any drives; for example, hunger will motivate a person to eat and thirst will motivate a person to drink. Satisfying the drive will then reinforce those behaviors, and the person will be more likely to engage in the same behavior when the drive presents itself in the future (i.e., conditioning).

One criticism of drive reduction theory is that it does not explain behaviors that do not address a drive. Many people eat when they are not hungry, which this theory cannot explain. Additionally, the theory does not adequately address secondary reinforcers and how they affect motivation. Secondary reinforcers do not meet physiological needs. Money is a secondary reinforcer; on its own it does not reduce hunger, but it can be used to purchase food and reduce the hunger drive indirectly. Despite not directly reducing drives, secondary reinforcers are still powerful motivators (e.g., money or pleasurable experiences). Although it later fell out of favor, drive reduction theory had a great influence on how many psychologists viewed motivation. Many later theories either expand on drive reduction theory or present an alternative viewpoint to it.

Incentive Theory

Although drive reduction theory focuses on one's biological needs as motivation for behavior, incentive theory asserts that external rewards are the primary motivation for action. There are some similarities between incentive theory and operant conditioning, in which the subject performs behavior to avoid punishment or to achieve rewards/reinforcement. In the case of incentive theory, however, the desire for the reward comes first, whereas in operant conditioning, the subject learns of the consequence of his/her actions only afterward. Compared to drive reduction theory, incentive theory works in the opposite way. Drive reduction theory posits that the individual seeks to remove an uncomfortable stimulus (e.g., hunger or pain), whereas incentive theory posits that the individual is motivated by a desire to add a positive stimulus.

Another response to drive reduction theory is Maslow's theory of the hierarchy of needs. This is discussed in great detail in a previous section.

Homeostasis

As mentioned in the section on drive reduction theory, homeostasis describes the need of an organism to maintain a certain stability. Homeostasis requires that the organism have a set point (e.g., for temperature, energy level, weight, etc.), an ability to determine if it is or isn't currently at the set point, and physiological and behavioral responses that will help revert to the set point.

Internal and External Cues

Internal, or physiological cues (such as hunger, thirst, or desire) direct us to eat, drink, and pursue sex, but this is only one type of cue. Other cues can also influence a person to eat, even without the physiological signals to do so. External cues can be either sensory or normative. External sensory cues include taste, smell, the way something looks, or even a written description. External normative cues look to consumption norms and expectations of the culture. In our culture, it is expected that people finish the food on their plates, so larger portion sizes can lead to people eating more. In the United States we tend to have larger portion sizes, from candy bars, to soft drinks, to yogurt cartons, which leads to our eating more than our counterparts in other countries. Social cues are another external cue that signals to us that it is time to eat or drink (e.g., eating or drinking with others). Stress also leads people to pursue food or other things without the physiological need for them. Stress tends to change a person's appetite, whether increasing or decreasing it.

In the brain the hypothalamus acts as the link between the neurological system and the endocrine system. When part of the hypothalamus is stimulated a person will feel hunger, thirst, and so on. It also helps the body maintain its set point for weight and sends fewer hunger cues when the body goes above its set point (and likewise sends more hunger cues when the body falls below its set point). The hypothalamus manages these internal cues, but an individual may not pay attention to them and may instead be distracted by external cues for eating or drinking.

Social Motives

The Five Core Social Motives model was developed by Susan Fiske and summarizes social motivations that affect a person's behavior. The five motives are belonging, understanding, controlling, enhancing self, and trusting. According to this system, the root need is belonging, and all others work to facilitate social functioning in groups. Fiske describes the five motives as follows:

> *Belonging*—people are motivated to bond and affiliate with one another
>
> *Understanding*—to belong, people are motivated to create sufficient shared social understanding

Controlling—people are motivated to feel effective and competitive in both animate and inanimate environments

Enhancing self—people hope that others see them as socially worthy

Trusting—when people view the world as benevolent, they are able to participate in group activities without unnecessary suspicion or vigilance

Theories of Emotion

The James–Lange theory of emotion asserts that the physiological effect comes first and leads to the perception of emotion. Although not working together, both psychologist William James and physiologist Carl Lange, although working separately, proposed that emotions are the result of physical experiences and that the person then interprets the physical experience to determine he/she is feeling an emotion. For example, if a person sees a threat, such as a vicious dog or a bear, he/she will exhibit physiological symptoms—perhaps quickened breath and heartbeat or trembling. The brain then interprets these physical occurrences as the emotion one is feeling—in this case, fear. Expectedly, the James–Lange theory has been met with challenges since it was first asserted. James himself acknowledged that his theory is counterintuitive.

In response to the James–Lange theory, Walter Cannon and Philip Bard developed their own theory of emotion, known as the Cannon–Bard theory or the thalamic theory of emotion. Their theory asserts that the physiological response and the emotional response occur simultaneously; one does not lead to the other. Cannon conducted experiments on the connection between the viscera (internal organs) and emotions. He found that separating the viscera from the central nervous system (by cutting the neural connection) does not change the individual's emotional response. This contradicts the James–Lange theory's assertion that the viscera are responsible for emotions. Cannon also found that the same reactions in the viscera can be seen in both emotional and nonemotional states (such as illness). Finally, Cannon determined that artificially stimulating changes in the viscera (like one would have during an emotional experience) does not produce emotions. The Cannon–Bard theory asserts that both the physiological response and the emotional response are due to the thalamus being stimulated (e.g., from seeing something threatening).

Another theory that seeks to explain the process of emotion relating to physical arousal is the Schachter–Singer Two Factor theory. Stanley Schachter and Jerome Singer asserted that two factors interact and result in an emotion. The theory purports that after experiencing a stimulus, the individual will have a physiological response, which will be cognitively interpreted based on context. A person's past experiences and existing knowledge help form the cognitive interpretations. Schachter and Singer conducted experiments in which they injected subjects with epinephrine (adrenaline). Some subjects were told what side effects they might experience, and others were not. Some subjects were placed with another person who either acted angry or euphoric. Schachter and Singer hypothesized that for the subjects who did not know to expect the side effects of the adrenaline (i.e., arousal), they would seek to explain their physiological state through context and would be more influenced by the person they were with who was in a euphoric or angry state. They found their experiment to support their hypothesis, but there has been later criticism of their theory including that emotions may be experienced before one thinks about them at times.

A final theory of emotion is *the facial feedback hypothesis*. This theory asserts that facial movement can influence emotional experience. The most common example used is that a person who is forced to smile during an unpleasant event will actually find the event more enjoyable. Among the first to suggest that physiological changes can have an impact on an emotion rather than just being the consequence of that emotion was Charles Darwin. He contended that the very expression of an emotion intensifies it and that even the imitation of an emotion can provoke it in one's mind. Later William James wrote, "Refuse to express a passion, and it dies." About a century after Darwin, the facial feedback hypothesis was developed. Modern research primarily focuses on the effects of facial muscular activity. There are two versions of the facial feedback hypothesis. The weak version, which Darwin introduced, is that the physical feedback intensifies or reduces an emotion already present. The strong version of this hypothesis alleges that facial feedback on its own can create the whole emotion.

Role of the Limbic System in Emotions

The entire central nervous system helps control emotions, but the limbic system and autonomic nervous system are especially influential. The limbic system makes up a curved border around the cerebral cortex and the diencephalon. The entire limbic system, which includes the hippocampus, hypothalamus, and amygdala, helps control many emotional, voluntary, endocrine, and visceral responses to the environment. The limbic system is believed to be one of the oldest and most primitive areas of the brain, and similar systems are also found in most other animals, including reptiles. Whereas the limbic system, as a whole, controls what is basically termed *emotions*, the hippocampus helps the brain form and retain memories, which have a central role in learning and development.

There is not 100% consensus regarding which specific brain structures are part of the limbic system. There is much neural overlap among areas of the brain, and so it is difficult to perfectly classify cortical areas. Most scientists consider the limbic system to be made up of the following:

- *Hippocampus*—associated with memory, focus, and motor control
- *Amygdala*—associated with fear and anxious emotions
- *Hypothalamus*—responsible for regulating hormones and maintaining homeostasis
- *Septal nuclei*—connected to pleasure and learning through reinforcement and/or reward
- *Cingulate cortex*—involved with memory and emotion
- Parahippocampal gyrus—helps with memory
- *Mammillary bodies*—connected to the amygdale and hippocampus
- *Fornix*—connects other parts of the brain, including the hippocampus and mammillary bodies

Functions of the limbic system include the following:

- Controlling emotions such as anger and fear
- Regulating eating, hunger, and thirst
- Responding to pleasure and pain
- Controlling the autonomic nervous system (i.e. pulse, blood pressure, breathing, and arousal)
- Sensing sexual satisfaction
- Controlling violent or aggressive behavior
- Responding to sensory information, in particular the sense of smell

Fight-or-Flight Response

Stress is the physiological and psychological response produced when a person experiences something unpleasant or circumstances requiring change and adaptation. Often the person feels strained by the stressor and may even worry that he/she does not have the ability or resources to deal with it.

The fight-or-flight response is also known as hyperarousal or the acute stress response. It is a physiological reaction in response to a perceived threat and is a general discharge of the sympathetic nervous system, which prepares the person or animal for either fighting or fleeing. The physiological changes that occur in the body during the fight-or-flight response are meant to give the body increased speed and strength. There is increased blood flow to the muscles, which is diverted blood flow from other parts of the body. Blood pressure, heart rate, blood sugars, and fats increase to supply the body with extra energy that may be needed. Blood clotting speeds up to prevent excessive blood loss in case of an injury. Increased muscle tension provides extra speed and strength. Physical signs of fight-or-flight that may be apparent to others include rapid heart rate and breathing, pale or flushed skin, dilated pupils, and trembling. After the stressor is gone, it takes the body between 20 and 60 minutes to return to its pre-arousal state. The fight-or-flight response is part of the first stage of general adaptation syndrome.

Selye's General Adaptation Syndrome

Hans Selye's theory describing the stress response among vertebrates is known as the general adaptation syndrome. This model is also called the classic stress response and revolves around the concept of homeostasis. The three stages of general adaptive syndrome are the alarm reaction, the stage of resistance, and the stage of exhaustion.

The alarm reaction occurs when the stressor first appears and the body gathers resources to deal with it. The pituitary gland begins releasing hormones (adrenaline, cortisol, and norepinephrine) into the bloodstream. These hormonal changes increase energy levels and muscle tension, reduce pain sensitivity, slow down the digestive system, and cause blood pressure to rise. In the stage of resistance, the body continues to build up resistance until either the physical resources are depleted or the stressful stimulus is removed. When the body uses up increasing amounts of its resources, the individual becomes increasingly tired and vulnerable to illness. Psychosomatic disorders first begin to appear in the stage of resistance. In the stage of exhaustion, the body is completely drained of resources and the hormones it was using to manage the stressor. The individual will now exhibit behaviors like irritability, avoidance of responsibilities and relationships, anxiety, poor judgment, and self-destructive behavior.

Effect of Stress on Immune System and Cardiovascular Health

The high level of arousal that humans experience when dealing with daily problems and micro-stressors is often unnecessary. Experiencing this level of arousal on a regular basis is associated with many health issues. The constant hormonal upheaval of chronic stress leads to serious health problems like hypertension, diabetes, and heart disease. Ongoing stress is so damaging because, during the stress response, the hormones that get us ready for emergencies also severely depress our immunity and reduce the immune system's ability to fight off antigens. As an example, cortisol decreases inflammation but also decreases white blood cells and NK cells that kill cancer, increases tumor development and growth, and increases the rate of tissue damage and infection. Stress effects are cumulative and build on themselves day by day.

Researchers have found links between stress and headaches, infectious illness, cardiovascular disease, diabetes, asthma, and gastric ulcers. As stress increases the heart rate and raises blood pressure, hypertension becomes more likely. Hypertension is a major risk factor in coronary heart disease. Stress increases blood cholesterol levels through the release of free fatty acids by adrenaline and noradrenaline. Increased cholesterol buildup leads to a raised heart rate. High blood pressure can lead to lesions on artery walls, in which cholesterol tends to get trapped.

Indirectly, stress affects the immune system when individuals use unhealthy coping strategies to deal with stress, such as alcohol or tobacco use, poor diet and lack of exercise due to lack of time, lack of sleep, and others.

Non-Physiological Effects of Stress

Reactions to stress are not only physical but can also be seen in effects on one's cognition, behavior, and emotions. Cognitive signs of stress include mental slowness, confusion, general negativity, persistent worrying, racing thoughts, difficulty concentrating and forgetfulness, and a general sense of overwhelm. Emotional signs of stress include irritability, frustration, overexcitability, feeling overwhelmed and overworked, feeling of helplessness, and apathy. Behavioral indications of stress include a sense of loneliness, decreased sex drive, decreased contact with family and friends, and avoiding others and social isolation.

Without satisfactory methods for handling stress, it can lead to a heightened sense of dysfunction. This can result in increased anxiety or depression, which if they persist for long periods of time, may require professional help to address them. Escalated stress and anxiety without a sufficient coping system are linked to multiple conditions, often accompanied by psychological distress. These include sleepwalking and other sleep disorders, amnesia and other memory problems, generalized anxiety disorder, obsessive-compulsive disorders, phobias, multiple personality, or hypochondriasis.

Sources of Stress

One particular type of stress is role conflict. This occurs when incompatible demands are placed upon a person so that fulfillment of both would be difficult if not impossible. Role conflict occurs when a person tries to respond simultaneously to the demands of different positions one holds (i.e., parent and employee). Role conflict can be experienced for either short or long periods of time and can be situational.

Another significant stressor is caregiver burden. This is an all-encompassing term that describes the physical, financial, and emotional toll of providing care for another person. Caregivers are nonprofessionals who give support and help to family members or others who need regular care. Caregiver burden is a subjective burden; how the caregiver perceives the situation determines the amount of caregiver burden. Four aspects of caregiving that can cause particular strain are having too little time for the caregiver's interests, sadness over the prognosis of the person they are supporting, too much energy being expended for care, and desire for recovery.

Another, more complex source of stress stems from socioeconomic status (SES). This is partly due to the fact that the feeling of lack of control over one's circumstances tends to decline as one descends the socioeconomic ladder. Researchers have found that the more helpless one feels in the face of a given stressor, the more toxic that stressor's effects are. Those with the lowest SES are more than three times as likely to die prematurely as those at the top. For these people depression, heart disease, and diabetes are much more likely as well. This has been called status syndrome, describing the fact that the higher one is in the social hierarchy, the better his/her health is. Even those who experience poverty in childhood, but later attain higher SES, experience consequences of the poverty they experienced into later life. They are more prone to illness and chronic inflammation, which increases the risk of degenerative diseases. Having little to no control over one's circumstances, as those with low SES and more limited resources do, leads to a strain from learned helplessness. Learned helplessness can result from experiencing a fight-or-flight response that continues indefinitely. When this response is activated chronically, it ravages the body.

Strategies for Coping with Stress

Given all the physiological and nonphysiological effects of stress, it is worthwhile to know ways to manage one's stress and reduce its effects. There are multiple strategies that have been proven to reduce the body's stress response, some of which come from the cognitive-behavioral school of thought.

- *Diaphragmatic breathing*—also called deep breathing, this has a physiological effect on the nervous system by activating the hypothalamus, which connects to the pituitary gland, to send neuro-hormones that trigger a relaxation response in the body.
- *Progressive muscle relaxation*—in this exercise, a person alternates between tensing and relaxing different muscle groups throughout the body. A more complete relaxation of muscles is found this way.
- *Self-monitoring*—this is a way to manage stress and anxiety by bringing awareness to one's thoughts and feelings. It involves writing down whenever one has uncomfortable or unpleasant thoughts and feelings, also noting the situation that led up to the feelings and writing out the current emotions one is going through. Some people also rate their feelings on a scale based on how intense the feelings are.
- *Behavioral activation*—this is a strategy that teaches people to be more active in enjoyable and pleasurable areas of life through identifying goals. This increase in activity and connection can help with mood and stress management.
- *Cognitive restructuring*—this cognitive-behavioral coping strategy helps reduce cognitive distortions such as catastrophic thinking.
- *Perceived control*—this is the extent to which a person believes that he/she has control over a situation. It may help reduce stress and offer other health benefits; however, the loss of perceived control or the idea of control being overemphasized can have adverse consequences on health.

Abnormal Psychology

Psychological Disorders

Problems with mental health often have a variety of causes: genetic factors, environmental stresses, biochemical imbalances, or a combination. Mental illness is often physical as well as psychological and emotional. Researchers do not know the exact cause of most mental illnesses; however, it is becoming increasingly clear through increased study that a combination of many factors contributes to them. Although in the past it was believed that mental health problems were caused by personal weakness or defects of character, scientists now know that at their root are genetic, biological, environmental, and psychological causes.

Many mental illnesses seem to run in families. This suggests that they may be passed on from generation to generation genetically. This does not mean that a child of a person with mental illness will necessarily have one as well. Heredity in this case means that a person is more likely to have the condition than if he/she did not have an affected family member. Additionally, researchers have come to believe that many mental health conditions are linked to issues in multiple genes, not merely one. This helps explain why a person can inherit a susceptibility to a mental disorder, but the disorder doesn't always manifest itself. A combination of genes and other factors, including environmental stressors and psychological trauma, can trigger a mental illness in a person who has inherited susceptibility to it.

A link has been found between some mental illnesses and an abnormal balance of neurotransmitters, which are chemicals in the brain. Neurotransmitters assist in communication among brain cells, and if they are out of balance or aren't working as they should, this communication may break down. This can lead to symptoms of mental illness. In some cases, defects in or injury to the brain have been linked to some mental illnesses.

Common Symptoms of Mental Disorders

Generally speaking, one or two symptoms are not enough for a mental health diagnosis. Rather, those with mental illness typically present a collection of symptoms. These symptoms must be persistent and interfere with daily life and work. What follows is an educational and informational tool and is not a diagnostic instrument. Some general symptoms are associated with mental health problems and psychological disorders.

In adults we might see the following:

- Social withdrawal
- Prolonged depression (which can manifest as sadness or irritability)
- Excessive worries, anxieties, or fears
- Obvious changes in sleeping or eating habits
- Feelings of extremes—both highs and lows
- Confused thinking
- Strong anger
- Suicidal thoughts
- Delusions or hallucinations
- Substance abuse
- Increasing inability to cope with problems and activities of daily life

- Denial of obvious problems
- Unexplained physical ailments

In children or pre-adolescents, we might see the following:

- Changes in school performance
- Poor grades in spite of great effort
- Changes in sleeping and/or eating habits
- Persistent worry or anxiety
- Persistent disobedience, aggression, or defiance of authority
- Frequent temper tantrums
- Excessive complains of physical ailments
- Frequent outbursts of anger
- Inability to cope with daily activities and problems
- Persistent negative mood, sometimes accompanied by thoughts of death
- Hyperactivity
- Persistent nightmares

Major Categories of Mental Illnesses

There are many different types of mental illness as the definition is so broad. The most recent edition of the *Diagnostic and Statistical Manual of Mental Disorders* (DSM-5) divides mental illness into five different types. These five different types are collections of disorders based on developmental and life span factors as well as the nature of the disorders themselves. The five broad categories of the disorders described in the DSM-5 are as follows:

1. *Neurodevelopmental disorders*—these are brain and nervous system disorders that have their onset during the early stages of development.
2. *Internalizing disorders*—these primarily manifest internally; symptoms are turned inward within the person. These include anxiety disorders, depressive disorders, and sometimes eating disorders (which can also be externalizing).
3. *Externalizing disorders*—these manifest externally with the behaviors turned outward toward the world. These include conduct disorder, substance abuse, and the manic phase of bipolar disorder.
4. *Neurocognitive disorders*—disorders and diseases of the brain can contribute to a decline in cognitive processing and functioning.
5. *Other disorders*—these are other conditions that do not meet the required diagnostic criteria for a specific mental illness such as a mood or anxiety disorder; however, these do cause significant dysfunction and disruption.

These five categories are simply a framing device to help organize the many disorders that are covered in the DSM. What follows is further discussion of many of these disorders.

Neurodevelopmental Disorders

Neurodevelopmental disorders are usually diagnosed early in life—during infancy, childhood, or adolescence. They involve problems during development, particularly with the brain. Some examples of neurodevelopmental disorders include the following:

- *Attention deficit hyperactivity disorder (ADHD)*—constant and long-standing behavior pattern evidenced by problems with inattention, a tendency toward impulsiveness, and hyperactivity. These symptoms make it difficult for a person to perform appropriately in two or more areas of life, beginning before age 12.
- *Autism spectrum disorder*—consists of a wide array of symptoms affecting social interactions, communication, and behavioral patterns. It begins in early childhood and can cause repetitive or restrictive behavior, including compulsive behavior, repetitive movements, and resistance to change. Because it is a spectrum disorder, severity varies widely, and individuals may have different levels of functioning.
- *Intellectual development disorder*—individuals have low IQ levels (at or below 70, possibly as high as 75), problems with cognitive functioning, and limitations in basic life skills (i.e., self-care, social skills, etc.). The disorder begins before age 18 and sometimes goes along with other medical symptoms (syndromic, such as Down's syndrome) or without any other issues (non-syndromic). Previously this was referred to as mental retardation. Before the age of 5, children may be temporarily diagnosed with global developmental delay, until which time their IQ can be tested.
- *Other neurodevelopmental disorders*—these include learning disorders (also called learning disabilities), communication disorders (such as stuttering or language disorders), motor disorders, and traumatic brain injury.

Schizophrenia Spectrum and Other Psychotic Disorders

The primary symptom in this category is psychosis, or an episodic break from reality, primarily hallucinations (sensing things that are not there) and delusions (believing things that aren't true). Other symptoms include incoherent speech, abnormal reasoning, and social withdrawal. Examples of these disorders include delusional disorder, brief psychotic disorder, schizophrenia, and schizoaffective disorder.

Depressive Disorders

These disorders are characterized by prolonged depressed mood, loss of interest in activities, changes in appetite or weight, changes in sleeping habits, feelings of worthlessness, impaired memory or concentration, fatigue, and thoughts of suicide. Disorders in this category include major depressive disorder (both single episode and recurrent), persistent depressive disorder (dysthymia), and premenstrual depressive disorder.

Bipolar Disorder

In the past, bipolar disorder was called manic depression as those who have it experience shifts between depression and mania, which is marked by an elevated, even hyper mood and increased energy levels among other symptoms. People experiencing mania often act in risky ways that may have lasting consequences, such as gambling, sexual promiscuity, and uncontrolled spending, among others. Bipolar II disorder presents with a less severe form of mania called hypomania, along with depression. Those with bipolar can have episodes (of either depression or mania/hypomania) that last for months; they can cycle rapidly, experiencing multiple cycles during one day or anywhere in between.

ANXIETY DISORDERS

The disorders in this category cause distressing and frequent periods of fear and apprehension lasting 6 months or more. Symptoms include panic attacks, physical symptoms (nausea, pain, and headaches), obsessive thoughts, difficulty sleeping, nightmares, and fear of leaving the house. Examples of anxiety disorders include the following:

- *Generalized anxiety disorder*—a quite common disorder, particularly in older adults, it is marked by persistent and nonspecific anxiety and also excessive worry about everyday things. It can cause impairment in making regular decisions, difficulties with memory due to poor concentration, and also physical symptoms such as fatigue and sleep problems.
- *Panic disorder*—panic attacks are brief episodes of extreme fear and anxiety that often include physical symptoms such as difficulty breathing, dizziness, nausea, and so on. People with panic disorder experience panic attacks, often with no known trigger, and may live in dread of the next attack. People with panic disorder may spend much time and energy attempting to stave off attacks or avoid possible triggers. The panic attacks themselves become a source of anxiety.
- *Social anxiety disorder*—this disorder involves fear of social situations in which one may be watched, judged, and/or embarrassed. It can cause difficulties with making friends and can lead to social isolation when the person seeks to avoid the triggering situation (i.e., social situations).
- *Separation anxiety disorder*—although separation anxiety is normal in infants and children, an excessive or inappropriate anxiety upon separation from a caregiver or other person or place qualifies as a disorder. Both children and adults have this disorder, but it tends to be more severe in children.
- *Agoraphobia*—closely connected to panic disorder, people with agoraphobia have a fear of public spaces, or a place where they are unable to escape or get help. Panic attacks can trigger agoraphobia as the individual seeks to avoid activities or places where he/she may have an attack.
- *Specific phobias*—this is the largest category of anxiety disorders and involves fear of specific situations or things. People experience fear far out of proportion to the actual risk. Different types of phobias include those of natural events (such as storms), medical issues (such as certain procedures or instruments), animals (such as spiders or dogs), and situational (such as flying or enclosed spaces).

OBSESSIVE-COMPULSIVE AND RELATED DISORDERS

Disorders in this category are characterized by extreme recurrent thoughts or preoccupations that are connected to either mental or behavioral behaviors, which are done to alleviate the obsessions. In addition to obsessive-compulsive disorder, examples include hoarding disorder, body dysmorphic disorder, trichotillomania (hair-pulling disorder), and excoriation (skin picking disorder), among others.

TRAUMA- AND STRESSOR-RELATED DISORDERS

Disorders in this category were previously grouped with anxiety disorders but are now in a distinct category of their own. They involve exposure to a stressful or traumatic event and are mental disorders resulting from outside forces that impact or alter the brain itself. Examples include the following:

- *Reactive attachment disorder*—now subdivided into two distinct disorders, reactive attachment disorder and disinhibited social engagement disorder, both are caused when a child does not form a healthy attachment to his/her primary caregiver in the first few years of life. Symptoms of reactive attachment disorder include withdrawal and lack of social engagement, social and emotional disturbances, listlessness, and sadness. Disinhibited social engagement disorder causes a child to not have discomfort with strangers and not see the caregiver as a safe and secure person, which can lead to dangerous situations.
- *Adjustment disorder*—this is an abnormal response to a life stressor or sudden change, such as death of a loved one, divorce, job loss, or another setback. Despite struggling to adjust, the person experiences impacts in multiple areas of life, such as relationships and work.
- *Posttraumatic stress disorder (PTSD)*—following a disturbing and stressful life event (either experienced or witnessed), some people develop symptoms such as re-experiencing the event (i.e., flashbacks), negative thoughts and mood (i.e., depression), heightened arousal (i.e., hypervigilance and sleep disturbances), and avoidance. PTSD can greatly interfere with one's life, even leading to social isolation, substance abuse, and increased risk for suicide.
- *Acute stress disorder*—similar to PTSD, this disorder occurs 3 days to 1 month after the precipitating event. Some people with acute stress disorder go on to develop PTSD but not all.

Dissociative Disorders

Dissociation is a coping mechanism albeit a pathologic and involuntary one. After a stressful or traumatic situation (either repeated or a one-time incident), a person may experience a break in normal awareness and may have a changed sense of memory, consciousness, or even identity. These disorders are much more common than once thought, and they are frequently diagnosed as other disorders. Every area of cognitive functioning can be affected by dissociation. Types of dissociative disorders include the following:

- *Dissociative identity disorder*—formerly called multiple personality disorder and caused by repeated and continuing trauma occurring before age 9
- *Dissociative amnesia*—caused by a trauma or stressful event and now includes dissociative fugue
- *Depersonalization disorder*—characterized by feeling detached from one's own self or one's surroundings

Somatic Symptom and Related Disorders

Formerly called somatoform or somatization disorders, these involve physical symptoms for which there is no obvious physical or medical cause as well as distress in response to the symptoms. The diagnosis requires that the person have experienced the symptoms over at least 6 months (although not necessarily for the entire time). Forms of somatic symptom disorder include the following:

- *Somatic symptom disorder*—an individual has one or more symptoms that are disrupting normal functioning and cause great distress. Onset is usually before or by age 30.
- *Illness anxiety disorder*—involving a disproportionate worry about having an undiagnosed medical condition, individuals are often excessively preoccupied about how they feel and about their bodily functions. It was previously called hypochondriasis.

- *Conversion disorder*—this disorder involves actual neurologic symptoms such as blindness, paralysis, or numbness.
- *Factitious disorder*—this occurs when a person consciously creates symptoms for a physical or mental illness, such as by self-injury. Individuals do not create symptoms for any practical benefit, such as a lawsuit; instead the benefit is psychological—they need to be seen as sick or hurt. It was previously called Munchausen syndrome.
- *Factitious disorder imposed on another*—previously called Munchausen by proxy, this disorder involves claiming or causing injury or illness in another person, often a child or another dependent.

Feeding and Eating Disorders

Feeding and eating disorders describes conditions in which there is an extreme preoccupation with weight and food, and this preoccupation causes physical and mental health problems. These disorders often co-occur with anxiety disorders or obsessive compulsive disorder. These disorders can cause significant medical problems, including weakened bones, cardiovascular problems, dental problems due to binging, and even loss of brain mass. Proper nutrition is essential to life, and so these disorders can affect every part of a person's health. Types of eating and feeding disorders include the following:

- *Anorexia nervosa*—individuals with this disorder often believe themselves to be of a much higher weight than they actually are. Characterized by an extreme fear of being fat, anorexia nervosa can cause one to greatly restrict food intake, exercise obsessively, and even create bizarre and complex rules for oneself around eating and food.
- *Bulimia nervosa*—individuals with bulimia nervosa will eat large amounts of food and then engage in some activity to compensate for it. Many force themselves to vomit or abuse laxatives and diuretics; others exercise excessively.
- *Binge eating disorder*—this is the newest category of eating disorder but also thought to be the most common. Individuals with this disorder will eat an extremely large amount of food over a short period of time, often in response to an emotional state. Those who have this typically feel they have a lack of control around food and are caused great distress by their binging.
- *Pica*—most typical in children and people with developmental disabilities (although not exclusively), this disorder is characterized by eating nonfood substances such as dirt, paper, soap, chalk, and so on.
- *Rumination disorder*—individuals with this disorder regurgitate food they have just swallowed and re-chew it. They then either spit it out or re-swallow it. Like pica, it mostly occurs in children or adults with developmental disabilities. Because of the repeated regurgitation, individuals can develop serious dental problems and malnutrition, among other issues.

Disruptive, Impulse-Control, and Conduct Disorders

Individuals with disorders in this category are frequently unable to control their emotions or behaviors and experience disruption in multiple areas of their lives. Unlike most of the other disorders discussed here, individuals with these disorders direct their disruptive behavior toward others, often violating others' rights and experiencing great conflict with both peers and authorities.

Males are more likely to experience these types of disorders than females. Types of these disorders include the following:

- *Oppositional defiant disorder (ODD)*—this disorder begins in childhood or adolescence, before age 18. It is characterized by a chronic refusal to comply with rules and open defiance of authority figures. Individuals with ODD often blame others for problems they have caused and often seek to deliberately aggravate others.
- *Conduct disorder*—although similar to ODD, this is a more serious disorder and is characterized by more violent and aggressive behavior. Individuals with conduct disorder are more likely to be violent with people or animals and are more likely to destroy property, along with other violations of rules and norms. It can often lead to serious legal problems and great difficulties with forming healthy relationships.
- *Intermittent explosive disorder (IED)*—individuals with IED exhibit sudden bouts of unpremeditated rage and even violence disproportionate to the situation that prompts the explosion. It can begin in childhood, adolescence, or young adulthood and sometimes co-occurs with other disorders, such as bipolar disorder or anxiety disorders.
- *Kleptomania*—individuals with kleptomania have an uncontrollable urge to steal things, often unnecessary items of little value. Despite not wanting to steal, those with this disorder find themselves unable to resist the impulse to steal. Kleptomania can cause significant legal and social problems for these individuals.
- *Pyromania*—individuals with this disorder are preoccupied with setting fires and often endanger themselves and others. As with other impulse-control disorders, individuals with pyromania experience a building tension and then a release after setting a fire.

Substance-Related and Addictive Disorders

Substance-related disorders occur when a person's use of substances increases and begins to affect other areas of their life. These substances may be prescription, over-the-counter substances, legal recreational substances, or illegal recreational substances. These can include alcohol, opioids, hallucinogens, tobacco, and stimulants, among others. The DSM-5 also includes gambling in this addictive disorders category because gambling stimulates the same reward system in the brain that substance misuse does.

Neurocognitive Disorders

Previously referred to as dementia, neurocognitive disorders are characterized by a deterioration of mental abilities that impacts one's daily life. The DSM-5 describes these disorders as either minor or major, depending on their severity. Symptoms include difficulties with cognition, including memory, planning abilities, focusing, and social interactions. Alzheimer's is the largest category of these disorders, but there are multiple other disorders that affect cognitive functioning in a similar way. Some of these disorders also affect the body in other ways, including the ability to control motor skills. Neurocognitive disorders include the following:

- Alzheimer's disease
- Parkinson's disease
- Lewy body disease
- Frontotemporal degeneration
- Huntington's disease
- Prion disease
- Traumatic brain injury (TBI)
- Vascular disease
- Neurocognitive problems caused by HIV

Personality Disorders

The DSM-5 places personality disorders in a separate section than other mental illnesses due to there being a lack of consensus about the nature of these disorders. Personality disorders involve a rigid pattern of behaviors that is in conflict with cultural and social expectations. People with personality disorders exhibit destructive ways of thinking, behaving, and interacting with other people. Personality disorders can co-occur with other disorders, particularly substance abuse disorders and depression.

There are three groupings of personality disorders in the DSM-5. The first group or cluster includes personality disorders that involve eccentric or odd behavior and thinking. Cluster A includes the following:

- Paranoid personality disorder
- Schizoid personality disorder
- Schizotypal personality disorder

Cluster B includes personality disorders that involve erratic, unpredictable, and dramatic thoughts and behavior. Cluster B includes the following:

- Antisocial personality disorder
- Borderline personality disorder
- Histrionic personality disorder
- Narcissistic personality disorder

Cluster C includes personality disorders that involve anxious and fearful thoughts and behavior. Cluster C includes the following:

- Avoidant personality disorder
- Dependent personality disorder
- Obsessive compulsive personality disorder (differs from obsessive compulsive disorder)

Additional Disorders

Other disorders not included in these categories include the following:

- *Sleep-wake disorders*—the sleep-wake cycle is disrupted in some way, affecting how a person is able to function during waking hours.
- *Gender dysphoria*—a person experiences him/herself as a gender other than the one that was assigned to them at birth.
- *Sexual dysfunctions and disorders*—the prevent a person/couple from experiencing sexual pleasure and include arousal disorders, desire disorders, pain disorders, and orgasm disorders.
- *Paraphilic disorders*—these sexual behaviors (including fantasies) involve atypical situations or objects and cause distress or threaten the well-being of another person.
- *Elimination disorders*—these involve the passing of urine (*enuresis*) or feces (*encopresis*), deliberately or not, in an inappropriate way (into clothing, onto the bed or floor, etc.).

Utilizing the DSM-5

The newest version of the *Diagnostic and Statistical Manual of Mental Disorders* (DSM) is the DSM-5, published in 2013. Perhaps the most significant change to this version of the DSM is the discontinuation of the Axis system used in previous editions. Instead, the DSM-5 has 20 chapters of related disorders, arranged more or less in life-span fashion. The DSM-5 consists of three sections. The first provides an introduction to the edition and information about how it is organized. Also, in Section I is information about revisions, field trials, and reviews—public, professional, and expert. In Section II one can find the diagnostic criteria and codes. The coding in the DSM-5 is based on the *International Classification of Diseases, 9th edition, Clinical Modification* (ICD-9-CM) and takes into account the changes made in the ICD-10-CM. The disorders in Section II are summarized in previous sections. The third section deals with measures of assessment, cultural formulations, a glossary, and conditions that call for further study.

Treatment of Psychological Disorders

Psychologist and others who treat psychological disorders typically rely on one or more theoretical frameworks of psychotherapy. These frameworks serve as a type of road map for practitioners and guide them through the process of both understanding their clients and developing solutions. There are five broad categories or theoretical frameworks.

- *Psychoanalysis and psychodynamic therapies.* This framework centers on changing problematic feelings, thoughts, and behaviors through studying their unconscious motivations and meanings. In this approach there is a close working partnership between patient and therapist, and patients learn about themselves through exploring their interactions in this partnership.
- *Behavior therapy.* This method centers on the role of learning in developing behaviors, both normal and abnormal. Pavlov discovered classical conditioning, otherwise known as associative learning. Desensitizing can be called classical conditioning in action—a therapist can help a client work through a phobia or trauma through repeated exposure to the cause of the anxiety. E. L. Thorndike discovered operant conditioning, which relies on rewards and punishments to influence people's behavior. The most common current version of this therapy is cognitive-behavioral therapy, which focuses on both thoughts and behaviors of the patient.
- *Cognitive therapy.* This framework highlights what the patient thinks rather than what they do. Cognitive therapists believe that dysfunctional emotions or behaviors are a result of dysfunctional thinking. These practitioners seek to change their patients' thoughts and by so doing change how they feel and what they do.
- *Humanistic therapy.* This therapeutic approach focuses on a person's ability to make rational choices and develop to his/her maximum potential. Important themes in this framework include concern and respect for others. Key influences for this type of therapy include Jean-Paul Sartre, Martin Buber, and Soren Kierkegaard. There are three types of humanistic therapy that are especially influential: client-centered therapy, Gestalt therapy, and existential therapy.
- *Biological therapies.* This approach focuses on the biological causes of psychological disorders and seeks to eliminate or alleviate symptoms. Biological, or biomedical, therapies are often used in conjunction with psychotherapy. Many practitioners assert that biomedical approaches can enhance the effectiveness of other therapeutic approaches in many cases. The three primary forms of biomedical therapies are pharmacotherapy, or the use of medications in biomedical treatment; electroconvulsive therapy (ECT), or the use of electrical current in the brain; and psychosurgery, a type of neurosurgery in which a small piece of brain matter is destroyed or removed.

Antipsychotics

Antipsychotics are prescribed most often for the treatment of psychosis, such as in schizophrenia. Some side effects include drowsiness, restlessness, tremor, muscle spasms, dry mouth, and blurring of vision. A long-term side effect is tardive dyskinesia (TD), which is a disorder in which a person experiences involuntary movements most often in the mouth, lips, and tongue but sometimes other parts of the body. Typical antipsychotics include the following:

- Thorazine (chlorpromazine)
- Trilafon (perphenazine)
- Stelazine (trifluoperazine)
- Serentil (mesoridazine)
- Prolixin (fluphenazine)
- Navane (thiothixene)
- Moban (molindone)
- Mellaril (thioridazine)
- Loxitane (loxapine)
- Haldol (haloperidol)

There are also atypical antipsychotics whose side effects include dry mouth, blurred vision, constipation, dizziness, lightheadedness, and weight gain. They also sometimes can cause problems sleeping, fatigue, and weakness. Some atypical antipsychotics also have the long-term side effect of TD. Atypical antipsychotics include the following:

- Abilify (aripiprazole)
- Clozaril (clozapine)
- Geodon (ziprasidone)
- Risperdal (risperidone)
- Seroquel (quetiapine)
- Zyprexa (olanzapine)

ANTIDEPRESSANTS

Antidepressants are a large category of medications used to treat depression. There are several different types of antidepressants. Selective serotonin reuptake inhibitors (SSRIs) gradually increase the amount of the neurotransmitter serotonin in the brain. Side effects include nausea, diarrhea, insomnia, and fatigue. Examples of SSRIs include the following:

- Celexa (citalopram)
- Lexapro (escitalopram)
- Luvox (fluvoxamine)
- Paxil (paroxetine)
- Prozac (fluoxetine)
- Zoloft (sertraline)

Another category of antidepressants are monoamine oxidase inhibitors (MAOIs). These are less common than SSRIs, and are used to treat complex, treatment-resistant depression. Side effects include dry mouth, headache, nausea, insomnia, dizziness, low blood pressure, sexual side effects, and weight gain. Some examples of MAOIs include the following:

- Emsam (selegiline)
- Marplan (isocarboxazid)
- Nardil (phenelzine)
- Parnate (tranylcypromine)

Tricyclics (TCAs) are another type of antidepressant that isn't used much currently. Their side effects include a drop in blood pressure, sedation, dry mouth, blurred vision, dizziness, and weight gain. Some examples include the following:

- Anafranil (clomipramine)
- Asendin (amoxapine)
- Elavil (amitriptyline)
- Norpramin (desipramine)
- Pamelor (nortriptyline)
- Sinequan (doxepin)
- Surmontil (trimipramine)
- Tofranil (imipramine)
- Vivactil (protriptyline)

Serotonin norepinephrine reuptake inhibitors (SNRIs) are another type of antidepressant that works by slowly increasing the amount of norepinephrine in the brain. Side effects include nausea, somnolence, constipation, dry mouth, dizziness, nervousness, increased heart rate, hypertension, and sexual dysfunction. Examples include the following:

- Pristiq (desvenlafaxine)
- Effexor (venlafaxine)
- Cymbalta (duloxetine)

Anti-Anxiety Medications

Anti-anxiety medications are used to treat numerous chronic and acute anxiety issues. One type of these medications is benzodiazepines. Also known as tranquilizers, they work quickly and can be effective for panic attacks. They can be quite physically addictive and are not recommended for long-term treatment. Side effects of benzodiazepines include drowsiness, dizziness, poor balance and coordination, slurred speech, difficulty concentrating and memory problems, confusion, stomach upset, headache, and blurred vision. Examples of benzodiazepines include the following:

- Xanax (alprazolam)
- Klonopin (clonazepam)
- Valium (diazepam)
- Ativan (lorazepam)
- Librium (chlordiazepoxide)
- Serax (oxazepam)
- Tranxene (clorazepate)

Buspirone (BuSpar) is another, newer anti-anxiety medication that also acts as a mild tranquilizer. Buspirone is slower acting than benzodiazepines but is not as sedating and does not impair memory and coordination. It seems to work well for generalized anxiety disorder but not other types of anxiety disorders. Side effects include nausea, headaches, dizziness, drowsiness, weight gain, upset stomach, nervousness, constipation/diarrhea, and dry mouth.

Beta blockers are often used to treat the physical symptoms of anxiety, especially social anxiety. They are used to control rapid heartbeat, shaking, trembling, and blushing for several hours. They are generally safe for most patients and have few side effects; however, they sometimes cannot treat stronger symptoms enough to cause relief. They do lower blood pressure and slow heart rate. Examples of beta blockers used for anxiety are Inderal (propranolol) and Tenormin (atenolol).

STIMULANTS

Stimulants are typically prescribed to individuals with attention deficit hyperactivity (ADHD) as they help regulate disorganized thought processes. Side effects include appetite loss, sleep problems, and mood swings. Examples include the following:

- Adderall (amphetamine and dextroamphetamine)
- Dexedrine (dextroamphetamine)
- Ritalin (methylphenidate)
- Strattera (atomoxetine)
- Focalin (dexmethylphenidate)
- Vyvanse (lisdexamfetamine)

MOOD STABILIZERS

Mood stabilizers are a type of psychotropic medication that are typically used to treat intense, repeated shifts in a person's mood. They are commonly used for patients experiencing bipolar, schizophrenia, or borderline personality. Mood stabilizers help balance neurotransmitters in the brain, which control emotional states and behavior. They can be used to treat mania and to prevent a return of both manic and depressive episodes. Some of these medications are known as anticonvulsants as they are also used to treat some types of seizures. Side effects include nausea and stomach upset, trembling, increased thirst, weight gain, and drowsiness. Examples of mood stabilizers include the following:

- Lithium
- Lamictal (lamotrigine)
- Tegretol or Equetro (carbamazepine)
- Depakote (valproic acid)

TYPES OF MENTAL HEALTH PROFESSIONALS

Types of mental health professionals work with people dealing with psychological disorders and other mental health problems.

A psychiatrist is a medical doctor and is the only mental health professional who can prescribe medications (other than some psychiatric nurses). Other doctors also prescribe medications for mental health diagnoses, but they do not have specialized training in mental health. Most psychiatrists focus their practice on finding and prescribing the best medications to help their patients. There are a few who do psychotherapy as well.

Psychologists have a doctorate degree but are not medical doctors. Their degrees are usually either a PhD or a PsyD. PhD programs focus on either clinical or research work, and the amount of clinical experience a given psychologist has can vary greatly from program to program. In contrast, PsyD programs usually focus on clinical practice, and a psychologist with this degree will likely have thousands of hours of clinical experience before entering practice. Beyond clinical training and research, psychologists receive training in psychological assessment, diagnosis, and a wide variety of psychotherapies.

A clinical social worker has completed a master's degree in social work (MSW) program and may also carry the Licensed Clinical Social Worker (LCSW) designation, particularly if he/she is doing psychotherapy. MSW programs focus on direct work with clients and give their students many opportunities to do fieldwork. Requirements for LCSW certification require thousands of hours of direct clinical experience and passing a licensure exam.

Generally, psychiatric nurses first train to be a registered nurse (RN) and then go on to get specialized training in psychiatry and some forms of psychotherapy. They generally get up to 500 hours of direct clinical experience during their training. In many states psychiatric nurses also carry prescription privileges, and they can prescribe the same types of medications that a psychiatrist can.

Marriage and family therapists usually have a master's degree, although not all states require this. They generally have hundreds to thousands of hours of direct clinical experience. This designation varies widely from state to state; therefore, the quality of the work by each practitioner may also vary significantly from person to person.

A Licensed Professional Counselor (LPC) has completed a master's or doctoral degree and is trained to work with individuals and groups in the mental health field. Like MSWs their program focuses on direct work with clients, and they have many opportunities to do fieldwork. They must complete at least 3,000 hours of post-degree supervised clinical experience and pass a licensure exam. In some states they are referred to as licensed clinical professional counselors or licensed mental health counselors.

Issues Around Confidentiality

The American Psychological Association's code of ethics affirms that psychologists (and other mental health professionals) may share only the minimum information necessary when disclosing information. Additionally, practitioners should have express, written permission to share any information. Confidentiality is not unlimited, however. The law requires practitioners to report information in specific situations. Examples of these situations include the following:

- Receiving a court order
- To report ongoing domestic violence or to report any abuse or neglect of children, the elderly, or persons with disabilities
- To protect the patient or the public from serious harm—in cases in which a client discusses plans to harm themselves or another person

This last example refers to a practitioner's duty to warn, which is the responsibility to inform third parties or authorities of a threat (either to the client him/herself or to another person). Two important legal cases established the obligation of therapists to breach confidentiality in case a client poses a risk to self or others. The first is *Tarasoff v. Regents of the University of California*, in which a therapist did not inform a young woman and her parents of specific death threats that a client made against her. The therapist did inform police that the client posed a danger to himself and others, but the person against whom he made the threat was not warned, and he eventually murdered her. The courts ultimately ruled that confidentiality is trumped by the need for public safety.

The second case is that of Jablonski by *Pahls v. the United States*. This case further extended the responsibilities of duty to warn. A review of records for previous violent behavior was deemed necessary for a complete risk assessment. In this case a doctor conducted an assessment of a potentially violent client but did not review the client's history of violence. As a result, another person, a girlfriend, was not warned about the client's history of violent behavior. The client murdered the girlfriend.

Duty to warn gives therapists and other counselors both the obligation and the right to breach confidentiality if they believe a client poses a risk to another person. The therapist is protected from prosecution for breach of confidentiality if he/she made the breach in good faith and had reasonable suspicion that the client might be a danger to self or others.

Developmental Psychology

Continuity Versus Stages

There has been some debate among developmental psychologists as to whether the process of development occurs smoothly over time or through age-specific periods. This can be referred to as continuity versus stages or continuity versus discontinuity. Some theorists assert that changes in development are just a matter of quantity; children come to display more of certain skills as they develop. Several major theorists outline series of stages in which skills or traits emerge during certain periods of development. Examples of these stages include Erikson's psychosocial development theory or Freud's psychosexual stages.

Critical Periods

Critical periods are time of increased and favored sensitivity to certain aspects of development. For example, the critical period for language occurs in early childhood. Young children are able to acquire languages easily during this time, whereas adults usually struggle to learn a new language.

Stability Versus Change

The issue of stability versus change addresses the question of how much one's personality traits are set and remain stable in expressions throughout a lifetime versus how much these traits can fluctuate throughout the life span. Some theorists assert that personality traits are relatively set in childhood and may become only more pronounced over time. There is evidence that support both sides of this issue. One of the first psychologists to emphasize the importance of early experiences on later development was Freud. He asserted that these early experiences play a formative role in a person's later development.

Human Development

Human development continues throughout the life span; it does not stop once adulthood is reached. The changes seen in babies and children are usually more dramatic and observable, but the progression from young adulthood through middle and late adulthood is no less momentous. The main developmental stages are outlined as follows:

- Infancy takes place from birth through about two years old. During this stage the infant is quite dependent on caregivers for most things; however, there are many psychological characteristics developing. The bond between the infant and caregiver during this stage has great impact on the infant's later emotional development.
- Childhood takes place between the ages of 2 to 10 years old. Throughout childhood, individuals become increasingly independent from their parents and caregivers as they gain more self-control and learn to carry out tasks for themselves. Children's cognitive skills develop throughout this stage in addition to their developing of understanding right and wrong.
- Adolescence takes place between the ages of 10 and 20. Puberty's onset indicates the beginning of adolescence. This stage is dominated by developing one's own identity and seeking independence from parents. Adolescents' thought processes are more logical, complex, and idealistic than those of children.
- Early adulthood takes place between the ages of 20 and 40. Throughout this stage, the individual establishes both personal and financial independence and seeks to consolidate a career. This is also typically the stage in which the individual selects a partner and begins a family.

- Middle age takes place approximately between the ages of 40 and 65. Throughout this stage of life, individuals expand personal and social involvements and responsibilities, advance their careers, and support their offspring in their path to becoming mature individuals.
- Older adulthood takes places from age 65 on. During this stage, the individual must make considerable adjustment to changes in life and self-perception. For many older adults, this stage can be a liberating time when day-to-day responsibilities of caring for children or working have lessened.

Sensation and Perception

The process in which a sensory receptor is stimulated is known as sensation. In this process, nerve impulses travel to the brain. The brain then interprets the impulses as a sound, a visual image, a taste, an odor, touch, or pain. In a process called transduction, the physical stimulus in the environment emits energy that is absorbed by a sensory organ. This causes sensation to occur.

Perception refers to the brain's organization of information it gets from the neural impulses which it then translates and interprets. Perception allows the individual to make sense of the information relayed by the physical stimulus. When the brain processes information to give meaning to it (by emotions, memories, etc.), perception occurs.

Sensation and perception work together for a person to be able to identify and create meaning from stimuli-related information. The two elements complement and balance one another. Perception is not possible without sensation; without perception, sensations are left unknown and not understood as there would be no mental processing of what one senses.

One element of growth that is vital to a child's development is that of sensory experiences. Young children learn to integrate the sensations from muscles and joints as well as sensations received through different parts of the body (e.g., hands, knees, mouth, and ears). The sensation of gravity is integrated into a child's learning, and different movements help organize the brain. All of these sensory integrations will be used for play, learning, speech, and motor skill mastery.

The different senses are gustatory (taste), tactile (touch), auditory (hearing), visual (sight), olfactory (smell), proprioception (feedback from the joints and muscles), and vestibular (equilibrium or balance). These last two are what's known as movement-based senses.

Another level of development has to do with a child's ability to receive, interpret, and respond successfully to sensory information. This is known as perceptual motor development. With the sensory motor skills as a foundation for learning and control of the body, the child gathers more sensory information while moving through his/her environment and practices skills to develop coordination and small motor development. Through increasingly complex experiences, the child develops more complex hand-eye coordination, visual-spatial perception, and auditory language skills, which are the foundation for skills needed for daily living as he/she grows into adulthood.

Piaget's Moral Development in Children

(For a more complete discussion of Piaget's theory of cognitive development, please see the section on Piaget in "Methods, Approaches, Ethics, and Assessment.")

Jean Piaget was primarily interested in children's moral reasoning (i.e., what they think about questions of morality) more than what they actually do. The three main areas of children's moral reasoning that interested Piaget were their understanding of rules, moral responsibility, and justice. He noted that children's ideas about all of these aspects of morality evolved as they grew older and that the children passed through stages of moral development, similar to stages of cognitive development. The two types of moral reasoning that Piaget described are heteronomous morality, or moral realism, and autonomous morality, or moral relativism.

Heteronomous morality is morality that is imposed from the outside, such as by parents, teachers, or God. Children in this stage of moral development believe that breaking the rules will lead to immediate and severe punishment and punishment is given to make the guilty suffer in relation to the severity of their wrongdoing. In heteronomous morality, rules are absolute and unchanging, and intentions or reasons for behavior are not taken into account. A small amount of deliberate damage is not as bad as a large amount of accidental damage.

As children mature, they experience a radical change in their attitude toward moral questions. Children who have entered the stage of autonomous morality recognize that morality depends not on consequences but on intentions and that there is no absolute right or wrong. By the age of 9 or 10, children become able to see things from others' point of view and also understand that rules are created by people and can be changed. Older children start to realize that a well-intentioned act that had bad results will likely garner less punishment than malicious intentions that do less harm. Unlike younger children who view punishment as retribution, older children start to see punishment as restitution and that it is necessary to put things right and not just have the guilty suffer. Older children are also more focused on justice and believe that it is always wrong to punish the innocent for others' misdeeds.

Vygotsky

In contrast with Piaget's stages of cognitive and moral development, Vygotsky developed a socio-cultural approach to cognitive development. He asserted that social learning precedes and even leads to development and that community plays a central role in the process of creating meaning. Unlike Piaget, Vygotsky assumes that cognitive development varies across cultures, and he emphasizes the effect of culture on cognitive development. Vygotsky emphasized social factors in development and asserted that children's environment influences how they think and what they think about. He also emphasizes the role of language in cognitive development, which he sees as resulting from an internalization of language.

Havighurst

Robert Havighurst established the theory of human development known as the developmental task concept. This theory asserts that the individual needs to achieve certain tasks at different points in life to continue to develop into a happy and successful adult. Havighurst divides these tasks into three categories: those influenced most by the individual's biology (physiological maturation and genetic makeup), psychology (personal values and goals), or sociology (culture in which the individual belongs). An example of a task influenced most by biology is that of a child learning to crawl, which becomes necessary as a small child matures physically. How an individual establishes his/her self-concept is an example of a task influenced most by psychology or personal values and goals. An individual who lives in an agricultural community will likely seek an occupation such as that of farmer; this is an example of a task influenced most by sociology, or the culture of the individual.

Havighurst proposed a list of common critical tasks categorized into six developmental stages. A few examples from each stage are listed as follows:

Infancy and Early Childhood (Birth to 5 Years)

- Learning to walk
- Learning to control bodily functions

- Learning to talk
- Learning to develop relationships with others

MIDDLE CHILDHOOD (6–12 YEARS)

- Developing physical skills for playing games
- Learning school-related skills such as reading, writing, and counting
- Developing values and conscience
- Becoming more independent

ADOLESCENCE (13–17 YEARS)

- Attaining emotional independence from parents
- Developing skills needed for productive occupation
- Establishing mature relationships with peers of both sexes

EARLY ADULTHOOD (18–35 YEARS)

- Choosing a partner
- Establishing a family
- Managing a home
- Establishing a career

MIDDLE AGE (36–60 YEARS)

- Maintaining economic standard of living
- Performing social and civic responsibilities
- Relating to a spouse or partner as a person
- Adjusting to physiological changes

LATER MATURITY (OVER 60 YEARS)

- Adjusting to deteriorating health and physical strength
- Adjusting to retirement
- Meeting social and civil obligations
- Adjusting to death or loss of spouse

JOHN BOWLBY AND ATTACHMENT THEORY

John Bowlby defined attachment as the "lasting psychological connectedness between human beings." He theorized that infants possess an innate need to form an attachment bond with a caregiver, most likely a parent. Bowlby's work with emotionally disturbed children led him to assert a link between early infant separations from the primary caregiver and later maladjustment. Bowlby observed that children experienced severe distress when separated from their mothers, and even when they were fed by other caregivers their anxiety did not diminish. This appeared to contradict the behavioral theory of attachment, which had been dominant. Bowlby showed that the behavioral theory underestimated the bond that a child has with his/her primary caregiver and that children become attached to their caregivers not only because they are fed by them but because of the "lasting psychological connectedness" that they have with their caregivers. Bowlby asserted that feeding itself is not the basis or purpose of the attachment bond. A child can develop a sense of trust in the world when attachment figures are available and reliable. Once this happens, the child is able to rely on the caregiver as a secure base from which he/she can explore the world.

Bowlby established that the attachment bond forms in a series of stages—preattachment, attachment-in-the-making, clear-cut attachment, and formation of reciprocal relationships. During the pre-attachment phase, babies can recognize the primary caregiver but do not yet have an attachment formed. Through the caregiver's meeting the infant's needs, by about the age of 3 months, the child will begin to recognize the caregiver more and will develop a sense of trust. During attachment-in-the-making, the infant will show a preference for the primary caregiver as well as for certain secondary caregivers. In clear-cut attachment, a child forms a strong attachment to one individual and will experience separation distress and anxiety when separated from that person. Finally, in the formation of reciprocal relationships, the child will begin to develop strong attachments to people beyond the primary caregivers.

Bowlby's colleague, Mary Ainsworth, identified three types of attachment that a child can demonstrate: secure, avoidant, and resistant/ambivalent. Later Mary Main identified a fourth type—disorganized attachment.

Attachment Theory and the Strange Situation

Despite John Bowlby's belief that attachment was an all-or-nothing process, research has shown that there are individual differences in attachment quality. As mentioned, Mary Ainsworth determined that there are several distinct types of attachment. She came to this conclusion through her research involving an assessment technique called the Strange Situation Classification. This research was conducted to examine how attachments might vary among children. In this study the researchers investigated the security and style of attachment in 1- to 2-year-olds by observing the behavior of infants in various situations including with mother, with baby and a stranger, with baby alone, with mother and baby alone, and with baby and stranger. The children were observed for different types of behaviors including contact seeking and maintaining, avoidance of proximity and contact, exploratory behaviors, and affect displays such as crying or smiling.

Through this study Mary Ainsworth identified three primary attachment styles: secure, insecure avoidant, and insecure ambivalent/resistant. Ainsworth concluded that these different styles were the result of early interactions with the primary caregiver. Ainsworth's colleague Mary Main identified a fourth attachment style, disorganized attachment, at a later time.

Securely attached children show some stranger anxiety (i.e., avoiding a stranger when alone but are friendly when mother is present), are somewhat distressed when their mother leaves them, and are positive and happy when she returns. They also use their mother or primary caregiver as a secure base from which they explore their environment.

Children with an ambivalent or resistant attachment show more significant stranger anxiety and avoid the stranger with or without their caregiver present. They show intense distress when the caregiver leaves and shows interest in him/her but resists contact with him/her when he/she returns, even pushing him/her away at times. A child with this type of attachment cries more and explores less than children of the other two types.

Children with an avoidant or insecure attachment show no distress at a stranger's presence and play normally when the stranger is there. These children show no signs of distress when their caregiver leaves and little interest when he/she returns. If upset, both mother and stranger are able to comfort the child equally well.

The category of disorganized or disoriented attachment was developed when researchers, including Ainsworth, had difficulty fitting some of the children into one of the three categories, and the fourth classification was later added. In the Strange Situation study, the attachment system is generally expected to activate when the caregiver leaves and then returns. If the child's behavior does not appear to be coordinated in a smooth way through the different phases of the study to achieve some kind of proximity with the caregiver, then it is considered disorganized. Disorganized attachment indicates a disruption or flooding of the attachment system, such as by fear. Many of the so-called disorganized infants, however, continue to approach the caregiver and seek comfort from him/her and can cease their distress without ambivalent or avoidant behavior.

Ainsworth concluded that a child's attachment style is dependent on the behavior that his/her caregiver shows toward him/her. Sensitive caregivers are more responsive to their child's needs and respond correctly to their child's moods and feelings. They are more likely to have securely attached children. This is contrasted with caregivers who are less sensitive towards their child, who respond to the child's needs incorrectly, or who are impatient or ignore the child. These caregivers are more likely to have insecurely attached children. These findings of Ainsworth's provided the first empirical evidence for Bowlby's attachment theory.

Approaches to Language Development

The learning theory (behaviorism) approach to language acquisition proposes that language is learned through reinforcement and conditioning. An early explanation for the acquisition of language was given by behaviorist and psychologist B. F. Skinner. Skinner explained the phenomenon of language development as a result of environmental influence. He argued that children learn language due to behaviorist reinforcement by associating words with meaning. He attributed learning to positive reinforcement given to correct utterances, such as asking for milk and receiving it. Children will find the outcome of receiving what they have asked for rewarding, which will enhance their language development. Behaviorism does not fully explain language development as children are able to come up with unique sentence structures on their own and not just those that have been specifically reinforced. It is possible that reinforcement, imitation, and modeling are supplementary to language acquisition instead of the rule.

The nativist approach to language development addresses some of the issues with the learning theory approach to language development. It suggests that learning language is an inborn process and that humans have an innate ability to learn and understand language as well as its more complex structures. Neural cognitive research supports the nativist approach as it has found brain structures related to and responsible for language as well as a gene related to language. Noam Chomsky, the world's most famous linguist to date, heavily criticized Skinner's language development theory. Chomsky argued that language input alone was insufficient to explain how children acquire the tools needed for processing an infinite number of sentences. Chomsky instead proposed his theory of Universal Grammar, which is a scheme of innate biological grammatical categories (such as a noun category and a verb category) that make possible language development in children and language processing in adults. Chomsky theorized that each individual has an innate Language Acquisition Device, which encodes Universal Grammar into a child's brain. Chomsky proposed that the task of the child is to learn the words of his/her particular language; children will instinctively know how to combine nouns and verbs into a meaningful correct phrase due to their inborn Language Acquisition Device.

Finally, the interactionist approach combines different language development theories and suggests that different factors, including both genetics and socialization, are involved in language acquisition. This perspective suggests that there are innate mechanisms in the brain responsible for language development but that they must be activated by environmental and social factors.

The Critical Period Hypothesis proposes that language can develop readily during the first few years of life, and after this time has passed language acquisition is much more difficult or even impossible. There appear to be two distinct cutoffs for the critical period, one around age 5 and the other around the onset of puberty. Those individuals who had little or no language input in their early years (including sign language for deaf individuals) were still able to achieve some fluency if they began exposure to language by the age of 12 (although often not full proficiency). Additionally, early language exposure increases the ability to learn a second language later in life.

Stages of Language Acquisition

Pre-linguistic stage. The first year of life is a pre-speech stage, but the child is developing aspects of communication related to speech, such as gestures, eye contact, sound repartee with the caregiver, cooing, babbling, and crying.

Holophrastic or one-word sentence. A child typically reaches this stage between 10 and 13 months of age. The single-word utterance is also supplemented by the context as well as nonverbal cues, such as pointing.

Two-word sentence. Children typically reach this stage by 18 months, and their utterances usually contain a noun or verb plus a modifier. Sentences can be declarative (car fast), interrogative (where Mommy?), negative (no bread), or imperative (more cake!). Like in the holophrastic stage, context and nonverbal communication support the meaning of the utterance.

Multiple-word sentence. Between the age of 2 and 2 1/2, the child will reach this stage. Use of grammatical morphemes like prefixes or suffixes can be used when changing meanings or tenses. Additionally, the child can now form sentences with a subject and a predicate. The examples from the previous stage might be expanded thusly: car is fast, where is Mommy?, that is not bread, I want more cake. Examples of utilizing a prefix or a suffix are: I catched it, I falling.

More complex grammatical structures. A child will reach this stage between approximately 2 1/2 and 3 years old. At this time, they will start to use more complex and intricate grammatical structures; additional elements such as conjunctions are added, embedded, and permuted within sentences, and prepositions are used. Some examples include conjunction (throw it, my ball), embedding (where is Brother?), permutation (I can't play), and preposition (Take me to the park).

Adult-like language structures. This level is reached by the typical 5- to 6-year-old child. Utterances now include more complex structural distinctions, such as with ask, tell, or promise, and word orders are changed appropriately (ask him where they went, she promised to help me).

Emotional Development

Emotional development in children is strongly connected to cognitive development. Although people often see the two as distinct parts of learning and becoming, in reality they are intertwined. Childhood emotional development depends quite strongly on the quality of relationships that a child has with his/her caregivers and teachers and on the interactions with those adults. Healthy emotional development affects the ability of a person to function successfully as an adult not only in social spheres but also academically and professionally.

Aspects of emotional development include understanding a person's own feelings, perceiving and understanding the feelings of others, dealing with one's feelings in a healthy way, being able to manage one's behavior, learning to have empathy for other people, and developing and sustaining healthy relationships with others. As children grow from infancy to adulthood, both the complexity of their emotions increases as well as their ability to deal with more and more ambiguity in their own and others' emotions.

In the first 3 months of a child's life, emotional development centers around learning about one's own self as well as about the other people in one's surroundings. At this stage, an infant is starting to learn that he/she is an individual and separate from those around him/her. Infants at this age also learn about their own bodies (looking at their hands, sucking on their fingers, and paying attention to parts of their body that a caregiver is touching), how different kinds of touch feel, how different parts of their body are attached (i.e., arms and legs), how caregivers can soothe and comfort them, and how to enjoy social stimulation.

As infants grow, they have a base of understanding about their own bodies, and social interaction becomes more and more important. Infants from 3 to 6 months of age smile, laugh, and even learn their own name and respond when they hear it. The game of peekaboo comes into play at this stage. As they grow, they begin to prefer familiar people over those they don't know as well. Children from ages 6 to 9 months of age know the difference between members of their family and strangers. They also respond when people speak or gesture to them. Their emotions start to become more complex, and they can express anger, happiness, fear, and sadness, among others. Children who are between 9 and 12 months of age not only show a preference for their caregivers, but they actually show distress when separated from them. At this age they are learning more self-regulation along with more complex physical skills such as feeding themselves and imitating others.

Children between 1 and 2 years of age increase the amount of self-awareness that they have. They can recognize themselves in a mirror. They also take part in many new play activities, including initiating play, playing independently, and imitating caregivers' actions in their play. They can express pleasure when they accomplish things, express frustration or anger, and even try to give others directions.

Between ages 2 and 4 years old, children greatly increase their self-confidence and independence. Just as they are able to successfully complete more and more complicated physical tasks, they are also able to interact socially and emotionally in increasingly complex ways. Children at this age express their preferences for many things, including food and toys. They say "no," are possessive of their belongings, and increasingly learn to share with others. They can have rapid mood changes. They learn to follow directions, play with other children, and take part in pretend games.

As children move out of the preschool years, they have increasing awareness of others. They make friends with other children and become much more responsive to the feelings of others. They learn about good and bad actions and learn to compare themselves to others. Early childhood brings an understanding of what embarrassment is and more attention paid to the responses of others. As children grow older into middle childhood and pre-adolescence, they increasingly seek to establish their own identity. They can still be childlike and silly at times but can also be selfish and argumentative as they start learning to increase their independence. Pre-adolescents have a greater ability to process cognitive complexities, and this is mirrored in their ability to navigate more and more complex social situations as well. They can differentiate among different expressions of themselves with different social groups (i.e., family, close friends, and acquaintances).

As kids move into adolescence, they are able to think more logically, although they may be quite moody and often need privacy. The opinions of peers become even more important to them, and the opinions of caregivers and family members take on less importance. Adolescents may "try on" different personality traits or style choices in attempts to figure themselves out. In seeking independence from parental figures, adolescents typically become emotionally distant. This is all a part of individuation and learning to become a healthy and competent adult, although the process may be painful for both adolescent and parent.

KOHLBERG'S THEORY OF MORAL DEVELOPMENT

Twenty-five years after Piaget presented his theory of moral development, Lawrence Kohlberg put forward his own theory of moral development. At the time, behaviorism and psychoanalysis were the primary psychological approaches; these both attributed morality to the internalization of family and societal rules through reinforcement or identification with authority. In contrast, Kohlberg emphasized the importance of an individual's own reasoning in making moral judgments.

To study moral development, Kohlberg would introduce moral dilemmas to people in his studies. Based on their responses, he would place them in one of six stages, which are split into three levels. The three levels are pre-conventional morality, conventional morality, and post-conventional morality. As a person advances through the stages, Kohlberg would assert that they are increasingly better at dealing with moral dilemmas than they were in previous stages.

Pre-conventional moral reasoning is mostly seen in children, although not exclusively. This level is less about right and wrong than about the consequences brought about by the actions in question. The stages in this level are (1) obedience and punishment orientation and (2) self-interest orientation. In Stage 1 the individual seeks to avoid immoral behavior because he/she may be punished. The severity of the punishment determines how bad or immoral an action may be. In Stage 2 the individual begins to pay attention to others' needs but only as far as the individual's own interests are advanced. This level does not take into account the greater community interest but rather only the interests of the individual.

Conventional moral reasoning is the usual level for adults and adolescents. As a person comes into this second level, he/she comes to accept what the greater society declares to be right or wrong. He/she may follow rules somewhat strictly without examining whether the rules are just or right. The stages in this level are (3) good interpersonal relationships and (4) maintaining the social order. In Stage 3 the individual wants others to see him/her as good, and he/she begins to determine how moral an action is based on its effects on relationships with others. The person in Stage 3 does not want others to disapprove of him/her, and so he/she tries to follow the rules. In Stage 4 the individual does not depend on the individual approval of others, as in Stage 3. The person in Stage 4 sees the greater importance of following societal rules and norms for the good of society as a whole.

Post-conventional moral reasoning takes the focus off of society's rules and norms and shifts it to the individual's own moral perspective. In this level, the individual may end up disobeying rules when they conflict with his/her own ethical principles. For people in this level, rules can be questioned and even disobeyed when they are deemed to be unjust. The stages in this level are (5) social contract and individual rights and (6) universal ethical principles. The person in Stage 5 sees rules and laws as social contracts and not as unbending mandates. He/she would change rules that are unjust or that serve to harm individuals or groups. The person in Stage 6 sees rules or laws that are unjust as invalid. He/she believes that he/she is obligated break or defy unjust rules, even if he/she must face societal or legal consequences for doing so.

The most famous moral dilemma that Kohlberg used in his research is that of Heinz, a man with an ill wife. The drug that she needs has been priced far above what Heinz can afford and many times more than what it cost to produce. After unsuccessfully pleading with the pharmacist to sell him the drug at an affordable price or allow him to pay later, Heinz decides to break into the laboratory to steal the drug so that his wife can have it and be cured. The question for research participants was whether or not Heinz should have broken in to steal this drug. How participants answer this dilemma and their stated reasoning for their answer determines their stage of moral reasoning.

Gilligan's Theory of Moral Development

Carol Gilligan has pioneered the field of gender difference psychology, which argues that men and women tend to think differently, in particular about moral problems. She asserts that these differences are likely due to gender conditioning and social influences. She argues that women's ways of thinking are often undervalued by society compared to those of men.

Gilligan is best known for her adaptation of Kohlberg's theory of moral development. Kohlberg found that more men reached the highest levels of moral reasoning. He also found that men strongly focused on justice. Gilligan criticized Kohlberg's theory as biased in favor of men. In her research, Gilligan found that women place a stronger emphasis on the role of caring in moral decision-making, something that Kohlberg's theory does not allow for. Because of this, women often fail to reach Kohlberg's so-called higher stages of moral reasoning.

Gilligan asserts that a woman's morality is influenced by her relationships and that women take into account how their decisions will affect others when forming their moral and ethical foundation. Like Kohlberg, Gilligan believes that women develop morality in stages, and she utilizes Kohlberg's phrasing of pre-conventional, conventional, and post-conventional. She has, however, based her stages on her research with women, and they vary from Kohlberg's stages significantly. In Gilligan's pre-conventional morality stage, the goal is individual survival. The individual then transitions from a focus on selfishness to a feeling of responsibility for others. In the conventional stage, self-sacrifice is seen as goodness. The individual then transitions from this focus on goodness to the truth that she (the individual herself) is a person, too, and worthy of caring. In the post-conventional stage, women emphasize taking responsibility for the consequences of their choices and gaining control of their own lives. Caring for others remains a strong component of this highest stage of moral development.

Factors That Interact With the Process of Development

There are many factors that affect the social and emotional development rate of children. These factors include the following.

- *Environmental risk factors:* unsafe living conditions or community, low-quality child care, lack of community resources, lack of policies supporting children and families, and so on. Maternal use of alcohol or drugs while pregnant can have a strong impact on a child's development by causing fetal alcohol syndrome or other issues.
- *Family risk factors:* maternal depression, mental illness or substance abuse in the family, family violence, poverty, and so on. Many of these stressful factors can actually affect the growth in parts of the brain involved in stress regulation, emotional processing, and memory.
- *Within-child risk factors:* fussy temperament, developmental delay, and serious health issues. Developmental delays can have genetic causes (such as Down syndrome), complications of pregnancy and birth (such as prematurity or infections), or unknown causes. Some causes of developmental delay are reversible if caught early enough, such as hearing loss from chronic ear infections.

Intelligence Theories and Testing

Although there is no standard definition of what intelligence is, many researchers have come up with different explanations. Some assert that intelligence is a single, general ability; others believe that it includes an array of aptitudes, talents, and skills. Definitions of intelligence vary greatly, but a general understanding of intelligence is that it involves the ability to learn, recognize problems, and solve problems. Different mental abilities that intelligence encompasses include logic, reasoning, problem-solving, and planning. Intelligence is a topic that is highly researched but also generates great controversy, for example, the use of testing to screen job applicants or to identify children who need academic help.

The first intelligence tests were developed by Alfred Binet to assist the French government in identifying schoolchildren who needed extra help with schoolwork. German psychologist William Stern first coined the phrase *intelligence quotient*, or IQ, in the early 1900s.

Over the past hundred years, researchers have formulated the following theories of intelligence.

General Intelligence

Charles Spearman, a British psychologist, believed that there was an underlying intelligence factor that influenced outcomes in types of cognitive tasks. He called this general intelligence or the *g* factor. Spearman found that people who do well in certain cognitive areas (such as math) also tend to do well in other areas (such as reading) and likewise for those who perform poorly. He asserted that this "general intelligence" can be measured and described numerically. In pursuit of understanding the *g* factor, Spearman helped develop the statistical theory called factor analysis.

Other Theories of Intelligence—Sternberg, Thurstone, and Gardner

Some theorists have posited that intelligence is not a singular factor but as a more nuanced and varied set of abilities. Instead of one particular quality determining how intelligent a person is in various domains, these different domains each represent their own type of intelligence.

Robert J. Sternberg's triarchic theory of intelligence describes mental functions as a set of metacomponents or triarchic components. These three factors or components include the following:

- Problem-solving ability or analytical intelligence
- Experiential or creative intelligence, which deals with the ability to react to new situations and challenges
- Practical intelligence, which deals with creating the best fit between oneself and the environment, also known as "street smarts"

In a similar vein, Louis L. Thurstone proposed the theory of primary mental abilities. This set of abilities stands in contrast to the *g* factor. In any single individual, different abilities may be stronger or weaker, leading to a more diverse view of intelligence. Thurstone's primary mental abilities include the following:

- Verbal comprehension
- Word fluency
- Numerical ability
- Spatial relations, memory
- Perceptual speed
- Reasoning

Howard Gardner posited a theory of multiple intelligences that he believed more fully represents the varied abilities of people. Different cultures value distinct skills and abilities to varying degrees. Gardner's eight intelligence modalities include the following:

- Visual-spatial
- Musical-rhythmic and harmonic

- Verbal-linguistic
- Bodily-kinesthetic
- Interpersonal
- Intrapersonal
- Logical-mathematical
- Naturalistic

Questions Remain

Much about intelligence and IQ testing is theoretical and unproven. Some important questions about this area of study include the following:

- How much of intelligence is a single ability, and how much encompasses a multitude of abilities and skills?
- What roles do genetics and environment play in intelligence?
- What biases may intelligence tests have?
- Can intelligence scores predict something about people, and if so, what?

Stanford-Binet Intelligence Scales

This series of tests helps assess cognitive strengths and weaknesses and is a tool used to evaluate if a student has a learning disability. The Stanford-Binet can be used with people from ages 2 to 85. It measures five different factors of cognitive ability:

- Fluid reasoning
- Knowledge
- Quantitative reasoning
- Visual-spatial processing
- Working memory

The Stanford-Binet is used to diagnose a wide range of developmental disabilities and is also useful in the following contexts:

- Clinical and neuropsychological assessment
- Early childhood assessment
- Psycho-educational evaluations for special education placement
- Providing information for interventions like Individual Education Programs, career assessment, adult neuropsychological treatment, and others
- Adult social security and workers' compensation evaluations
- Forensic contexts
- Research on abilities and aptitudes

Wechsler Adult Intelligence Scale (WAIS)

The Wechsler Adult Intelligence Scale (WAIS) is established on David Wechsler's idea of intelligence, which he describes as "the global capacity of a person to act purposefully, to think rationally, and to deal effectively with his environment." Wechsler asserted that intelligence was comprised of specific elements that can be isolated, defined, and measured. He did not see these elements as independent but rather as interrelated. He argues that general intelligence is made up of specific and interrelated functions that can be individually measured.

These ideas about intelligence varied significantly from the Binet scale, commonly seen as the highest authority in intelligence testing at the time. Wechsler strongly advocated for the concept of non-intellective factors, and he asserted that the 1937 version of the Binet scale was lacking in its failure to incorporate these factors into the scale. Non-intellective factors include things like lack of confidence, fear of failure, attitudes, and so on and contribute to the overall score in intelligence but are not in and of themselves intelligence-related items. Other criticisms Wechsler had of the Binet scale include the single score that it gave, its design being for children not adults, and the emphasis on speed.

A critical difference from the Binet scale was the nonverbal performance scale. The Binet scale had been relentlessly criticized for emphasizing language and verbal scales. Because of this, Wechsler created an entire scale that allowed the measurement of nonverbal intelligence, which became known as the performance scale. In essence, this scale required the subject to perform a task (like copy symbols or point out a missing detail) rather than simply answer questions. This development in assessment was important as it attempted to overcome biases caused by language, education, and culture. Additionally, the performance scale allowed clinicians to observe subjects completing a type of behavior that required something physical as well as a longer interval of sustained effort and attention.

The Wechsler-Bellevue scale was first released in 1939 and has been revised several times. The current version is the WAIS IV. Many of the original concepts that Wechsler advocated for have now become standards in psychological testing.

Wechsler Intelligence Scale for Children (WISC)

Although the Wechsler Intelligence Scale for Children (WAIS) is used for persons 16 and older, the WISC is aimed at persons between 6 and 16 years of age. It can be used to determine if a child is achieving below what one would expect, which may be explained by learning disabilities. Evaluators also use the WISC to compare a child's age with his/her cognitive development and can help identify intellectual weaknesses and strengths, including "giftedness." From the results of the WISC, both a "full-scale IQ" as well as five primary index scores are given. The five indices are: verbal comprehension, visual spatial, fluid reasoning, working memory, and processing speed.

Cultural Bias in Testing

Categories of testing bias include construct-validity bias, content-validity bias, and predictive-validity bias.

Whether a test accurately measures what it was designed to is known as construct-validity bias. For example, students who are English language learners may encounter words they haven't yet learned on intelligence tests, and therefore the test results may be reflective of their English language skills rather than intellectual abilities.

When the content of a test is comparatively more difficult for one group of students than for others it is known as content-validity bias. This occurs in the following scenarios: when members of a subgroup of test takers (e.g., ethnic minority groups) have not had the same opportunity to learn the material that is being tested, when scoring is unfair to a group (e.g., when answers that make sense in one group's culture are scored as incorrect), or when the wording of questions is unfamiliar to test takers because of cultural or linguistic differences. A subcategory of content-validity bias is item-selection bias. This refers to the use of individual testing items that are more appropriate for one group's language and cultural experiences than to others.

A test's accuracy in predicting how well a group of test takers will perform in the future is known as predictive-validity bias or bias in criterion-related validity. An example of this would be a test's being considered unbiased if it was able to predict future academic and test performance equally well for all groups of students.

Some believe that certain tests are culturally loaded and that their language and content give an unfair advantage to test takers of the dominant culture. Some believe that many tests do not actually measure aptitude but rather the knowledge of mainstream white culture. Those who support this view acknowledge that minority children and children from the dominant culture are raised in different environments and learn different values and skills that are needed to succeed in their respective cultures. Some assert that a universal, unbiased test is not possible to achieve. Those on the other side of this argument assert that testing is valid and accurately measures intelligence and predicts future achievement.

Health Psychology

Health

Definition of Health

Quite simply, health is the state of being sound in mind, body, and spirit. According to the World Health Organization, health is not only the absence of disease, but the presence of physical, mental, and social well-being. When assessing an individual's health, a professional is likely to examine him or her from a physical, psychological, spiritual, social, intellectual, or environmental standpoint. Although every individual has his or her own standard of health, it is common for people to recognize the following characteristics as healthy: an optimistic outlook in life, the ability to relax, a supportive home life, a clean environment, a satisfying job, freedom from pain and illness, and the energy necessary to enjoy life.

Psychological Health

According to health professionals, maintaining optimal psychological health is not just a matter of avoiding major disorders or illnesses. In order to achieve excellence in this domain of health, a person has to take active measures to become aware and accept both his or her own feelings and the feelings of others. Achieving optimal psychological health also means developing the ability to express complex emotions, to be independent and not have to rely on anyone else for validation, and to be able to cope efficiently with the normal stress of life. Of course, reaching this state in the psychological domain depends on making progress in the other domains; that is, psychological growth depends on physical, spiritual, social, intellectual, and environmental health.

Physical Health

Many health professionals view physical health as a continuum of possible conditions. On the extreme negative end of the continuum is premature death, while at the extreme positive end is optimal wellness. Optimal wellness is defined as the state in which the individual feels and performs at their personal best. Most individuals fall somewhere in between the extremes on the physical wellness continuum. Indeed, health professionals assert that a person will remain somewhere in the middle unless he or she takes active steps to improve his or her physical health. To do this, he or she must eat better, exercise more regularly, avoid dangerous and destructive habits, and protect himself or herself from injury and illness.

Social Health

When health professionals refer to social health, they mean the ability of an individual to interact with other people effectively, to develop positive relationships, and to adequately fulfill social roles. Individuals who are socially healthy contribute to the affairs of the community, live peacefully among other people, and are sexually healthy. Social health has major effects on all the other aspects of a person's life. Studies have shown that individuals without strong social ties are more likely to abuse substances, to have heart disease, and even to develop cold infections. Furthermore, individuals who become ill are more likely to recover if they have support from friends and family.

Spiritual Health

It is inaccurate to assume that spiritual health means being involved in an organized religion. Many people have a quality spiritual life all by themselves. According to health professionals, an individual has achieved excellent spiritual health if he or she has a defined purpose in life, has learned to experience love, joy, and peace, and is able to help themselves and others achieve these positive feelings. For many people, spirituality is defined as feeling connected to something greater than themselves or their own personal interests. Many recent studies have indicated that the relaxation and behavioral practices associated with spirituality are conducive to physical and psychological health, as well. Many doctors have even gone so far as to classify a lack of religious practice as a risk factor for physical health.

SUBSTANCE ABUSE

Substance abuse is a disorder in which an individual begins to overuse or becomes dependent on a particular drug or a group of drugs that ultimately has a negative impact on his or her health and human development.

- Substance abuse, especially when the individual becomes addicted to or dependent on the drug, can affect the individual's ability to interact both socially and physically
- His or her ability to communicate intelligibly or even to complete relatively simple tasks can be severely hindered
- After an individual has become chemically dependent on a particular drug, his or her body develops a physical need for the drug, and the individual will experience the effects of withdrawal if he or she is unable to meet that need
- Substance abuse not only affects a person by causing health problems, it also severely hinders an individual's ability for social development, as the individual often has difficulty improving social skills because of his or her inability to control behavior, actions, and even basic speech

ILLEGAL DRUG USE ON THE UNBORN CHILD

This is a brief summary of the effects of illegal drug use on the unborn child.

- All these drugs contribute to miscarriage, premature birth, and low birth weight
- Babies born addicted can suffer various withdrawal symptoms
- Marijuana smoke contains carbon monoxide that prevents the fetus from getting enough oxygen
- Carbon monoxide in the blood causes developmental delays and behavior and learning problems
- Cocaine can cause severe bleeding, birth defects, and fetal death
- Babies can have genital, kidney, and brain defects
- They may also have learning disabilities in later life
- Heroin can cause breathing problems, hypoglycemia, intracranial hemorrhage, and infant death. When a mother uses dirty needles, babies can be born HIV positive
- PCP and LSD cause poor muscle control, brain damage, and birth defects
- These hallucinogens can cause violent behavior, which can lead to the mother harming herself and the baby
- Methamphetamine causes less oxygen to reach the fetus
- Babies can have genital, kidney, and brain defects, and they may also have learning disabilities later in life

DRUG ADDICTION EFFECTS

Drug addiction is the prolonged use of and psychological and physiological dependence on a chemical substance that affects the central nervous system.

- Drug addiction is a complex physical and mental disease
- It is characterized by psychological and physiological cravings, which persist even when the person is aware of the serious consequences of the drug's use

- Prolonged use of a controlled substance causes problems with brain function, which can cause aberrant behavior
- Abuse of drugs also causes chemical changes in the body
- A woman who uses drugs while pregnant risks serious damage to her unborn child because the drugs are transferred to the developing fetus
- Nicotine has been connected to premature births, and children of mothers who use alcohol can be born with severe developmental problems
- Research is ongoing to discover the effects of mothers using tobacco and alcohol on the fetus before and during pregnancy and on the child after birth

ALCOHOLISM

The National Council on Alcoholism and Drug Dependence considers alcoholism as a disease that is influenced by social, environmental, and genetic factors. The common features of alcoholism are the inability to control consumption, continued drinking despite negative consequences, and distorted thinking patterns (like irrational denial). It is important to note that alcoholism is not simply the result of a weak will but is a physiological state that requires medical treatment so that it can be controlled. Many individuals may have a problem with alcoholism but not realize it if they are still functioning well overall and only drink in social situations. Alcoholics tend to be those who, even when they aren't drinking, place an undue amount of psychological emphasis on alcohol.

EFFECTS OF ALCOHOL

Alcohol has a number of effects on behavior and judgment. It is known to impair sensory perceptions: the eye is less able to adjust to bright lights, and the ear has difficulty distinguishing sounds. The senses of smell and taste are also diminished by excessive consumption of alcohol. Alcohol will decrease sensitivity in general, making it possible for individuals to feel comfortable in extreme temperatures that may be hazardous to their health. Intoxication typically causes an impairment of motor skills, meaning that activities performed with the muscles cannot be done with any precision or coordination. Intoxication usually has a negative effect on sexual performance, even though it may increase interest in sexual activity.

From the moment it is consumed, and even before the individual notices any of the psychological effects, alcohol is at work in the human body. It is almost immediately absorbed into the bloodstream through the walls of the stomach and the upper intestine. Typically, it takes about 15 minutes for the alcohol in a drink to reach the bloodstream and, usually, about 1 hour for the alcohol to reach its peak. Once in the bloodstream, alcohol is carried to the liver, heart, and brain. Although alcohol cannot leave the body until it is metabolized by the liver, it is a diuretic that accelerates the removal of other liquids from the body; thus, alcohol has a dehydrating effect. Alcohol also lowers the temperature of the body.

ALCHOHOL AND THE BRAIN

When consumed in low volume, alcohol alters the areas of the brain that influence behavior in a way that makes the individual feel more relaxed and less inhibited. Of course, this is accompanied by deficits in concentration, memory, judgment, and motor control. Heavy drinkers may experience long-term intelligence and memory impairment. This occurs because alcohol depresses the central nervous system and slows down the activity of the neurons in the brain. This dulling of mental reactions increases in proportion to the amount of alcohol consumed and can culminate in unconsciousness, coma, or even death. Although one or two drinks may have a pleasant tranquilizing effect, many more can entirely snuff out central nervous system activity.

Response to Alcohol

Several things determine the severity of an individual's response to alcohol. Obviously, the more alcohol consumed, the higher the individual's blood-alcohol concentration will be. Also, since the liver can only process half an ounce of alcohol every hour, heavy drinking results in a higher level of intoxication than moderate drinking. More potent forms of alcohol, like liquor and fortified wine, get into the bloodstream more quickly than less concentrated beverages, like beer, especially if the liquor is accompanied by a carbonated beverage. Heavy individuals tend to get drunk more slowly as they have an excess of water with which to dilute the incoming alcohol. Typically, women tolerate alcohol less well than men because they have less of the stomach enzyme that neutralizes alcohol. Older individuals tend to have less water and so are more affected by alcohol. The effects of alcohol are seen more quickly if it is taken on an empty stomach, if tolerance to it has not been built up, or if it is accompanied by a prescription medication.

Recommended Level of Alcohol Consumption

Alcohol is not entirely bad for the body; in fact, there is consistent evidence that suggests a single drink every day can reduce an individual's risk of heart disease. This is more true for men than for women. The National Institute of Alcohol and Alcohol Abuse suggests that men should have no more than two drinks every day, and women should have no more than one. This amount should be adjusted, depending on an individual's weight or age. Many individuals, including pregnant women, people with ulcers, people on certain prescription medications, or those operating heavy machinery, shouldn't drink at all. The health risks associated with alcohol increase in proportion to the amount of alcohol that is consumed.

Alcohol and the Cardiovascular and Immune Systems

Alcohol is thought to have some positive effects on the cardiovascular system. Light drinkers seem to have healthier hearts, fewer heart attacks, lower cholesterol levels, and, thus, a lower risk for heart disease than those who abstain altogether. In contrast, excessive drinking will weaken the heart muscle, and this is particularly true if alcohol is used in combination with tobacco and cocaine. Chronic alcohol use will inhibit the creation of white blood cells (which help fight infection) and of red blood cells (which carry oxygen around the body). It is dangerous for a person suffering from an infection (like a cold or the flu), to drink alcohol because it will suppress the immune system's ability to fight the infection.

Alcohol and the Digestive System

The first stop for alcohol is the stomach. It is partially broken down there, and the remainder of it is absorbed into the bloodstream through the stomach lining. While in the stomach, alcohol stimulates the release of certain chemicals that tend to irritate the lining; it is for this reason that heavy drinking often causes nausea and chronic drinking may contribute to ulcers. The alcohol in the bloodstream moves on to the liver where, for the most part, it will be converted into fat. If an individual consumes four or five drinks a day for a few weeks, the liver cells will accrue a large amount of fat. Heavy alcohol use may eventually cause white blood cells to attack the liver, which can cause irreparable damage.

Alcohol-Related Death

Alcohol can kill those who abuse it in various ways. The main cause of death is injury, generally sustained in auto accidents involving drunk driving. In fact, alcohol is involved in at least half of all traffic fatalities (as well as being involved in half of all homicides and a quarter of all suicides). After injury, the second most common cause of death related to alcohol is cirrhosis of the liver and other digestive disease. Health professionals believe that about half the people admitted to the hospital have a health problem related to alcohol. As would be expected, young drinkers are more likely to die from injury and older drinkers more likely to succumb to alcohol-related illness.

Alcohol When Consumed with Other Drugs

The dangers of alcohol may be magnified greatly if it is consumed in combination with other drugs, whether legal or illegal. Indeed, more than half the most frequently prescribed drugs contain one or more ingredients that react with alcohol. In most cases, this is because the ingredient affects the same areas of the brain as alcohol, thus increasing the pharmacological effects. Particularly, the synergistic combination of alcohol and an antidepressant or anti-anxiety medication can be fatal. One commonly used drug that is thought to have negative consequences when taken with alcohol is aspirin. Although many people take aspirin to alleviate the negative consequences of drinking, research has shown that aspirin may diminish the stomach's ability to process alcohol.

Social Drinking

Though there are no set standards for the varying degrees of alcohol consumption, there are a few basic patterns of drinking that are agreed upon by health professionals. Light drinking is usually defined as having three or fewer alcoholic beverages every week. Infrequent drinking is having less than one drink a month, but more than one drink in a year. Infrequent drinkers can often be those who rarely drink but, on the occasions when they do, are apt to drink four or more drinks. A moderate drinker is one who has approximately 12 drinks a week but is not impaired in any life domain. Social drinking is not defined by a particular quantity; rather, it is drinking at a level consistent with one's peer group, whether this level is high or low.

Reasons for Alcohol Consumption

Alcohol has been popular throughout history because it depresses the central nervous system and makes people feel more relaxed. People also often drink in celebration or when meeting with friends because alcohol tends to reduce inhibitions and make conversation easier. People who drink alcohol often report feeling smarter, sexier, or stronger, even if studies indicate the opposite. Alcohol is also used by many people as a way to escape personal problems or a bad mood. It is also true that many people drink because they are swayed by the massive advertising campaigns launched by brewers; indeed, the effects of alcohol advertising on underage consumers remains a controversial topic. Finally, many people drink in order to emulate people they admire, whether celebrities, family members, or peers.

Interventions

Brief interventions are short, intense training sessions that teach alcoholics the skills they will need to battle their drinking problem. These programs, which typically last about 8 weeks and center on topics like "assertiveness" and "self-esteem," are best suited for individuals who do not have a physical dependence on alcohol. Moderation training, another form of treatment, tries to equip drinkers with the skills to manage their drinking, by showing them ways to reduce consumption and avoid problematic situations. This method is somewhat controversial because critics assert that the only good choice for chronic alcohol abusers is abstinence. However, advocates of moderation training point out that their programs are designed for less severe cases and that their goals are more realistic than those found in other programs.

Detoxification

Whenever an individual with an alcohol problem begins treatment, the first step is detoxification, the gradual removal of alcohol from the system. Most of the time, detoxification does not produce major withdrawal symptoms. However, those who have been drinking heavily for a long period may develop severe symptoms, including seizures and delirium tremens (also known as DTs).

Delirium tremens is a condition in which the individual becomes agitated and may have delusions, a rapid heartbeat, sweating, vivid hallucinations, fever, and trembling hands. This condition is most likely to strike those alcoholics who also suffer from malnutrition, depression, or fatigue and usually ceases after a few alcohol-free days.

Treatment of Alcoholism

If alcoholism is caught in its early stages, doctors often prescribe antidepressant or anti-anxiety medication. These drugs increase the amount of serotonin in the brain and are believed to reduce painful cravings for alcohol. Doctors also recommend that recovering alcoholics take vitamin supplements to remedy the malnutrition that prolonged alcoholism may cause. For especially severe cases, doctors may prescribe Antabuse (the commercial name for the drug disulfiram), which causes an individual to become nauseous or ill when they consume alcohol. Individuals on this medication must also be careful to avoid foods that have been marinated or cooked in alcohol; indeed, some sensitive individuals may even have an adverse reaction to the alcohol in shaving lotion. Although Antabuse is effective in forcing an individual to stop drinking, it does not treat any of the psychological or social causes of drinking.

Inpatient and Outpatient Treatment for Alcoholism

For a long time, a four-week stay at a psychiatric hospital or residential facility was considered necessary for a recovering alcoholic. This inpatient treatment was usually successful, too: over 70% of those who complete such a treatment remain sober for five years afterward, according to one study. Unfortunately, inpatient treatment is expensive, and insurance companies have been increasingly unwilling to pay for it. So outpatient treatments like group therapy, family therapy, interventions, and organizations like Alcoholics Anonymous have become more popular in recent years. Some studies have indicated that intensive outpatient treatment can be as effective as inpatient care, especially if the individual continues it for at least a year.

Recovery from Alcoholism

Defeating alcoholism is often the most difficult challenge an individual will face in his or her lifetime. Relapse into drinking is common; some studies estimate that 90% of recovering alcoholics will drink again within a year after quitting. The people who tend to be successful at abstaining are those who have something to lose: that is, parents of children and people with important jobs. Almost every recovering alcoholic will experience mood swings and an occasional temptation to drink. More and more, relapse prevention is a part of treatment. Relapse prevention involves giving the individual the information and skills to cope with the temptations of alcohol, as well as providing a support network that the individual can rely on in times of stress. Exercise and a general reduction in stress seem to be the most helpful treatment techniques for creating a permanent life away from alcohol.

Tobacco and Nicotine

Smoking or otherwise ingesting tobacco creates an immediate effect on the body and brain. The primary active ingredient in tobacco is nicotine, a colorless, oily compound. Nicotine can be poisonous if it is ingested in a concentrated form. Inhaling cigarette smoke into the lungs causes about 90% of the nicotine to be absorbed into the body. Nicotine stimulates the cerebral cortex, enhancing mood and alertness, but, paradoxically, it can act as a sedative if taken in large doses. At the dose levels found in cigarettes, nicotine triggers the production of adrenaline, thereby increasing blood pressure and speeding up heart rate. Nicotine also decreases hunger, dulls the taste buds, and prevents the creation of urine. The FDA classifies nicotine as a dangerous and addictive drug because it is known to contribute to heart and respiratory disease.

Psychological Addiction to Tobacco

Tobacco creates in the user certain psychological changes that may become addictive over time. For instance, nicotine is known to stimulate the part of the brain that generates feelings of satisfaction or well-being. Nicotine is also known to temporarily enhance memory, the performance of repetitive tasks, and the tolerance of pain. It is also credited with reducing hunger and anxiety. Individuals suffering from depression may also seek relief through tobacco. Studies have consistently shown that depressed individuals are far more likely than others to develop a smoking habit. Even more troubling, the effects of depression make it much more difficult to quit smoking, so the interdependent relation between tobacco use and depression is likely to continue for a long time.

Drug Abuse

A drug is any chemical substance that changes the way a person acts or feels. Drugs may affect a person's mental, physical, or emotional state. Though many drugs are taken to improve the condition of the body or to remedy personal problems, drugs can also undermine health by distorting a person's mind and weakening a person's body. According to the World Health Organization, drug abuse is any excessive drug use that is not approved by the medical profession. The use of some drugs in any quantity is considered abuse; other drugs must be taken in large quantities before they are considered to have been abused. There are health risks involved with the use of any drug, legal or illegal, insofar as they introduce a foreign substance into the balanced system of physical health.

Drug Dependency

A psychological dependence on drugs may begin as a craving for the pleasurable feelings or relief from anxiety that the drug provides. However, this craving can soon turn into a dependency on the drug in order to perform normal mental operations. A physical dependency, on the other hand, is said to occur when the individual requires increasing amounts of the drug to get the desired effect. Many drugs, like marijuana or hallucinogens, do not cause withdrawal symptoms; others, like heroin or cocaine, may be extremely painful to stop using. Individuals with a severe chemical dependency will eventually use a drug like this simply to avoid experiencing the effects of withdrawal. Typically, an individual with a severe dependency will try to stop many times without success.

Non-Biological Reasons for Addiction

Some individuals are at a higher risk of addiction because they lack self-control, have no moral opposition to drugs, have low self-esteem, or are depressed. Research has also shown that individuals who live in isolation or in poverty are more likely to become addicted to drugs. People who associate with drug users are more likely to become users themselves. Drugs that produce a short-lived but intense state of intoxication (cocaine, for instance) are more likely to be addictive, as are those that have especially painful withdrawal symptoms. Most of the people who will experiment with drugs do so during adolescence. Although many have suggested that drugs like alcohol, tobacco, and marijuana lead to use of harder drugs, most research on this subject has been inconclusive.

Relapse Prevention

Most substance abusers will relapse several times after kicking the habit. This is important for both the user and the user's support group to know so that they do not become too frustrated at the setbacks on the road to recovery. Some therapists even say that these relapses can strengthen self-understanding and make it more likely that future relapses can be avoided. Over time, substance abusers should be able to recognize the stimuli that make them susceptible to using drugs, and they should learn to avoid these people, places, and situations. It is also important to make the distinction between a minor and a major relapse; often, it is a huge victory for a recovering addict to keep a minor relapse from turning into a major one.

IMMUNITY AND STRESS RELATIONSHIP

There is a well-documented link between an increased level of stress and the diminished activity of the immune system. Whenever a person becomes stressed out, certain chemicals are released by the body in order to organize the response to the stressful event. These chemicals, however, dampen the effectiveness of the immune system. This is evidenced by research that indicates people who have recently suffered a personal loss are more likely to contract an infection. Persistent stress also gradually weakens an individual's response to pathogens. On the other hand, research suggests that a low-stress life, coupled with support from friends and family, can have a bolstering effect on the immune system.

OBESITY

Obesity is defined by health professionals as the state weighing 20% or more than the ideal body weight. Mild obesity means the person is between 20% and 40% higher; moderate obesity means the person is from 41% to 100% heavier than they should be; and severe obesity indicates a body weight more than 100% higher than the ideal. Every segment of American society has cases of obesity, although it is especially high among African American and Mexican American women. Of particular concern is child obesity, which has increased by about 50% in the last 20 years. Obesity in children increases the risk of heart disease, diabetes, and osteoporosis later in life. Obesity is often the result of slow and steady weight gain over a number of years rather than sudden change in lifestyle, so individuals should be on guard against developing obesity.

OBESITY RELATED HEALTH RISKS

There are numerous dangers to health associated with obesity. Obese individuals are almost three times as likely as their fellows to have diabetes or high blood pressure. For women, obesity can lead to heart attacks, chronic chest pain, higher blood pressure, ovarian cancer, and breast cancer. For men, obesity may contribute to heart disease and to cancer of the colon, rectum, and prostate. More generally, obesity is often at the root of psychological problems like depression, guilt, and anxiety. However, many studies have shown that the differences in health between obese and non-obese individuals seem to grow smaller with age, raising the question of whether mild or moderate obesity can be condemned entirely.

CAUSES OF OBESITY

When obese individuals claim they have no control over their weight, they may be somewhat correct. There is a protein in the brain responsible for limiting food intake and signaling satiety; if this gene is defective, obesity can be the result. Obesity may also be caused by the individual's failure to eat properly or get enough exercise. Impoverished people are more likely to be obese, partly because they are not taught about nutrition and because a diet rich in fruits and vegetables can be expensive. Some individuals may be predisposed to obesity by overfeeding during childhood; their fat cells are large and numerous, and this is more likely to contribute to obesity. People who suffer from psychological disorders like depression and chronic anxiety are also more inclined to obesity.

SEXUAL ADDICTION

Sometimes people may come to rely so heavily on sex for relief from restlessness or low self-esteem that it becomes a physical addiction. Most health professionals consider a person to be addicted to sex when his or her desire to engage in sexual activity crowds out or damages other areas of his or her life. Sex addiction is not limited to any class, gender, or sexual orientation. Oftentimes, individuals with a sexual compulsion have been physically or sexually abused and seek love in repeated sexual encounters. Individuals with this trouble will often spend a great deal of time trying to procure sex and will use sex to hide from larger problems in their life. A person who feels he or she may be addicted to sex should consult a health professional.

Insomnia, Narcolepsy, Sleep Apnea

Sleeping disorders are common in adults. Insomnia is the sleeping disorder in which the individual either cannot fall asleep or has difficulty staying asleep. Of note, it is common to wake up in the middle of the night, but this does not necessarily indicate insomnia.

Narcolepsy occurs when an individual quickly moves from being awake to REM sleep. This is problematic, because this occurs unexpectedly and can be dangerous.

Sleep apnea is a sleeping disorder in which the individual stops breathing while sleeping. Individuals with this disorder are typically chronic snorers and will be awakened after short periods of not breathing.

Information Processing, Physiological Function, and Activation Synthesis

Information process dream theory applies dreams in order to help an individual better process or make sense of their waking life. This is accomplished by delving into the dream in order to assess life events and memories.

Physiological function suggests that REM sleep helps develop and increase neural pathways, they increases brain functioning and processing. While this theory offers an explanation for the use of dreams, it does not provide any information to explain what the dreams mean.

Activation synthesis suggests that dreams are formed based on memories that are brought into the sleeping mind via neural connections triggered during REM sleep.

Stages of Sleep

Most individuals experience 5 stages of sleep, 1-4 and REM. Stages 1-4 are differentiated by the brain waves that are most active during that stage and include: beta, alpha, theta, and delta. Also associated with these four states of sleep are difference in muscle activity, temperature, and blood pressure. Beta waves are high frequency waves (18-24 cycles/second) and are most prevalent while awake. Alpha waves are slower (8-12 cycles/second) and occur during states of relaxation. Theta waves occur ever 4-7 cycles/second and indicate the transition from alpha, relaxation, to sleep (Stage 1). Stage 2 sleep occurs when the body falls into a deeper sleep and the body and brain continues to slow. Stages 3 and 4 are indicated by very deep sleep and delta waves. The final stage of sleep is referred to as REM sleep, also called rapid eye movement. It is during REM that dreaming occurs.

Manifest Content and Latent Content

Manifest content, according to Freud is the part or the story line of an individual's dreams that they remember. This is the information that is present in the conscious after the individual wakes up from a dream. This may include events from an individual's day or previous experiences.

Latent content is the information in an individual's dream that they do not remember. According to Freud, latent content is the underlying meaning or theme of the dream. From a psychological point of view, the latent content may be revealed to identify problems or issues in an individual's life.

Hypnosis, Posts Hypnotic Suggestions, and Disassociation

Hypnosis is a therapeutic technique in which an individual is in a semi-unconscious state; however, is fully alert. While in this stage, one individual, the therapist, can make subtle suggestions to the individual in the hypnotic state.

Post hypnotic suggestions are those subtle suggestion that are made during hypnosis and are intended for the individual to act on when not under hypnosis. Of note, post hypnotic suggestions are never things the individual would not do on their own.

Disassociation occurs when an individual's conscious is split between two levels of consciousness. During this type of disassociation, an individual may be able to

CDC Findings

Drug Abuse

The Center for Disease Control maintains that adolescent drug abuse is an ongoing problem that needs to be addressed. Besides the health risks associated with the drugs themselves, the CDC asserts that persistent drug use contributes to failure in school, fights, antisocial behavior, and unintentional injuries. Prolonged drug use can also be responsible for depression and anxiety. The CDC also maintains that drug use contributes to the HIV epidemic, insofar as those who share needles are liable to contract the virus, and drug users in general tend to engage in risky sexual behaviors. The statistics kept by the CDC state that marijuana use among teenagers decreased from 26% to 22% between 1997 and 2003.

Alcohol Abuse

The Center for Disease Control not only considers alcohol destructive to adolescent health in itself, but believes that it contributes to other behaviors that are damaging to adolescent health. Specifically, the CDC suggests that alcohol contributes to unintentional injuries, fights, academic problems, and illegal behaviors. Over time, alcohol may lead to liver disease, cancer, cardiovascular disease, neurological damage, depression, anxiety, and antisocial tendencies. The rate of alcohol abuse among adolescents has fluctuated a bit in the past years: whereas 50% of high school students admitted to regular drinking in 1999, only 45% said that they were regular drinkers in 2003. Of these, 28% stated that they engaged in regular heavy drinking.

Unintended Pregnancy

According to the CDC, teens who become pregnant immediately decrease their chances for success in life. Teen mothers have a reduced chance of finishing high school, and are more likely to spend their lives in poverty. The good news on this subject is that better contraceptive practices and more responsible behavior by adolescents have led to a reduction in the number of teen pregnancies, abortions, and birth rates over the past decade. However, these rates are still higher in the United States than in other developed countries, and they are especially high among African-Americans and Hispanics. The CDC has approved a number of programs that they say do a good job of educating and encouraging teens to make less risky decisions.

Tobacco

According to the Center for Disease Control, every day about 4000 American teenagers try smoking for the first time. Assuming that conditions remain as they are today, about 6.4 million of today's children will eventually die from a smoking-related illness. The CDC reports that in 2003 22% of high school students smoked cigarettes regularly, and 15% smoked cigars on a regular basis. In addition, about 10% of high school students were users of smokeless tobacco. For the most part, students seem to be more likely to smoke cigarettes if they are from a poor background and if they have parents or friends who are smokers. White males are far more likely to use smokeless tobacco than are any other demographic group.

Sexually Transmitted Disease

Because they are more likely to engage in risky sexual activity with multiple partners, adolescents are more likely to contract a sexually transmitted disease. The CDC believes that adolescents are particularly at risk if they are frequent drug users and if they do not have access to contraceptives or to sex education. In order to meet the ongoing needs, the CDC has developed programs to present important information to adolescents so that they can protect themselves, as well as so that they can seek treatment if they do contract an STD. Part of the CDC's mission is to increase the level of parental involvement in the lives of adolescents. The CDC has published a number of statistics indicating that when parents actively supervise their children's lives, the children are less likely to engage in dangerous sexual behavior.

Managing Nutrition Services

The CDC offers some suggestions for how schools can manage the nutrition services provided to students and staff. First, health education at the high school should include some instruction on basic nutrition. Most high schools benefit from participating in the USDA National School Lunch Program, and many of these participate in the breakfast program as well. Schools should make sure to order the following healthy foods: skim or low-fat milk, fruit juice, vegetables, baked goods that are low in fat, and fresh fruits. In order to best serve students, schools should employ a full-time nutritionist and food service manager. All food-service employees should receive some training in nutrition.

School-Provided Health Services

In order to provide adequate health services, the CDC recommends that every school have a coordinator of health services, a full-time physician, a nurse, and health aides. Schools should have policies in place to deal with students who have HIV/AIDS. Staff should be allowed to administer medication to students, provided students have the appropriate documentation. Moreover, students should be allowed to self-medicate with prescription inhalers and insulin injections as long as they are supervised by staff and have filled out the necessary paperwork. In order to fully serve students, many schools will need to form partnerships with local health agencies, organizations, or health professionals.

Mental Health and Social Services

The Centers for Disease Control has provided some basic guidelines for schools seeking to provide adequate mental health care and social services to students. It is recommended that each school have an employee to oversee mental health and social services; some schools may benefit from having a guidance counselor, psychologist, or social worker. Many states require schools to provide a Student Assistance Program (SAP) for all students. Schools that lack either the population or money for such services should partner with local health agencies. Schools that can provide counseling services to students may benefit from offering assessments as well as family, individual, and group counseling.

Health Promotion

The Centers for Disease Control outlines a few ways for schools to promote the health of the faculty and staff. Many schools have an employee in charge of overseeing health promotion for faculty and staff. Most schools allow the faculty and staff to use the exercise facilities maintained for students. Unfortunately, too many schools fail to provide physical examinations to employees. If possible, employees should also receive a tuberculosis test and screening for illegal drugs. Many school districts provide funding for alcohol treatment, HIV testing, nutrition counseling, stress management therapy, and weight management therapy for employees.

Family and Community Health

The Centers for Disease Control has issued some basic guidelines for schools to incorporate families and the community into school health programs. First, schools need to communicate their health programs and services to families. It is important for parents to know what materials and services are available to their children. Many schools have a specific employee charged with acting as a liaison between the school and the community. A number of schools benefit from a close working relationship with external health organizations and professionals. Many schools also open up school exercise facilities to members of the community. Schools should have a protocol in place in the event that a health educator needs to contact a student's family immediately.

Amount of Exercise

According to the Centers for Disease Control, individuals should engage in a minimum of 30 minutes of moderate exercise at least five days per week. By "moderate," the CDC means any level of activity in which oxygen consumption is increased to between three and six times the amount required during rest. Thirty minutes of moderate physical activity is roughly equivalent to a fast walk of about 2 miles. Fulfilling this exercise requirement does not necessarily mean starting a planned, regimented fitness program; a person can get 30 minutes of exercise simply by playing with a child or pet or by cleaning vigorously. Indeed, it may be better for individuals who are out of shape to get used to exercise gradually by introducing it into their normal lives.

Code of Ethics for the Health Education Profession

Preamble

The preamble to the Coalition of National Health Education Organization's Code of Ethics states that the health education profession is dedicated to promoting individual, family, and community health. Furthermore, it states that health educators should embrace a multicultural perspective and respect the worth of all students. The fundamental values underlying the Code of Ethics are respect for autonomy, promotion of social justice, promotion of good, and avoidance of harm.

Article 1

Health teachers are responsible for educating the general public about good health practices. In order to do this, they must support the rights of individuals to make informed decisions; encourage social policies that promote health; communicate the consequences of health services and programs; act on issues that can damage public health; be honest regarding their qualifications and limitations; protect the dignity and privacy of individuals; and actively work to involve individuals, groups, and communities in the educational process so that health issues are understood by all.

Article 2

Health educators are responsible for their own professional behavior, for the reputation of their profession, and for promoting ethical conduct in the profession. In order to do so, health educators must continuously maintain and expand their professional competence through study and training; join professional organizations; model and encourage nondiscriminatory behavior; encourage critical discourse that protects and enhances the profession; share the processes and results of their work; avoid conflicts of interest; and avoid violating the rights of others.

Article 3

Health educators must recognize the boundaries of their own professional competence and be accountable for their own activities and actions. In order to do this, they must accurately represent their qualifications and the qualifications of those they recommend; use appropriate standards, theories, and guidelines when carrying out professional duties; accurately represent potential outcomes to employers; anticipate and disclose competing commitments, conflicts of interest, and endorsement of products; openly communicate any job expectations that conflict with professional ethics; and maintain competence in their areas of practice.

Article 4

Health teachers must exercise ethical behavior in the delivery of health education. Health educators need to respect the rights, confidentiality, and worth of all people by adapting effective strategies for a diverse community. In order to do this, health educators must be sensitive to social and cultural diversity and in accordance with the law; stay informed of the latest advances in theory, research, and practice; stay committed to program evaluation and the methods used to achieve results; empower individuals to adopt healthy lifestyles; and communicate the potential outcomes of proposed services, strategies, and decisions to all relevant individuals.

Article 5

Health educators must contribute to the health of the population through research and evaluation and do so in accordance with federal and state law. They should support research practices that do no harm to individuals or the environment; ensure that participation in research is based on informed consent; respect the privacy and dignity of research participants; treat all information received from participants as confidential unless otherwise required by law; take credit only for work they themselves have performed; discuss the results of research or evaluation only with those for whom the service is performed, unless withholding information would jeopardize someone's health or safety; and report the results of research objectively, accurately, and in a timely manner.

Article 6

Health educators who are involved in the training of new health educators are required to provide their students with a quality education that benefits both the profession and the public. Health educators must select students based on merit and on a system of equal opportunity; strive to make the educational environment and culture conducive to overall health; engage in adequate and effective preparation; present up-to-date and appropriate material; give fair feedback to students; state reasonable objectives; conduct fair assessments; provide objective counseling; and provide adequate supervision and meaningful opportunities for professional development.

Laws

Individualized Education Program

The Individuals with Disabilities Education Act mandates that any disabled student will have an Individualized Education Program (IEP) created specifically for him or her. IEPs are created by teams of specialists, including school psychologists, parents, and special education teachers. The point of an IEP is to assess the student's performance and determine appropriate goals and methods for further schooling. Typically, it will include schedule modifications, necessary accommodations for transportation, and a vision statement indicating hopes for the student's future. For many students, an IEP will include the critical health information teachers may need to know in case of an in-class emergency.

Controlled Substances Law

For the most part, the law of the United States takes a stern view of the growth, use, and distribution of controlled substances, such as marijuana, cocaine, and heroin. These drugs are illegal in any quantity, and individuals carrying a certain minimum amount can be charged with possession with intent to sell, which carries a much stiffer penalty. Individuals will also receive a much stiffer penalty if they are discovered carrying drugs across state lines. The minimum age for purchasing tobacco products is 18 years of age in most states. Retail carriers can be fined substantially for selling to underage individuals. Moreover, more places are becoming off-limits to smoking every year; recently, the city of New York banned smoking in all of its bars and restaurants.

American Disability Law

For the most part, American disability law is regulated by the Americans with Disabilities Act of 1990 (ADA). This law prevents discrimination against disabled individuals with respect to housing, employment, education, and access to public services. Interestingly, the ADA includes alcoholism as a disability. The ADA asks that reasonable accommodations be made to provide equal opportunities to disabled individuals. States are not forbidden from passing their own disability laws, so long as they do not contradict the ADA. A number of other acts have been created as spin-offs to the ADA, eg, the Fair Housing Act, the Air Carrier Access Act, and the Individuals with Disabilities Education Act.

Immunization Laws

Every state sets specific immunization laws for children seeking to attend public school. Most states require children to be immunized for diphtheria, tetanus, pertussis, influenza, measles, mumps, rubella, polio, and hepatitis B. Some states will also require immunization against chickenpox. Though many schools offer these immunizations on-site, parents can also have them performed elsewhere and then provide documentation. There are no mandatory immunizations for adults, unless they are entering the military service. Individuals seeking to permanently migrate to the United States must receive immunization for every disease which is preventable by vaccine.

Inclusion and Public Law 94-142

A great deal of time is spent trying to equip teachers to handle students labeled "exceptional" for one reason or another. Furthermore, Public Law 94-142 mandates that schools must identify those students that require special treatment, whether for being extremely gifted or because of a disability. Many schools, however, feel that the best way to handle exceptional students is simply to include them in the regular classroom. Advocates of this program assert that specialists can come into the class and help exceptional students as necessary and that otherwise these students will benefit from being in contact with students from a wide range of abilities. However, this approach can overwhelm classroom teachers.

Mainstreaming

United States law indicates that students are to be educated in the least restrictive environment possible; that is, they should be allowed to join the highest level class in which they can participate. For many high-functioning disabled students, this means being "mainstreamed," or put into a class with normally-functioning students. The success or failure of such students often has a great deal to do with the expectations of the teacher; students who are ignored or who are made to feel they do not belong are more likely to have trouble. The AAHPERD states that it is "cruel" to place students in activities they are not equipped to handle, but it is "criminal" to exclude them from those in which they could contribute. The best strategy for teachers is to learn as much as possible about students and their disabilities before determining their level of participation.

Affirmative Action

Affirmative action is the set of programs that have been developed in the United States to try to offset the discrimination of the past. This policy was put into action by various government agencies after the passage of the Civil Rights Act in 1964, and is currently enforced by the Equal

Employment Opportunity Commission. Specifically, affirmative action policies allocate jobs and resources to specific groups that were discriminated against in the past, such as minorities and women. In the profession of physical education, this means not only that schools are prohibited from discriminating against formerly-oppressed groups, but that schools are required to hire qualified members of these groups whenever possible. This has led some to charge that affirmative action creates reverse discrimination. This issue has been batted about in the courts for decades, although affirmative action continues to apply.

OSHA

In the United States, work safety is overseen by the Occupational Safety and Health Administration (OSHA), which was created in 1970 by the Occupational Safety and Health Act. The major changes that have been effected by OSHA are placement of guards on all moving parts in industrial operations, regulation of chemical exposure to employees, enforcement of employee dress codes including protective equipment, mandatory disconnection of electrical equipment before repair, and specific requirements governing procedures for working in enclosed spaces. OSHA sets many other guidelines for specific businesses and routinely inspects worksites to ensure that they are safe for employees and visitors.

Types of Negligence

Several types of negligence are chargeable offenses. Malfeasance occurs when the teacher has committed some act which is against the law. Misfeasance, on the other hand, occurs when the teacher obeys the law but not well enough to prevent injury. Nonfeasance occurs when a teacher has failed to perform some act which could have prevented an injury to a student. Contributory negligence occurs when the injured student is, in part, to blame for the injury. Finally, comparative (or shared) negligence is said to have occurred when both the injured student and the teacher are to blame. In this latter situation, the student must prove that the teacher was more to blame in order to receive compensation from the teacher.

Lawsuit

No matter how responsible and cautious they are, many physical educators will be charged with negligence for a student injury at some point in their career. In order to avoid having their professional life seriously damaged by such allegations, teachers should make sure that they have liability insurance. This is typically provided by the school district. Often, a good liability insurance policy allows the teacher to settle cases out of court. Teachers should also be sure to keep good records of any accidents, as records are vital to a legal defense. Finally, teachers should create and maintain a comprehensive checklist of safety and emergency care guidelines so that they will be prepared in the event of any injury and can demonstrate an intention to protect students.

Sport Psychology

Sense of Effort

As a growing human being develops, he or she will learn how to gauge the degree of effort or force that is required to perform a given task. Anyone who has ever been swatted in the nose by an infant will recognize that children are not always aware of the effort necessary to get someone's attention. As this sense of required effort develops, one will be able to determine whether a given movement requires fast or slow performance, and whether the force behind it must be strong or weak. A slightly more complicated case arises when an individual is somehow constrained. Free movements, in which the only resistance is air and the limitations of the human body, will always require the same scale of effort; constrained motion, however, requires an accurate assessment of the strength of the constraint.

Open-Loop Motor Control Theory

The theory of motor control known as open-loop control asserts that movements are made according to a preexisting motor program, a set of muscle commands laid out before the movement is begun. These movements are performed without any adjustment based on feedback, the sensory information transmitted to the brain. Open-loop motor control theory seems to explain many of the common movements that individuals make unconsciously, and there is excellent research evidence to suggest that animals often perform tasks in a way similar to the open-loop model. However, many scientists maintain that open-loop theory is only accurate in situations where the movement is too short for there to be any meaningful feedback.

There are three general criticisms that have been made of the closed-loop theory of motor control. First, some scientists suggest that if a perceptual trace must be developed for every possible movement of which a human is capable, then the volume of these perceptual traces would quickly grow larger than the space available for their storage. Another criticism of the theory is that it has no formula for how movements will be performed for the first time; indeed, closed-loop theory really only applies to movements for which the individual has already developed a perceptual trace. Finally, some scientists insist that many movements are too brief for feedback to play a significant role in their execution, and therefore these would seem to be performed without the assistance of any perceptual trace.

Closed-Loop Motor Control Theory

The closed-loop theory of motor control requires that there be two different states of memory in order for a body to be able to correct its mistakes. One of these is a program of movement that is remembered by the body and is called a memory trace. This memory trace is responsible for initiating a particular movement. The state of memory which carries more responsibility for learning and controlling movement is called the perceptual trace. The perceptual trace is basically a standard of correctness: if the feedback resulting from a motion initiated by the memory trace indicates a departure from the perceptual trace, a change in the movement is ordered. In this model, the quality of a movement is only as high as the quality of the perceptual trace.

Individual Differences Research

A whole field of motor learning research, known as individual differences research, is concerned with charting the various behavioral abilities of different people. In this field, individual differences are defined as stable, enduring differences among people that contribute to permanent differences in performance. Identifying advantages in motor learning requires not only observing repeated superiority in the performance of a task but in determining what particular ability accounts for the disparity in performance. For instance, it is not enough for a scientist to watch one person consistently make more successful free throws than another; in order to conclude that the first person has superior motor skill, the scientist must isolate the particular ability that is superior and collect data in support of the hypothesis.

Other Factors Affecting Motor Performance

It is the job of a physical educator to remind students that natural ability is only one of the factors that contribute to motor performance. Some individuals perform well because they have been given more opportunities to learn than an average person. Individuals with an active temperament seek out opportunities and tend to have better motor performance. Body type contributes to motor performance, also, in that healthy, flexible people are more able to take advantage of their natural abilities. A child who is raised in a family or community that supports athletic endeavor is more likely to develop good motor skills. Finally, motivation, competitiveness, and vigor cannot be underestimated as factors affecting motor performance. No individual can be successful at the highest level of competition simply by relying on his or her natural ability.

General Motor Ability Myth

In the early days of motor ability research, it was thought that all the abilities called into play in performing a task were part of the same ability, known as general motor ability. This idea became popular at the same time as the notion of the intelligence quotient, which claimed to be able to give a universal assessment of cognitive ability. Besides being convenient, the idea of a general motor ability seemed to be borne out in most cases. Subsequent research, however, has indicated that the motor abilities of an individual may vary widely between tasks. For instance, individuals with great muscular strength are often inflexible and incapable of performing precise tasks quickly. Indeed, recent tests have shown that there is a great degree of variability even within the category of balance.

Body Awareness

In order to successfully develop and implement basic motor patterns, the human body has to have an awareness of its own dimensions and potentials. For instance, the body must be aware of its current orientation: not only its location and position, but also the range of motions that are possible from its current position. For instance, one develops an intuitive understanding that it is difficult to jump from a sitting position. The body, as it matures, will also develop a sense of balance in its various parts, so that wild movements can be made with the limbs without throwing the entire trunk off balance. Similarly the body will develop the ability to automatically transfer weight for the best performance of a given movement.

Relationships with People and Objects

The full development of motor skills requires the ability to assess and adjust to the various relationships that affect motion. These can be classified as either relationships with people or with objects. In relationships with people, an individual needs to be able to determine whether his motion is to be matching or contrasting. For example, a child on a see-saw has to determine that he cannot make the same pushing motion at the same time as his partner. One also has to determine whether one is leading or following another and adjust movements accordingly. As for the relationships with objects, it is essential to be able to know the orientation of the object in relation to oneself, as well as to be able to determine whether one will need to go around, through, over, or under the object.

MOTOR ABILITY ASSESSMENTS

FIGURE EIGHT RUN AND BALANCE BEAM

In the assessment of motor ability known as the figure eight run, subjects are required to run around a small course that demands making several quick turns. This test is timed to determine an individual's degree of speed and agility. In the balance beam test, subjects are required to perform a few different movements (for instance, standing on one foot, raising arms above the head, or standing on the toes) while traversing a beam two inches wide and twelve feet long. Subjects are timed and awarded points based on the number of movements they are able to perform on the balance beam. There are a few other clinical tests designed to measure balance, but most of these require expensive equipment and are unsuitable for the classroom.

VERTICAL JUMP AND BAR SNAP

It has been difficult for scientists to create tests of motor ability that are general enough to measure something other than the performance of the specific activity of the test. The vertical jump test measures leg power by requiring the subject to jump straight into the air from a stationary position. The individual's score is measured as the difference between the individual's standing reach and the highest point touched during three trial jumps. The bar snap exercise measures agility, power, and coordination. In this exercise, the legs are lifted and swung forward as far as possible while the subject is holding onto an overhead horizontal bar. The bar snap exercise is considered to be quite challenging. It is therefore not appropriate for everyone.

SPEED AND REACTION TIME

Speed is one of the easier aspects of motor ability to measure. Typically, an individual's speed is tested by timing a fifty- or hundred-yard sprint. Some measures of speed seek to eliminate differences caused by acceleration and only measure time once the individual has reached top speed. In order to measure reaction time, special equipment must be purchased, allowing the measurement of time to the hundredth of a second. Scientists use a number of different movements as gauges of reaction time, ranging from a simple motion of the hand to a full-body response. There are extensive records of male and female motor skill norms so that physical educators can determine how students compare to the general population.

SPEED DEVELOPMENT

In order to train for running distances of up to two miles, athletes need to train the anaerobic fast-twitch muscle fibers. This is most easily done by interval training, in which distances of between 100 and 400 yards are run as quickly as possible, with a brief period of rest in between. In order to train for sports that require a burst of speed along with cardiovascular endurance, such as soccer or basketball, it is good to run continuously, occasionally breaking into a sprint. Most fitness professionals believe that training at distances slightly greater than those required for competition is the best way to prepare. Also, many athletes report positive benefits from assisted intervals, in which running is done downhill. Theoretically, this will teach the muscles to work more quickly than usual.

GENDER, CONDITIONING, AND THE DEVELOPMENT OF MOTOR SKILL

Research has consistently shown that there are basic differences in the motor performance of men and women. However, these differences have been discovered to be based on differences in conditioning and body structure rather than on innate differences in ability. Girls tend to have far fewer opportunities to develop motor skills than do boys. This phenomenon is blamed on a number of different factors, from sexism in society that discourages girls from playing sports to socialization that encourages girls to engage in more sedentary activities. In any case, female and male athletes who have the same number of motor experiences are found to develop at much the same rate. This information is especially valuable for physical educators who may have to confront the false assumption that girls are not meant to play sports.

Coordinative Structures and Motor Control

The concept of coordinative structures suggests that some motor programs can group together seemingly independent parts of the body for the easier performance of certain tasks. Formerly, theorists assumed that there must be particular commands for each independent muscle group when an action is to be performed. Although this more-recently understood feature of the motor system may relieve the body of some administrative stress, it can be problematic as well, as anyone knows who has tried to improve a bad golf swing. Scientific research has shown, however, that with practice individuals can develop the ability to uncouple their coordinated structures and restore independent control.

Characteristics of Skilled Movement

Sheridan asserted that four characteristics of skilled movement must be accounted for by any theory that professes to describe motor control. First, a skilled movement will display some flexibility of movement. In other words, there must be the ability to accomplish the same task with a variety of different muscles and bones. Second, a skilled movement must have a degree of uniqueness because it is physically impossible for any two movements to be exactly alike. Third, a skilled movement must display some consistency, i.e., the individual will perform it in a similar way in a variety of situations. Fourth, a skilled movement will have some degree of mutability, i.e., the individual will be able to make small adjustments during its performance.

Gender, Body Structure, and Motor Performance

Research into the differences in motor performance between men and women has revealed that most of the advantages claimed by either gender are the result of differences in body structure. Men, for instance, tend to have more muscle mass in their upper body, and so they are likely to develop superior performance in skills like throwing or striking. Women, on the other hand, are noted for having a lower center of gravity and therefore balance, and so they may be better than men in the performance of certain movements. Both genders are limited in motor performance by their flexibility, skeletal size, body composition, and overall level of fitness. It has been frequently observed that the difference in motor performance between the best and the worst man is much greater than the difference between the average man and woman.

Dynamic Systems Theory

The dynamic systems theory of motor control is also referred to as the ecological theory or action systems theory. It posits that there is a dynamic (constantly changing) relationship between the individual and the environment. Within this relationship, the individual perceives various things and reacts to them either reflexively or voluntarily. Movements are the result of the integrated interaction of many smaller systems of biological, muscular, skeletal, neurological, and cardiorespiratory agents. This integration is known in dynamic systems theory as self-organization. This theory allows for the fact that minute adjustments are made constantly during the performance of a movement.

Reflex Theory

The reflex theory of motor control states that movements are the result of rapid, automatic responses to stimuli in the individual's environment. According to this model, once the reflexes in the spinal cord are stimulated by the sensory receptors in the various parts of the body, the reflexes process the information and stimulate a muscular response. Over time, an individual becomes conditioned to respond in a similar way to common stimuli, and the individual's reactions become faster and more precise. This theory of motor control accounts for the consistency of movement, but it does not seem to make room for voluntary control of movement. Also, it does not allow for the minute adjustments that individuals seem to be able to make during the performance of a movement.

Ecological Theory

The ecological theory of motor learning is based on the dynamic systems theory of motor control. It asserts that movement is the result of an interaction between the individual and the environment. This interaction is in large part based on the individual's sensory and perceptual skills. According to the ecological theory of motor learning, individuals are constantly scanning their environment, looking for ways to improve their performance of movements. Over time, individuals become better able to isolate the important information in the immediate environment and respond precisely and appropriately to it.

Schema Theory

The schema theory was developed in part as a reaction to the closed-loop theory's inability to describe how new actions are performed, how motor programs are stored, and how feedback can be a part of even the shortest movements. As with closed-loop theory, there are two distinct memory states in schemata theory. These are called schemata (the plural of schema), and are abstract versions of commonly-performed movements. According to the schema theory, the body takes common actions and develops a motor program of the general features of common actions. Then, the body is able to use that abstracted program to perform any similar action. Also, the body will call up an appropriate program when it is called upon to perform a new action.

According to schema theory, performance of a given movement enables the body to make an abstract motor program of that movement so that it will be able to perform similar movements in the future. This is known as a generalizable motor program, and is composed of the invariant features of the movement: that is, the aspects of force and timing which do not vary in other performances of the motion. These features are scaled (or, in scientific terms, parameterized) so that they can be applied to different cases. These specific requirements are covered in the motor program as variant features, such as which muscles are to be used.

In schema theory, the body has four sources from which it can gain information about how best to perform movements. The first source of information is called the initial conditions, and is the current status of the individual: his or her posture, position of limbs, etc. The response specifications identify the unique requirements of the response, for instance which direction it will take, which limbs will be involved, etc. During the performance of this response, the body will receive the sensory consequences, giving it an idea of the status of the movement. Finally, the response outcome will give the individual a sense of the end result of the movement. All of these sources of information are used by the two schemata: the recall schema, which organizes the specific programs needed for a response; and the recognition schema, which evaluates the outcome and makes any adjustments.

Information-Processing Theory

According to the information-processing theory of motor learning, an individual receives information in the form of stimuli from the outside world, selects a response, and then executes that response. During the reception of information, the individual must determine the nature of the stimulus. This will be more or less difficult depending on the familiarity of the stimulus, the number of competing stimuli, and the individual's personal characteristics. In the next phase, the individual determines what response, if any, is required. Then, the individual organizes the appropriate motor response. The resulting movement is known as the output. One of the criticisms of the information-processing theory is that it fails to account for the role of memory or anticipation in motor performance.

Hierarchical Model

One theoretical model that scientists use to explain motor control is the hierarchical model. According to this model, there is a higher level in the motor system that adjusts according to feedback and a lower level that performs the commands of the higher. The lower level, like a low ranking soldier in battle, continues to execute a set of directions until the upper level gives a different order. This model is a hybrid of open-loop and closed-loop theory because it allows for both automatic and modifiable movements. Some studies have indicated that when learning a new task individuals begin by using a closed-loop motor control and gradually move to a more hierarchical style.

Inverted-U Principle

Researchers have spent a great deal of time trying to determine how arousal and anxiety affect motor performance. One of the principles that have emerged from this research is known as the inverted–U principle. It asserts that an individual's performance will increase along with arousal level for a while, but if arousal continues to increase, then performance will begin to decline. The principle gets its name from the shape it takes when represented on a graph. The range of arousal in which an individual performs best is known as the zone of optimal functioning. Different individuals have different zones of optimal functioning depending on their trait anxiety: that is, their general disposition to consider situations as dangerous or threatening.

Reaction Time

An individual's reaction time (RT) is the time observed between the presentation of a stimulus and the occurrence of the person's response. RT is especially important for the information-processing school of motor learning because it provides a direct measure of the time taken by a complete processing and response event. The number of stimuli presented is one of the common factors that influence RT: the fewer stimuli, the shorter RT is likely to be. RT will also tend to be shorter if there is good compatibility between stimulus and response, i.e., the desired response is appropriate to the situation and uncomplicated. Finally, RT is generally much shorter if the desired response is one that has been practiced and performed many times in the past.

Spatial and Temporal Anticipation

Researchers into motor performance have classified anticipation as being either spatial or temporal. When a person can predict what is likely to happen in a given situation, it is known as spatial anticipation. For example, if you are driving and the car in front of you brakes in advance of an intersection, you may suspect that the driver is going to turn. This is spatial anticipation. Temporal anticipation, on the other hand, occurs when an individual can predict when something is going to happen or the length of time that something will take to happen. This kind of information is useful in many kinds of settings, from gauging the speed of an oncoming object to anticipating the appearance of a certain stimulus. Most researchers, however, think that motor reaction is more dramatically improved by spatial anticipation than by temporal anticipation.

Hick's Law

Hick's Law was developed during the study of choice reaction time while investigating the amount of time it takes an individual to respond to an unanticipated stimulus. Basically, Hick's Law declares that choice reaction time will increase in proportion to the number of choices made available. This law, which seems a bit obvious on the surface, has become a fundamental principle of the study of motor performance because it has been able to establish such a clear predictive measure for reaction time. In fact, subsequent studies have shown that reaction time seems to increase by the same amount every time the number of choices is doubled. This law has found applications in everything from basketball to military tactics.

Cooperative Games

Many teachers find that cooperative games are a positive way to build teamwork among students while still developing motor skills and strategy concepts. There are five basic components that are emphasized by a cooperative game: fun, cooperation, equality, participation, and trust. A good cooperative game must be enjoyable, or else students will not want to continue. It must also require students to have faith in one another. and the active participation of all students. The goal of a cooperative game is to generate enthusiasm for physical activity, even among students who are normally reticent about joining in.

Competitive Games

A competitive game is any one in which players or teams vie to defeat one another. Competitive games can be a great motivator in physical education class, as long as the competition is seen as a chance for everyone to test their skills and improve, rather than as a chance for superior athletes to embarrass others. In order to keep the games fun for all students, teachers should make a point of assessing student abilities and ensuring that no unfair matchups arise. Also, teachers should stress that competition is a way to find the areas in which each person needs to improve

Invasion Games

Basics of Invasion Games

Invasion games are any team games in which players have to penetrate the territory of an opponent, and either enter a goal themselves or put a ball of some kind into a goal. Invasion games are a good way for students to get an appreciation for different strategies of attack and defense, to develop teamwork skills, and to improve whatever particular skills are required by the game. Some examples of invasion games are soccer, football, basketball, hockey, lacrosse, and Ultimate Frisbee. Invasion games force students to use both their mind and body in order to outwit and outmaneuver their opponents. For this reason, invasion games have been cited as beneficial to coordination, reflexes, and problem-solving skills.

Tactics

When teaching students to participate in invasion-style games, it is important to ensure that they understand the basic rules, strategies, and tactics of the given game. To this end, students should be taught when to pass and when to maintain control of the ball (passing, of course, should be done when one is defended). Also, students should begin to consider which places on the field are the easiest from which to score, and which places are the easiest from which an opponent can score. In most games that have a small goal at one end of the field, it is easiest to score from the middle of the field at that end. Students should also learn about different attack and defense formations, and the various merits of each. Finally, students should learn about the different roles of the members of the team; for example, the midfielders' responsibility to distribute the ball.

Developmental of Technical Skills

One of the objectives of teaching an invasion game is to improve certain skills, like passing, receiving, or shooting a ball. In order to accomplish this objective, teachers should give direct instruction to students on the techniques used in the game in question (for instance, teaching the bounce and chest passes in basketball), including the demonstration of how to position the body to best advantage. Students should also learn how to shield the ball from defenders, and how to quickly change speed or direction while maintaining control of a ball. In the end, students will have successfully met the skills objective if they can perform with accuracy, understand the basic skills for each game, and know how to keep score in each game.

Evaluation of a Student's Progress

When students have learned and understand the basic strategies of an invasion game, they should be capable of playing the game in a number of different formations and with teams of various sizes. They should also be able to determine the appropriate strategy for a given game situation; for example, they should know when to pursue a risky attack towards the end of a losing game). Students should also demonstrate the basic principles of defense, by marking opponents closely and keeping the ball away from dangerous areas. Advanced students will be able to look at a game and determine which areas need improvement, and what strategies might be more effective. These students will be able to describe the particular advantages of good players and will know the best tactics to take advantage of their team's talents.

Individual Psychology

Unfortunately, there are some aspects of a physical education class which may affect student participation and which cannot be changed. For one thing, sometimes there may be spectators at a class activity, and this may discourage some students from participating. Most research has shown that the presence of an audience only increases participation among those students who feel they are skilled at the activity. Another external factor that may influence participation is competition. Despite a teacher's most diligent efforts to make an activity non-competitive, sometimes students will compare themselves to one another, and those students who feel their performance is inferior may be discouraged from participation.

There are a few changes a physical educator can make to the classroom environment that will influence and encourage student participation. For one thing, he can institute a token rewards system, whereby students earn something by participating. These rewards might be food, candy, certain privileges, or just recognition. Setting goals for a class or for an individual student is also a good way to increase participation. Oftentimes, students will respond positively to an explicit goal, especially if it is one they believe they can attain. A teacher may also influence participation by creating an atmosphere of encouragement in the classroom. If the teacher is constantly exhorting students to achieve, more students are likely to want to participate.

Perceptual Differences

Studies have shown that differences in the quality of an individual's perception may directly affect the quality of the performance of certain tasks. One study assessed the effects of four kinds of visual perception: static visual acuity (perception of stationary objects), dynamic visual acuity (perception of moving objects), size constancy (perception of objects of different sizes), and depth perception. The study determined that for basketball players only static visual acuity was related to success in shooting free throws. For shooting a field goal at any other time, the only relevant visual perception was dynamic visual acuity. It was noted that inequalities among an individual's perceptual abilities were quite normal. For this reason, researchers have concluded that differences in perceptual ability may underlie inconsistencies in the performance of seemingly similar tasks.

Ability Patterns

As research has mounted suggesting that individuals may have an immensely detailed repertoire of abilities, it has become necessary for physical educators to refine their position on individual performance. Educators expect that individuals will display somewhat consistent patterns of performance: that is, their ability in a certain task will probably be consistent with their abilities in similar tasks. However, an individual's pattern of abilities is not the only factor that contributes to performance. Skill, motivation, and practice will also contribute to the performance of motor tasks in physical education class. Indeed, the most recent research in this field suggests that mood can be one of the prime determinants of success or failure in athletic competition.

ABILITY GROUPING

Many teachers, faced with a diverse class, resort to grouping students according to some variable. Most teachers are familiar enough with the law and with basic courtesy to know that it is inappropriate to divide students according to gender, ethnicity, or socioeconomic status. Nevertheless, many teachers persist in grouping students according to ability, despite consistent research suggesting that this practice is destructive. For one thing, ability grouping tends to reinforce differences in expectation levels and in the treatment of students. When this practice is used, the high-performing students tend to improve, while low-performing students only get worse. The only successful ability grouping occurs when students receive equal attention and have the opportunity to change groups based on their performance.

EDUCATOR ADJUSTMENT

It is important for physical educators to be aware that students will have different levels of ability for different tasks and to take this into account when guiding their students. It is not appropriate to set the same performance goals for every student. On the other hand, individuals should not be allowed to focus solely on those activities in which they excel. Rather, physical educators should strive to help students become self-aware and to work conscientiously on those areas of performance in which they have less natural ability. By maintaining a positive attitude while new skills are being acquired, educators can encourage students to improve their all-around performance.

CLASS PARTICIPATION

Some personal factors that discourage students from participating in physical education class are virtually impossible to change. One of the major factors that discourages participation is anxiety; students who are temperamentally prone to worrying about performance or obsessing over possible negative consequences of participation are more likely to stay on the sidelines. Some individuals have a higher level of stress during competitive activities, and they are more likely to avoid competitive situations. Often, these individuals perceive competitive situations as being more threatening then they really are. The good news for individuals who suffer from competition-related anxiety is that it seems to decrease with more exposure to athletic competition.

There are a number of personal factors that teachers can try to change in students in order to increase their class participation. It has been consistently shown, for instance, that a student's level of participation is directly tied to his or her impression of the incentives; in other words, if the student feels that he or she will gain something from participation, then he or she is more likely to join in. Part of successful motivation is persuading reluctant students that they have something to gain by participating. Students will also be more likely to participate if they have a natural affinity for the activity. This is a bit more difficult for a teacher to create, but many studies have shown that repeated exposure to an activity is likely to result in the development of appreciation for that activity.

Group Environment

When physical educators refer to group environment as a factor influencing the performance of a team, they mean the situational, physical, or geographical conditions that surround the group. These conditions may be either objective or subjective: a large audience, for instance, is only influential if the team perceives the audience to be large. Perhaps the classic example of environment as an influence on group dynamics is the so-called "home-field advantage." Research has shown that such an advantage does exist, and that it is virtually the same for every competitive sport. The reason for home-field advantage is believed to have something to do with the adverse psychological phenomena associated with playing in front of an unfriendly crowd.

Group Composition

In physical education, a group or team is defined as a collection of individuals who share a goal, have a structured way of interacting, have a shared identity, and consider themselves to be a group. One of the factors that influences the performance of such a group is the group composition: that is, the characteristics of the various people who make up the group. The characteristics might include the ages, sizes, aptitudes, skill levels, and genders of the members of the group. Many studies have shown that a beneficial arrangement of players on a team may influence success more than simply a high average skill level among the members.

Group Structure

The performance of a group is heavily influenced by the group structure, which is the position, status, and responsibility of each group member, and the standards for behavior (norms) held by the members of the group. The importance assigned to various group members is based on two factors: task dependence and propinquity. Task dependence is the degree to which a player must relate to the others during the course of a game. A catcher, for instance, is much more central to the action in a baseball game than is a left fielder. Propinquity is the extent to which a player has knowledge of and is seen to be a part of the action. For players in varying positions of responsibility, there will be varying chances for reward or recognition for good performance.

Cooperation

When physical educators refer to group cohesion as a factor influencing the performance of teams, they mean the degree to which a team can remain united and cooperate in pursuit of a common goal. There may be different reasons for group cohesion: in some cases, individuals with little social connection may all feel drawn to the common goal, while in other cases a group of close associates may feel loyal to one another without especially valuing the stated goal. In physical activities, cohesion and cooperation determine success. Interestingly, though, studies have shown that it is much more common for success to lead to cohesion than vice versa. Basically, winning teams tend to create better environments for cooperation and mutual advancement.

There are a few basic group processes that every team must perform: communication, the establishment of collective goals, the performance of various group tasks, analysis of success or failure, and the development of a collective identity. The degree to which the team is able to perform these tasks efficiently and positively will determine the achievement of the group. Recent research has centered on the existence of collective goals: that is, aspirations of the group that exceed any personal ambitions. In successful teams, there is often the willingness to put the welfare of the team first. Another determinant of team success is the degree to which team members recognize their own role in the performance of group processes and tailor their actions to be the most efficient within the context of that particular team. Sometimes, for instance, it is necessary for a would-be leader to step back and let someone else lead if that is what is best for the team.

Competition

When considering whether or not to make class activities competitive, teachers should consider a number of factors. For one thing, in competitive activities the level of participation is often uneven throughout the class, since successful players tend to play more and be involved in more games. On the other hand, surveys have shown that most students want to participate in competitive events, even if they do not expect to win. The personal investment of competition, along with the social training provided by winning and losing, can be a great advantage of competition. On the whole, most secondary physical education teachers seem to find that the most popular activities are those that combine recreation and competition.

Recreation versus competition

One of the perennial issues facing physical educators is whether activities should be promoted as forms of recreation or as competition. If competition is to be the dominant feature, then activities must have explicit rules, a formal way of keeping score, and identifiable winners and losers. When students are taught activities for competition, the emphasis will be on practicing specific skills, and avoiding mistakes as much as possible. When sports are taught as recreation, participation is the most important factor for students. Each student should get an equal amount of experience and performance time, regardless of his or her skill level. Although score is typically not kept in strictly recreational activities, students may receive certificates for good sportsmanship or diligent participation.

Specialization and generalization

One of the issues that has been consistently debated in physical education over the past few decades is the question of whether professional education should include specialized training, for instance driver education or health and safety education. Some educators feel that these subjects are naturally within the domain of physical education, and as such should be included in the curriculum. Others, however, worry that teachers will not be able to treat any one subject adequately if so many diverse topics are to be covered. At present the general consensus is that the primary responsibility of physical education is to develop physical activity in sport and exercise, and that other topics relating to the human body should not interfere with this mission.

Personal-social development

There are a few different conceptual models of how teachers can motivate students to participate in physical education. The personal-social development model asserts that students can be motivated by the incentive to improve their lives through cooperation and personal responsibility. This model is particularly popular among those theorists who envision physical education as merely a component of a total education. They claim that students will be motivated by the idea that physical activity can enhance all of the other areas of their lives. Personal-social models of development may center on self-esteem (participation will make students feel better about themselves), moral education (participation will teach students how to behave morally), and responsibility (participation will encourage students to take charge of other areas of their lives).

Participation

Recent research has indicated that a major factor in the success or failure of students is how they perceive the expectations of their teacher. Indeed, teacher expectations are a sort of "self-fulfilling prophecy": students tend to perform at the level at which they are expected to perform. Teachers form expectations from a number of sources, both static (gender, race, age) and dynamic (behavioral patterns, past performance). Subsequently, a teacher will pay more or less attention to a student depending on whether or not he or she believes that attention will be worthwhile. Even if expectations are not spoken , they are perceived by students, who are likely to perform in a manner consistent with expectations.

Skill Discrepancy

When teachers organize students for competitive activities, they need to strive for fairness and impartiality. It is important that every student feels that he or she has a chance to succeed. For this reason, it is a bad idea to organize one-on-one competitions in areas where the differences in skill are extreme. For the most part, team sports are the best way to combine players of different abilities, as being part of a team gives everyone a role and a chance to contribute. Furthermore, many times team sports have the effect of minimizing the differences in talent that may exist in a class. In other words, the best players on the team will have to depend on the worst, and vice versa. If this skill discrepancy is managed successfully by the teacher, it can be an excellent social skill-building exercise.

Creation of Fair Teams

When dividing students into teams, a physical educator should strive for heterogeneity; that is, teams should be composed of students of varying genders, ages, and skill levels, if possible. There are a couple of ways to create heterogeneous teams. One way is to select two students of similar skill level and have those students select teammates. However, rather than conducting this process in front of the other students, and risking hurt feelings for those students chosen last, the teacher should have the two captains pick their teams in private. Another way to ensure heterogeneous teams is to write the names of the students down in groups according to skill level, and then pick the names at random. In this way, each team can be assured of having the same number of players from each respective skill group.

Competition and Gender

For many years, female physical educators were discouraged by the extreme competitiveness of most men's athletic programs. For this reason, many women advocated non-competitive activities like dance and aerobics. Although many women still endorse this policy, there has been a recent trend towards competition in women's physical education. Specifically, the increase in popularity of such sports as soccer, basketball, and softball has led many women into the arena of competition. In many high schools, this trend has been credited with drawing more attention to female athletic excellence, and dispelling some stereotypes about the ability of women to compete at a high level. However, many female physical educators still decry what they see as an over-emphasis on winning and losing that excludes many girls from participating.

Research Methodology and Experimental Research

The Empirical Approach and the Scientific Method

Empirical science requires that one gains knowledge through experience (i.e., the senses), as opposed to rationalism, which asserts that one gains knowledge through logic and reason. The empirical approach (gaining knowledge through experience) led to scientific enquiry, in which facts and evidence are gathered through observation and experiments.

The definition of the scientific method in the *Oxford English Dictionary* states that it is "a method or procedure that has characterized natural science since the 17th century, consisting of systematic observation, measurement, and experiment and the formulation, testing, and modification of hypotheses." In essence, the scientific method is a process of developing and testing theories. Said theories may be formed in the process of conceptualizing problems. A hypothesis is a testable prediction that one arrives at logically from a theory. Psychological studies follow the scientific method, including experiments, case studies, and surveys. The scientific method requires critical thinking. Without critical thinking, one cannot utilize logic to make conclusions.

Theory and Hypothesis

A theory is a proposed explanation of a phenomenon or behavior that is typically based on observation or previous research. Theories are often not proven and through further research may be modified or completely rejected. A hypothesis is typically a one-sentence statement that aims to predict the certain phenomenon to be tested in the research experiment. Based on the results of the research, the hypothesis is either supported or not supported. Both theories and hypotheses are components that are tested or further explored for scientific research. Both components are essential in an experiment because they provide support for the purpose of the study as well as the focus of what the researcher hopes to or expects to find with the results.

Behavioral Psychology

The basis of behavioral psychology is that all behaviors are learned. This school of psychology, founded by John B. Watson, is based on the belief that behaviors can be measured, trained, and changed. This perspective became dominant in the early half of the 20th century due to the work of B. F. Skinner and John B. Watson. Watson's paper, "Psychology as the Behaviorist Views It," established the school of behavioral psychology in 1913. Behavioral psychology theorizes that all behaviors are acquired through conditioning, which occurs through interaction with one's environment.

Behaviorism asserts that one can study behavior in a systematic and observable manner and need not consider internal mental states. Behaviorism studies only observable behaviors and sees internal states, such as cognitions, emotions, and moods, as too subjective. The strict behaviorist would believe that any individual could potentially be trained to perform any task without regard to genetic background, personality, or internal processes as long as he or she experiences the right conditioning.

Critics of behaviorism assert that this approach is a one-dimensional way of understanding human behavior and that behavioral theories do not account for types of learning that occur without the use of reinforcement and punishment. They also do not account for the idea of free will and other internal influences like moods, thoughts, and feelings.

Behavioral psychology has brought us useful approaches to changing maladaptive or harmful behaviors through intensive behavioral intervention, behavior analysis, and token economies. Behaviorism is easier to quantify and collect data and information than some other schools of psychology when one is conducting research.

Cognitive Psychology

Cognitive psychology studies the mind, mental function, mental processes that affect behavior including learning, memory, attention, perception, reasoning, language, conceptual development, and decision-making. The work of cognitive psychology is present in other psychological disciplines, including social psychology, educational psychology, psychology of personality, abnormal psychology, and developmental psychology.

Humanistic Psychology

Humanistic psychology has five basic principles, which are as follows:

- Human beings cannot be reduced to components and, as human, surpass the sum of their parts.
- The existence of human beings is within both a uniquely human context and a cosmic ecology.
- Human beings are conscious; that is, they are both aware and aware of their awareness. This includes an awareness of self in relation to others.
- Human beings have choice and responsibility.
- Human beings seek creativity, meaning, and value. They seek goals, act with intention, and have awareness of their roles in future events.

The perspective of humanistic psychology rose in response to what adherents see as the limitations of the work of Sigmund Freud and his psychoanalytic theory and the behaviorism of B. F. Skinner. This approach emphasizes the natural drive of the individual toward self-actualization and creativity. It focuses on creativity, free will, and human potential and asserts that people are inherently good. An early source of humanistic psychology comes from the work of Carl Rogers, who in turn was deeply influenced by the work of Otto Rank (who broke away from Freud in the mid-1920s). Rogers coined the phrase "actualizing tendency," and this concept later led Abraham Maslow to study the topic of self-actualization as one of the needs that humans have. Maslow and Rogers worked in response to what they viewed as the overly pessimistic view of psychoanalysis. They introduced a more positive response in humanistic psychology, which some see more as a perspective on the human condition that informs psychological research and practice than as a discipline within psychology. One later development in psychology that would not have occurred without humanistic psychology is the idea of emotional intelligence.

Behaviorist Versus Humanistic Psychology

Behaviorist psychology focuses on the mind by observing human behaviors. This school of thought asserts that whereas one cannot measure or observe feelings, human actions can reveal emotions. Humanistic psychology focuses on the current environment of the individual in determining the reasons for behaviors. Humanistic psychology does not see looking into the past (as with psychoanalysis) as sufficient to obtain a clear picture of the individual. Both these fields of psychology focus on observing human actions; however, behavioral psychology focuses on objective observations with no consideration for internal mental processes of the individuals, whereas humanistic psychology focuses on the individual's potential for growth by determining what in their environment needs to be changed to improve functioning.

Biological Psychology

The biological approach to psychology is also known as behavioral neuroscience, psychobiology, or biopsychology. It applies the principles of biology, specifically neurobiology, to the study of developmental, physiological, and genetic mechanisms of behavior in both humans and nonhuman animals. This approach studies at the level of basic biological processes, neurons, neurotransmitters, and brain circuitry that lie beneath behavior, both normal and abnormal. Many experiments in this area of psychology involve animal (nonhuman) subjects such as rats, mice, and nonhuman primates but enhance the understanding of human pathology.

Principles of Biological Psychology

William James wrote *The Principles of Psychobiology* in 1890, and in it he asserts that psychology as a scientific study should be based on an understanding of biology. Many early psychologists, including James, had significant training in physiology. Biological psychologists explore similar themes as other psychologists but are limited by the need to use nonhuman animals. Because of this, much of the literature in this area of psychology explores mental processes and behaviors that are shared across species, including the following:

- Emotion
- Biological rhythms and sleep
- Memory and learning
- Movement control
- Motivated behavior (i.e., sex, hunger, thirst)
- Perception and sensation

Recent technological advances and the increasing sophistication of research methods allow biological psychologists to expand into other, classical, areas of psychology, including language, decision-making and reasoning, and consciousness. Biological psychology has a strong history of contributing to our understanding of medical disorders such as Parkinson's disease, Huntington's disease, Alzheimer's disease, clinical depression, schizophrenia, autism, anxiety, and substance abuse.

The Psychodynamic Approach

The psychodynamic approach, also referred to as dynamic psychology, studies the psychological forces that influence human behaviors and emotions. It explores the relationship between conscious and unconscious motivation. Psychodynamics studies the interrelationships of the mind, personality, and psyche as related to forces (mental, emotional, and motivational), particularly at the unconscious level. The psychodynamic approach can also refer to the psychoanalytical approach that Sigmund Freud and his followers developed, as inspired by the scientific theory of thermodynamics. Freud asserted that psychological energy was constant, with emotional changes consisting only of energy displacements.

Classical Freudian psychoanalysis tends to consist of treatment three to five times per week. In contrast, psychodynamic therapy can be less intensive and consist of only one to two sessions per week. Both of these types of therapy rely on a theory of inner, subconscious conflict and in which repressed feelings and behaviors rise to the patient's consciousness.

Psychodynamics studies changes in psychic energy among the id, ego, and superego, which are all aspects of one's personality. Freud asserted that the ego is at the heart of all psychological processes, and he sees the ego as contending with the id, the super-ego, and the world outside the self. The id is the unconscious reserve of psychic energy fueling instincts and psychic processes, otherwise known as the libido. The superego is the reservoir of an individual's morality and values and consists of both the internalization of society's most basic rules and norms (conscience) as well as the internalization of the individual's own goals (ego ideal). The ego operates as the administrator of personality and makes decisions about the pleasures that the id demands, keeping the individual safe, and the morality of the superego that it will follow.

Freud's model concentrates on the ever-changing interactions among id, ego, and superego and tries to explain human behavior in terms of these intrinsic forces or processes.

The Evolutionary Approach

The theoretical approach of evolutionary psychology endeavors to explain certain traits, both mental and psychological (including memory, language, or perception), as adaptations. In other words, evolutionary psychology views these traits as practical outcomes of the process of natural selection. A primary assertion of this approach is that the brain (also, mind) evolved to solve problems that humanity's ancient ancestors faced. In other words, this approach focuses on how evolution forms mind and behavior, primarily in humans but also in other organisms with a nervous system.

Certain behavior most likely developed as an adaptive process. In other words, individuals who adapt certain behaviors can be more likely to survive and reproduce or even to have the opportunity to reproduce (i.e., by appearing more attractive to potential mates). Evolutionary psychology can sometimes explain behaviors that may appear to make little sense (physical response to mental stress) or even those that are dysfunctional (mental illness).

Biopsychology

The biological aspects of behavior and mental processes are the focus of this subfield. Specialties within the subfield include *physiological psychology,* which studies the neural, cellular, and genetic mechanisms that cause specific behaviors by using animal models. Also included is *cognitive neuroscience,* which uses neural imaging tools to investigate the neural parallels of psychological processes in humans, and *neuropsychology,* which determines specific aspects and the extent of cognitive deficits caused by brain damage or disease through the use of psychological assessments.

Clinical and Cognitive Psychology

Clinical psychology studies and applies psychology to understand, prevent, and treat psychologically based dysfunction. Many clinical psychologists concentrate on psychological assessments and psychotherapy, and many primarily seek to promote well-being and personal development. Some clinical psychologists engage in other areas of practice, such as research, teaching, consultation, or forensic testimony. Within clinical psychology there are four primary theoretical approaches. These are psychodynamic, cognitive behavioral, existential-humanistic, and systems therapy approaches.

The subfield of cognitive psychology gives its attention to the mental processes that bring about mental activity. These mental processes include perception, attention, reasoning, problem-solving, memory, learning, language, and emotion. Within cognitive psychology we can find cognitive psychologists and neuroscientists, linguists, researchers in artificial intelligence and human-computer interaction, computational neuroscientists, logicians, and cognitive social psychologists.

Developmental and Learning Psychology

Developmental psychologists endeavor to understand the processes of the development of the human mind throughout the life span. This subfield of psychology examines how people perceive, understand, and behave within the world and how all of these change as they grow older. Developmental psychologists are particularly interested in cognitive, affective/emotional, moral, social, and neural development. Research in this area tends to focus on the ages that experience rapid change, such as infancy, adolescence, and older adulthood.

Learning psychology, more commonly referred to as educational psychology, is the subfield of psychology that deals with the scientific study of learning in human beings. Psychologists in this subfield examine individual difference in intelligence, cognitive development, affect, motivation, self-regulation, and self-concept and how all of these play roles in learning. Educational psychology is interested in the study of memory, conceptual processes, and individual differences in coming up with new strategies for learning processes in human beings. Theories that influence learning psychology are operant conditioning, functionalism, structuralism, constructivism, humanistic psychology, Gestalt psychology, and information processing.

Industrial-Organizational Psychology

Industrial-organizational (I-O) psychologists apply psychological concepts and techniques to improve human potential in the workplace. One area of I-O psychology, personnel psychology, seeks to utilize psychological methodology and principles to select and evaluate workers. Another subset of I-O psychology is organizational psychology, in which work environment and management styles are examined for their effect on worker motivation, job satisfaction, and productivity.

Subfields of Psychology

Personality Psychology

The subfield of personality psychology deals with long-lasting patterns of behavior, thought, and emotion in individual human beings. Different approaches to theories of personality include neo-Freudianism, trait theory, and social cognitive theory.

Sensation and Perception Psychology

The subfield of sensation and perception examines how elemental stimuli in the environment are translated into a complex psychological phenomenon, such as how light is translated into the human perception of color. All five senses are examined in this subfield as well as physiology of the sensory systems and theories of perception.

Social Psychology

The subfield of social psychology studies how human beings regard each other and how they relate to one another. This area of study deals with subjects like social influence, attitudes, prejudice, group dynamics, and social justice. Subtypes of social psychology include social cognition and social neuroscience. Social psychology is seen by many as a bridge between psychology and sociology.

Contributions of Wilhelm Wundt

Wilhelm Wundt is often called the father of psychology. He opened the first laboratory dedicated to psychology; its opening is thought of as the beginning of modern psychology. Wundt separated psychology from philosophy and studied the working of the mind in a more structured way than was previously done. In his studies he emphasized objective measurement and control. Wundt's background in physiology is evident in the topics he studied, such as the study of reaction times and sensory processes. Wundt founded the school of voluntarism, which is the process of organizing the mind. A follower of Wundt's later developed his theories and described the system as structuralism, which is the analysis of the basic elements that constitute the mind.

Wundt believed that the structure of the human mind and conscious mental states could be scientifically studied using introspection, which was a highly practiced form of self-examination. He developed a theory of conscious thought by training his psychology students to make observations that were biased by personal interpretation or previous experience. Although introspection was a great focus of Wundt's, it did not remain an elemental tool of psychological study past the early 1920s. Rather, Wundt's greatest contribution was showing that psychology could be a valid experimental science, which he did in part by conducting his research in carefully controlled conditions.

The three areas of mental functioning on which Wundt concentrated were thoughts, images, and feelings, which are the basic areas studied today in cognitive psychology. The study of perceptual processes is traced back to him, and he can be called the founder of experimental psychology.

Contributions of William James

William James has been called the "father of American psychology." He is best known for his association with the philosophical school of pragmatism, as a founder of functional psychology, as well as the James Lange theory of emotion. He himself struggled with depression for much of his life. He wrote *The Principles of Psychology* in 1890, which met wide acclaim. Some, however, were critical of the tone of the work, such as psychologist Wilhelm Wundt, who called it "beautiful, but . . . not psychology."

The psychological philosophy known as functionalism, or functional philosophy, views mental life and behavior in relation to active adaptation to the person's environment. Functionalism gives a general basis for formulating psychological theories that are not testable by controlled experiments. Functionalism surfaced in the United States in the late 1800s in response to structuralism and later helped lead to behaviorism.

Contributions of Ivan Pavlov

Ivan Petrovich Pavlov, a Russian physiologist, is best known for his work in classical conditioning. He won the Nobel Prize for Physiology or Medicine in 1904. Pavlov's most famous concept is that of the conditioned reflex, which he developed in 1901. He learned this concept when examining salivation rates among dogs. Pavlov showed that when food being presented to a dog is done so in coordination with a bell or other sound, the dog would eventually learn to salivate without the presentation of the food and only with the sound. The idea of conditioning as an automatic form of learning became a key component to the school of behaviorism. Pavlov's work continues to have huge influence in modern behavior therapy.

Contributions of John Watson

John Broadus Watson was an American psychologist who established the psychological school of behaviorism. Watson conducted research on child rearing, advertising, and animal behavior through his behaviorist approach. His best-known research is the "Little Albert" experiment, which was quite controversial. In this experiment, Watson conditioned a small child to fear a white rat by pairing Albert's seeing the rat with a loud, frightening noise. They showed that this fear could be generalized to other white, furry objects. The ethical criticisms of this experiment include the fact that the young child was never deconditioned.

Watson's theories purported that the human mind began as a tabula rasa, or blank slate. He believed that one could mold an infant into any type of person one wanted—doctor, lawyer, beggar, or thief—regardless of the child's background and ancestry. He believed psychology should focus on observable behavior only, not on introspection.

Contributions of Sigmund Freud

Sigmund Freud was an Austrian neurologist, primarily known as the father of psychoanalysis, which is a clinical method for treating psychopathology through dialogue (between patient and psychoanalyst). Credited to Freud are therapeutic techniques such as free association as well as the discovery of transference. The primary theory underlying Freud's theory of psychoanalysis is the Oedipus complex. Dream analysis had a large role in Freud's practice and contributed to his theory of the unconscious as a disruptive force to the conscious state of mind.

In his theory of psychosocial development, Freud posits that psychological development in childhood occurs in a series of predetermined stages. He referred to these stages as "psychosexual stages" because (in his view) each stage represents the focus of libido (which he described as the drive for pleasure, not just sexual pleasure). As the child grows physically, different areas of his/her body become the focus of potential pleasure, frustration, or both. If a stage is not completed successfully, a child may become fixated on that particular part of the body or erogenous zone and will either over- or under-indulge in adulthood.

Freud's Psychosexual Developmental Stages

Oral stage (birth to 18 months). During this stage, a child focuses on oral pleasures (i.e., sucking). If the child has too much or too little oral gratification in this stage, it can result in an oral fixation, which is indicated by a preoccupation with oral activities (e.g., smoking, drinking, eating, or nail biting). Those who have an oral fixation or oral personality may be overly dependent on others, perpetual followers, and gullible. Conversely, it is also possible that they fight their urges and become pessimistic and aggressive toward others.

Anal stage (18 months to 3 years). The focus of pleasure during the anal stage is on eliminating and retaining feces. The child must learn to control anal stimulation by means of society's pressure (typically via the parents). Those adults with an anal fixation can have a preoccupation with cleanliness, perfection, and control. This is known as anal retentive. Conversely, they can also become messy and disorganized, which is known as anal expulsive.

Phallic stage (3 to 6 years). In this stage, the focus of pleasure is the genitals. Freud posited that in this stage, a boy develops unconscious sexual desires for his mother and consequently becomes rivals with his father, seeing him as competition for his mother's affection. He also is afraid of castration by his father as punishment for these feelings of desire. Freud named this phenomenon the Oedipus complex. Later, other thinkers added to the theory that girls go through a similar situation but with the genders reversed (i.e., having sexual feelings for their fathers). Freud disagreed with this, but it has been named the Electra complex by other psychoanalysts. Fixation in the phallic stage can cause sexual deviancies (of both avoidance and overindulgence) and weak or confused sexual identity.

Latency stage (6 years to puberty). During this stage, children's sexual urges are repressed, and they interact and play primarily with peers of the same sex.

Genital stage (puberty onward). This last stage of psychosexual development begins with puberty, when sexual urges are reawakened (after the latency stage). Adolescents direct their sexual urges onto opposite sex peers, and the primary focus of pleasure is the genitals.

Id, Ego, and Superego

Freud also posited that the human psyche has more than one facet. He saw the psyche as constructed of three parts: the id, ego, and superego. Each of these develops at different stages of life. These are not physical parts of the brain but rather psychological systems.

The most primitive and instinctive aspect of personality is the id. It is the impulsive and unconscious part of the psyche. It responds directly and immediately to instincts. The newborn child's personality is all id. The id operates on what Freud termed the pleasure principle, which is the notion that every desired impulse should be satisfied immediately without regard to the consequences. The id engages in primary process thinking (illogical, primitive, irrational, and fantasy).

The ego is id altered by the external world. It develops as a mediator between the unreality of the id and the external real world. It is the decision-making component of personality and works by reason in contrast to the chaos and unreason of the id. The ego functions on the reality principle and works out realistic ways of satisfying the demands of the id. The ego can compromise or postpone satisfaction to avoid negative consequences. The ego makes decisions based on societal norms, etiquette, and rules of behavior. Freud compared the ego to the rider of the id's horse. The ego tries to manage and steer the id's desires. It engages in secondary-process thinking (realistic, rational, and problem-solving) and develops in the phallic stage.

The superego seeks to control the impulses of the id, particularly those of sexuality and aggression. Additionally, it seeks to persuade the ego to rely on moralistic goals instead of merely realistic goals. The two systems of the superego are the conscience and the ideal self. It is through the conscious that the superego punishes the ego through feelings of guilt (i.e., if the ego gives into the id's demands). The ideal self, also called the ego ideal, is an imagined picture of how a person ought to be. It represents career aspirations, how one wishes to treat others, and how one wishes to behave as a part of society. If an individual's ideal self is an unrealistic standard, then the individual will see whatever he/she does as a failure. Parental values and upbringing determine the ideal self and conscience.

Jung

Carl Jung's work has influenced philosophy, anthropology, archaeology, literature, and religious studies in addition to psychiatry. Jung's theory of psychological types led to the development of the Myers-Briggs Type Indicator, a highly popular personality test and psychometric instrument. Jung developed several important psychological concepts, which include the following:

- Introversion and extraversion (present-day definitions of these terms differ from the concepts he defined)
- The complex
- The collective unconscious
- Archetypes
- Individuation

Additionally, Jung was involved in spiritual concepts and believed that the journey of transformation (which he called individuation) is at the heart of all world religions. He defines this journey as a quest to meet the self and the divine. Jung is believed to have had an indirect role in the establishment of Alcoholics Anonymous due to his belief that spirituality could serve as a cure for alcoholism.

Although Jung held by Freud and his theories early on, they split after Jung publicly criticized Freud's theory of the Oedipus complex and how he emphasized the sexuality of the very young. Up to that point, their shared interest in the subconscious had brought Jung to support Freud. After separating from Freud, Jung later developed his own take on psychoanalytic theory. A significant portion of Jung's work reflects the theoretical differences that he had with Freud. For example, Jung asserted that libido was generalized psychic energy and not just sexual energy. Jung also believed that people are shaped by the future (i.e., their aspirations) as well as by the past and their childhood experiences.

Jung emphasized the unconscious more than Freud and proposed that the human psyche comprises three components—ego, personal unconscious, and collective unconscious. Jung's personal unconscious is analogous to Freud's unconscious. Jung's collective unconscious is a second, deeper layer that the individual shares with all other people. It comprises latent memories from our evolutionary and ancestral past. Jung referred to ancestral memories and images as archetypes and believed they are found in dreams, literature, art, and religion. Examples of important archetypes include the persona (social mask or public face), anima/animus (male and female sides), and the shadow (like Freud's id, animal urges, survival).

PIAGET

When Jean Piaget's ideas became widely popularized in the 1960s, the designation of development as a major subfield of psychology soon followed. His cognitive development theory has four major stages:

1. Sensorimotor stage (birth to age 2)—In this stage, the child experiences the world through movement and his five senses. A child is extremely egocentric in this stage and cannot perceive the world from others' viewpoints. During the sensorimotor stage, children come to develop object permanence.
2. Preoperational stage (ages 2 to 7)—Beginning with the child's learning to speak, this stage sees an increase in children's playing and pretending, primarily through symbolic play and manipulating symbols. Children in this stage continue to have difficulty seeing things from different points of view. The two substages of the preoperational stage are the symbolic function substage and the intuitive thought substage.
3. Concrete operational stage (ages 7 to 11)—In this stage children are beginning to think logically and are no longer egocentric. They greatly improve their classification skills and become more aware of logic and conservation.
4. Formal operational stage (ages 11 to 16)—This stage sees the development of abstract reasoning. Children in this stage develop abstract thought and can conserve and think logically with more facility. Children in the formal operational stage show more skills for problem-solving.

Piaget posited that there are three types of intellectual structures:

- Behavioral (sensorimotor) schemata—organized patterns of behavior that represent and respond to objects and experiences
- Symbolic schemata—internal mental symbols, including images or verbal codes, used to represent aspects of experience
- Operational schemata—internal mental activity performed on objects of thought

As Piaget described them, schemata are significantly important building blocks of development and are modified by ongoing experiences. They are continuously being modified or changed and can be a generalized idea based on prior knowledge or experience.

Review Video: Piaget's Cognitive Development Theory
Visit mometrix.com/academy and enter code: 100376

Erikson

A student of Anna Freud (daughter to Sigmund Freud), Erik Erikson saw human development as continuing throughout the life span. This is in contrast to Freudian theory, which posits that development is mostly completed by adolescence. Erikson built onto the Freudian model of and extended it throughout the entire life span into older adulthood. Erikson appears to attempt a linkage between individual development and the broader context of society. His early stages are linked to those of Sigmund Freud, but they are formulated on different lines of thinking. Erikson focuses more on ego qualities that emerge from each stage and less on sexual modes and their consequences (as Freud's theory does).

The Eight Life Stages of Erikson's Theory of Psychosocial Development Are as Follows:

Basic Trust Versus. Basic Mistrust—the period of infancy (first year of life), also most fundamental stage. A baby develops a sense of trust based on the parental relationship. This sense of trust serves as a foundation for the child's sense of identity. Failure to develop basic trust results in feelings of fear and that the world is unpredictable and inconsistent.

Autonomy Versus Shame—early childhood, 1 to 3 years old (approx.). In this stage the child attempts to master toilet training.

Purpose (Initiative) Versus Guilt—preschool, 3 to 6 years old (approx.). The child learns to do things on his/her own, such as dressing. Feelings of guilt about making his/her own choices can be overshadowed by a positive sense of accomplishment.

Competence (Industry) Versus Inferiority—6 to 11 years (approx.). In this stage the child compares self-worth to others and can recognize inequalities in personal abilities among peers.

Identity (Fidelity) Versus Role Confusion—adolescence, 12 to 18 years (approx.). The adolescent questions self: Who am I? How do I fit in? Where am I going in life? Per Erikson, if parents push conformity to their own views on the adolescent, he/she will face identity confusion, but if parents allow exploration, he/she will assume his/her own identity.

Intimacy Versus Isolation—early adulthood, 18 to 35 (approx.). The individual experiences love and intimacy through successfully forming loving relationships with others (dating, marriage, friends, and family). If the individual is unable to form lasting relationships, he/she may feel isolated and alone.

Generativity Versus Stagnation—middle adulthood, ages 35 to 64 (approximately). In this stage, some settling into one's own life often occurs. The individual makes progress in a career or determines he/she unsure if about continuing in his/her path. Also important in this stage can be raising of children and/or participation in other meaningful activities. Those uncomfortable with the way their lives are progressing may feel regret and a sense of uselessness.

Ego Integrity Versus Despair—older adulthood, age 65 on (approximately). Individuals approach and/or achieve retirement and the last chapter of life. Ego integrity signifies the acceptance of one's life in its fullness, both accomplishments and defeats.

Skinner

B. F. Skinner was an American psychologist who developed a philosophy that he called radical behaviorism. He believed that free will in human beings is an illusion and that all human actions come about as a result of consequences. With bad consequences, the action may be repeated. With good consequences, it is more likely the action will be more likely. This is what Skinner named the principle of reinforcement. Skinner accepted thoughts and emotions as subject to the same rules as overt behavior. This is in contrast to methodological behaviorism, which does not accept so-called private events such as thinking and unobservable emotions as causes of a being's behavior.

Maslow

Abraham Maslow sought to understand the motivations that drive people. He believed that human beings are motivated by systems other than those related to rewards or unconscious desires. Maslow developed a hierarchy of needs that he believed motivate human beings. Before a person can progress to higher-level growth needs, he/she must satisfy the lower-level, more basic needs. Different life experiences, such as loss or illness may cause a person to move between the different levels of the hierarchy. The highest level in Maslow's model is that of self-actualization. Maslow asserted that only one in 100 people become fully self-actualized because of society's focus on lower needs such as esteem, love, and other social needs.

Maslow's first hierarchical model included five levels as follows:

1. Biological and physiological needs (air, food, drink, shelter, and sleep)
2. Safety needs (security and stability)
3. Love and belongingness needs (friendship, intimacy, and love)
4. Esteem needs (independence, status, achievement, self-respect, and respect of others)
5. Self-actualization needs (self-fulfillment, personal growth, and realizing personal potential)

Maslow later expanded this five-stage model to include cognitive, aesthetic, and transcendence needs. The eight-level model is as follows:

1. Biological and physiological needs
2. Safety needs
3. Love and belongingness needs
4. Esteem needs
5. Cognitive needs (knowledge and meaning)
6. Aesthetic needs (appreciation and search for balance, beauty, etc.)
7. Self-actualization needs
8. Transcendence needs (helping others achieve self-actualization)

Maslow's focus on human potential and how human beings fulfill that potential led him to focus on more positive aspects of human behavior instead of psychopathology. Maslow believed a person continues "becoming" always with a need for personal growth and discovery present throughout life. He saw self-actualization as a continual process of "becoming" more than a perfect state that one may reach. Self-actualization is achieving one's potential, not being perfect. Maslow studied people he considered to be self-actualized (including Einstein and Abraham Lincoln), and he identified 15 characteristics of a self-actualized person. They are as follows:

1. Ability to perceive reality efficiently and tolerate uncertainty
2. Acceptance of self and others for what they are
3. Spontaneity in thought and action
4. Problem centered rather than self-centered
5. Sense of humor
6. Ability to view life objectively
7. High level of creativity
8. Resistant to greater culture, however, not purposely unconventional
9. Concerned for humanity's welfare

10. Capable of deeply appreciating basic life experience
11. Able to establish deep, satisfying relationships with a few people
12. Peak experiences
13. Need for privacy
14. Democratic attitude
15. Strong moral and ethical standards

Maslow identified the following behaviors that he believed lead to self-actualization:

- Childlike ability to experience life and to fully absorb and concentrate
- Willingness to try new things and not just stay with safe options
- In evaluating experiences, listening to one's own feelings instead of the voice of the majority, of tradition, or of authority
- Being honest and avoiding pretense
- Willingness to be unpopular if one's views do not line up with those of the majority
- Working hard and taking responsibility
- Identifying one's own defenses and being willing and courageous enough to give them up

Bandura

Albert Bandura originated social learning theory as well as the theoretical construct of self-efficacy. Social learning theory explains that people can learn not only through direct experience but also through observing others. He conducted the significant Bobo doll experiment. This was actually a collection of experiments in 1961 and 1963 in which he studied the behavior of children after they watched an adult model behave aggressively toward a Bobo doll. The most noteworthy of these experiments measured the behavior of the children who observed the adult model beat up the Bobo doll and then be rewarded, punished, or face no consequence. This series of experiments show that humans can learn through observing, imitating, and modeling and that they can learn by watching others face consequences (reward or punishment) and not solely by experiencing consequences themselves, as behaviorism posits.

Major Principles of Social Learning Theory

- Learning is not solely behavioral but rather a cognitive process taking place in a social context.
- Learning can occur by vicarious reinforcement, which is observing a behavior and its consequences.
- Learning includes making observations, extracting information from said observations, and coming to a decision about the performance of the behavior. Consequently, learning can take place without an observable change in behavior.
- Reinforcement is not entirely responsible for learning but does play a role in learning.
- Learning is an active process, and cognition, environment, and behavior all reciprocally influence one another.

Types of Modeling Stimuli

- Live model
- Verbal instruction
- Symbolic (i.e., through media such as television, Internet, etc., and can utilize real or fictional characters)

Bandura's Cognitive and Behavioral Processes Necessary for Learning

- Attention, which is affected both by characteristics of the observer (perceptual abilities, cognitive abilities, arousal, and past performance) and characteristics of the event (relevance, novelty, affective valence, and functional value)
- Retention, also affected by both the characteristics of the observer (cognitive abilities and cognitive rehearsal), and characteristics of the event (complexity)
- Reproduction, affected by observer characteristics of physical and cognitive capabilities and previous performance
- Motivation, including predicted consequences and internal values

Independent Variable and Dependent Variable

The independent variable is also referred to as the experimental variable. This is the variable that will change based on the experimental treatment. For example, in a study on academic interventions, the independent variable includes a traditional curriculum and a new academic curriculum. The dependent variable is the variable that is measured based on the independent variable. In this example the dependent variable may be academic performance, which will be measured based on which group the student is in—the traditional curriculum or the new academic curriculum group. In other words, the researcher seeks to find differences in the dependent variable (academic performance) based on which group the participants are in (independent variable: traditional vs. new curriculum). Therefore, if students perform better when placed in the new academic curriculum group compared to those in the traditional curriculum group, the researcher may determine that the new curriculum is more effective.

Sampling Techniques

Sampling is an efficient method to investigate an entire population. The researcher gathers data on a small part of the whole population. This is called a sampling frame and is used to inform what the data looks like for the whole population. What follows are different types of sampling techniques:

- *Simple random sampling*. Researchers choose a random sample through methods that ensure that each subgroup of the whole population has an equal probability of being chosen as part of the sample.
- *Stratified random sampling.* Researchers divide the whole population into sections or strata. The researchers then choose a random sample from each. These are then combined into the overall sample.
- *Multi-stage sampling*. Researchers use this method when a population is too large and/or scattered to be practical to make a list from which to draw a simple random sample. Researchers may have to break the population down by variables to take random samples from each.

Examples of non-probability sampling techniques include voluntary response sampling, judgment sampling, and convenience sampling. Probability and statistics cannot be used to analyze the results of these types of techniques.

Operational Definitions

Operational definitions are the researchers' specific definitions about the variable tested in an investigation. Specifically, for a variable to be operationally defined, the researcher must include information about the procedure used to determine the variable. For example, if a variable is low socioeconomic status, the operational variable may be that low socioeconomic status includes all individuals who fall under the poverty line according to the Department of Housing and Urban Development. It is important to define variables in such a way that future researchers can replicate the study. Using well-defined operational definitions will also increase the validity and reliability of a study.

Common Research Concepts

- *Experimental study* changes one variable in the environment.
- *Observational study* tries to change as little of the existing environment as possible.
- *Longitudinal study* observes a large group of individuals who were born around the same time over a long period of time.
- *Cross-sectional study* observes individuals of different ages.
- *Cross-sequential study* combines both longitudinal and cross-sectional methodologies by observing different age groups over a long period of time and noting both similarities and differences in and between the groups.
- *Correlational study* establishes if two variables are correlated or not. Three types of correlations that can be identified are positive correlation (increase in one variable leads to an increase in the other and vice versa), negative correlation (increase in one variable leads to a decrease in another and vice versa), or no correlation.
- *Survey research* includes any research methods that involve asking questions of respondents from short written feedback to in-depth interviews.
- *Double blind procedure* is one in which neither the participants nor the experimenter are aware of which group the participant is in.
- Placebo affect occurs when an individual who is given a placebo and is unaware of that fact experiences changes that are similar to those experienced by individuals given the actual treatment.
- *Experimental group* is the research group that is given the actual treatment.
- *Control group* is the research group that is given no treatment or is given a placebo. For example, in this study on depression and medication, the experimental group will be given the study drug to examine the effects of this trend on depressive symptoms. The control group will be given either a placebo or no drug and all. In a double blind procedure, neither the participant nor the researcher will know who received the actual drug.
- *Case study* is an in-depth exploration into one individual or entity to gather as much information as possible to support or develop a theory or support the hypothesis. Case studies are beneficial in exploring situations that may not be widespread. For example, research involving brain damage is often done through case studies because there is not a large sample population of individuals with brain damage to draw from. One limitation of case studies is that they cannot be generalized to a larger population. Similarly, characteristics of an individual from a case study cannot be generalized to another individual with a similar issue (e.g., two people with right hemisphere brain damage). The reason for this is because the case study could be an atypical case.

Mode, Median, and Mean of Statistical Scores

Mode is a frequency score and is the most common score among all participants. For example, if a study measures academic performance, and five students receive an A, seven students receive a B, two students receive a C, and one student receives a D, the mode for this statistical data set is B as this was the most frequent score achieved. Median is the middle point at which all scores are lined sequentially from smallest two largest. For example, if the total score possible on a test is a 5, and 10 students obtained the following scores; 1, 1, 3, 3, 3, 4, 4, 4, 4, 5, the median score is a 4 because the score is located at the midpoint. Mean is the average of all scores. In the above example, the mean score is a 3.2.

CORRELATION

Correlation is the extent to which two things are related to each other. For example, research may suggest that minutes spent reading per day is correlated to academic performance. In stating this correlation, the researcher will aim to obtain a correlation coefficient that states the degree to which two things are correlated as well as the direction, which may be positive or negative. For example, if two items have a positive correlation, that means as one increases, the other increases as well. On the other hand, if two items have a negative correlation, it means as one increases, the other decreases. For example, if minutes spent reading per day and academic performance are positively correlated, this means the more time a child spends reading, the better his/her academic performance. Likewise, stress in the home is negatively correlated with academic performance; therefore, the more stress a child experiences at home, the more academic performance will decrease.

MEASURES OF VARIATION

Range refers to the difference between the lowest and the highest score. For example, if the lowest score is a 70 and the highest score is the 100, the range of scores is 30. Standard deviation refers to the amount that one score defers or deviates from another score. This measure of variation tells the researcher if scores of an entire sample population are close together or widely disbursed. For example, a standard deviation of one indicates that one score typically defers from another by only plus or minus. As such, by looking at one score of 85, the researcher can be certain to find similar scores of 84 and 85. A **normal distribution**, also referred to as a bell curve, indicates that most scores will fall within the middle, and fewer scores fall on the upper and lower points. For example, IQ is often indicated by a normal distribution or a bell curve with the majority of people scoring at the midpoint, or around 100, and fewer people scoring either below or above this midpoint.

ETHICAL CONSIDERATIONS WHEN CONDUCTING PSYCHOLOGICAL RESEARCH

All researchers must first provide participants with an informed consent form that they must read and sign prior to beginning any psychological research. Contained within this form is information about the study, their responsibilities during the study, the researchers' responsibilities, information on confidentiality, as well a disclosure that the participant may quit the study without any negative repercussions. The researcher must also do everything possible to protect participants from harm. Researchers must maintain the confidentiality of all participants, which includes avoiding linking individual names or other identifying information to their study results. Finally, the researcher must fully debrief participants following the conclusion of the study. This includes providing them with any information that was not disclosed prior to beginning of the study as well as a brief discussion on the purpose of the study and what the results may be used for in the future.

DEVELOPMENT OF ETHICAL PRINCIPLES IN RESEARCH

There have been a number of important research studies that have influenced the development of ethical principles for research, for example, the Tuskegee Syphilis Study, conducted in the United States between 1932 and 1972. In this study, 400 African American men were left untreated for syphilis, even after penicillin became a proven treatment. The men were never told their diagnosis. Between 1939 and 1945 Nazi scientists conducted experiments on prisoners in concentration camps. The Nuremberg Code for research on human subjects was adopted after the end of World War II and was subsequently used to convict Nazi scientists of war crimes. The Obedience to Authority Study, published in 1974 by Stanley Milgram, proved that many people will do things they consider to be wrong morally if they are following an authority's orders. The World Medical Association's Helsinki Declaration established ethical principles for research on human subjects.

The National Research Act was passed by the US Congress in 1974 and authorized federal agencies to develop human research regulations.

Assessment

Through psychological assessment, psychologists use a combination of techniques to come to a conclusion about a person and his/her behavior and/or personality and capabilities. This is also called psychological testing or performing a psychological battery. Reliability is the extent to which an assessment instrument produces consistent and stable results. Validity is how well an assessment measures what it claims to measure. Psychological assessment should take place under standardized conditions with each person being assessed under basically identical conditions. Standardization is important because many test results are used to compare performance among participants. Assessment norms consist of data that enable the assessors to establish the relative standing of an individual person who has been assessed. A test score on its own means little. Usually, assessors must interpret a test score to determine one's position relative to others who have been assessed. Norms offer a basis to compare the individual within the group.

Limits of Psychological Assessment

Although psychological assessments can be useful, they do all have some limitations. One should take into account the way that the assessment tool is constructed. For example, some assessment tools rely heavily on the interpretation of the assessor and not on objective results. Other tests measure attributes not based on science, such as personality types. Another limitation of assessments can come through cultural bias. Many tests make assumptions of those being assessed, for example, that those being assessed will have similar experiences and language proficiency in English. Different cultures (even within one country, such as the United States) vary widely, and individuals from different cultures (majority culture, minority cultures) will likely interpret items in a psychological assessment quite differently due to upbringing and cultural perspectives. This can cause inaccuracies in the results. Another limitation of psychological assessments comes from the participants themselves, who may not give true responses. Some respondents may try to portray themselves in a more positive light and will distort their answers accordingly. A final limitation comes in the interpretation of the results. Assessors can make errors, even those with much skill and experience. This is more likely when the assessment involves either emotional or cognitive responses. These are more likely to get a subjective interpretation, and the same response may be scored differently depending on who the assessor is.

IB Practice Test

Want to take this practice test in an online interactive format?
Check out the online resources page, which includes interactive practice questions and much more: **mometrix.com/resources719/ibpsychology**

1. Though he was schooled in physiology, ____________was the first person to develop a psychology lab, in Leipzig, Germany.

    a. Sigmund Freud
    b. William James
    c. Ivan Pavlov
    d. Edward Titchener
    e. Wilhelm Wundt

2. This pioneer was known as the first to develop a psychology laboratory in the United States. His name was:

    a. Sigmund Freud
    b. William James
    c. Ivan Pavlov
    d. G. Stanley Hall
    e. Wilhelm Wundt

3. These early scientists were concerned about the study of mental processes. They relied on a technique known as introspection to examine mental experiences. These individuals were called:

    a. Functionalists
    b. Psychodynamic theorists
    c. Structuralists
    d. All of the above
    e. Cognitivists

4. Psychologists today utilize all of the following approaches to understand human behavior except:

    a. Behavioral
    b. Cerebral
    c. Psychodynamic
    d. Humanistic
    e. Cognitive

5. Sigmund Freud is associated with which of the following approaches?

    a. Behaviorist
    b. Humanistic
    c. Psychodynamic
    d. Evolutionary
    e. Cerebral

6. "Self-actualization" is a term associated with the ___________ approach to understanding human behavior.

a. Behaviorist
b. Humanistic
c. Psychodynamic
d. Cognitive
e. Biological

7. When participants in a control group experience changes because they believe they are getting a special treatment, this is known as:

a. A blind study
b. A double-blind study
c. The placebo effect
d. Case study
e. Cause-effect analysis

8. Which of these types of study would lend itself to studying only one person?

a. Case study
b. Correlational
c. Descriptive
d. Experimental
e. Survey

9. __________ is the study of how the different parts of the body interact with one another and how this communication affects behavior.

a. Behavioral neuroscience
b. Behaviorism
c. Humanism
d. Functionalism
e. Freudianism

10. A type of neuron that interacts or communicates with other neurons is referred to as:

a. Afferent
b. Association
c. Efferent
d. Motor
e. Sensory

11. Serotonin is a neurotransmitter that affects all of the following except:

a. Arousal
b. Mood
c. Sleep
d. Voluntary movement
e. Appetite

12. Which division of the nervous system controls voluntary skeletal muscle movements?

a. Autonomic
b. Parasympathetic
c. Peripheral
d. Somatic
e. Sympathetic

13. A patient is suffering from diabetes. The patient's blood sugar is elevated. Which division of the nervous system raises the blood sugar level?

a. Autonomic
b. Parasympathetic
c. Peripheral
d. Somatic
e. Sympathetic

14. Which subsystem of the nervous system regulates internal organs and glands?

a. Autonomic
b. Parasympathetic
c. Peripheral
d. Somatic
e. Sympathetic

15. What part of the brain deals with the functioning of memory?

a. Amygdala
b. Hippocampus
c. Hypothalamus
d. Reticular formation
e. Thalamus

16. __________ is the act of mentally developing a picture of one's outside environment.

a. Just noticeable difference (JND)
b. Perception
c. Sensation
d. Sensory adaption
e. Signal detection theory

17. Psychophysics is the part of psychology that deals with______________.

a. Just noticeable difference (JND)
b. Perception
c. Sensation
d. Sensory adaption
e. Signal detection theory

18. When my perception of the couch in my living room diminishes to the point where I barely pay any attention to it, I am experiencing:

a. Just noticeable difference (JND)
b. Perception
c. Sensation
d. Sensory adaption
e. Signal detection theory

19. __________ is dependent upon an individual's expectations, past experiences, and motivation.

a. Just noticeable difference (JND)
b. Perception
c. Sensation
d. Sensory adaption
e. Signal detection theory

20. Margaux listened to two CD players in a department store. She noticed that the first CD player sounded slightly clearer than the second CD player. The difference in sound that Margaux noticed is called:

a. Just noticeable difference (JND)
b. Perception
c. Sensation
d. Sensory adaption
e. Signal detection theory

21. People often misjudge how far an approaching train is from them. They usually think it is farther away than it is. This is because the farther away parallel objects such as train tracks are, the closer they appear to be to one another, distorting the distance perception. This is an occurrence of:

a. Difference threshold
b. Interposition
c. Linear perspective
d. Motion parallax
e. Weber's law

22. The train tracks seemed to be moving as I drove by the stationary train. Which of the following terms would explain this?

a. Difference threshold
b. Interposition
c. Linear perspective
d. Motion parallax
e. Weber's law

23. What prevents a person from physically acting out his dreams?

a. The brain stem prevents the transference of messages originating in the motor cortex.
b. The occipital lobes do not function during "s" sleep state.
c. The parietal lobes are in a temporary immobile state during REM sleep.
d. The cerebellum cannot coordinate motion when a person is asleep.
e. Sleep renders skeletal muscles immobile.

24. The dream state is usually characterized by:

a. Alpha waves
b. Delta waves
c. Hypnogogic sensation
d. REM
e. Slow-wave sleep

25. Which sleep disorder causes a person to involuntarily fall into sudden sleep modes throughout the day?

a. Activation-synthesis theory
b. Insomnia
c. Narcolepsy
d. REM rebound
e. Sleep apnea

26. According to Sigmund Freud, repressed sexual or aggressive desires that manifest themselves in dreams are referred to as:

a. Activation-synthesis theory
b. Dissociation
c. Latent content
d. Manifest content
e. REM rebound

27. Margie is under hypnosis, but she is fully conscious of all activities. This is known as a split in consciousness or ___________.

a. Activation-synthesis theory
b. Dissociation
c. Latent content
d. Manifest content
e. REM rebound

28. Which of the following is considered a type of associative learning?

a. Classical conditioning
b. Observational learning
c. Modeling
d. Behavioral replication
e. Differentiation

The following questions relate to how learning takes place in organisms. Use the following concepts to answer questions 29–35.

a. Classical conditioning
b. Observational learning
c. Operant conditioning
d. Behavioral conditioning
e. Differentiation

29. A person who learns by connecting two stimuli is a product of:

30. A neutral stimulus is part of which learning procedure?

31. An unconditioned stimulus that gets an unconditioned response is an aspect of:

32. Reinforcement is characteristic of which learning procedure?

33. In which type of learning does "negative" indicate that a stimulus has been removed?

34. Learning the consequences of behavior by watching what happens to others is considered what type of learning procedure?

35. Which of these does NOT require that a stimulus be directly introduced or removed?

36. Habituation is an example of:

a. Associative learning
b. Expectation
c. Instrumental conditioning
d. Non-associative learning
e. Sensitization

37. A researcher, Dr. Maggie George, started with the following hypothesis: Most bilingual students are Hispanic. Dr. George sought out information to prove her supposition while ignoring data that would disprove her hypothesis. She was engaging in what is known as:

a. The availability heuristic
b. Confirmation bias
c. Functional fixedness
d. Rehearsal
e. The representativeness heuristic

38. The inability to utilize old items in new ways is known as:

a. The availability heuristic
b. Confirmation bias
c. Functional fixedness
d. Rehearsal
e. The representativeness heuristic

39. __________ means that a person will choose the most vivid or most recent memory based on the ability the person has to quickly recall the information. It will be the first thing that comes to the person's mind.

a. The availability heuristic
b. Confirmation bias
c. Functional fixedness
d. Rehearsal
e. The representativeness heuristic

40. A two-word pattern where kids generally voice a noun and a verb together is part of:

a. The babbling stage
b. The concrete operations stage
c. Conservation
d. The formal operations stage
e. Telegraphic speech

41. Who is known for his belief that children possess a language acquisition device?

a. Alfred Binet
b. Noam Chomsky
c. William James
d. B. F. Skinner
e. Charles Spearman

42. Which of these concepts is NOT an example of a mnemonic strategy?

a. Acrostics
b. Attention
c. Automaticity
d. Chunking
e. Rehearsal

43. Permanent memories are kept in:

a. Long-term memory
b. Sensory memory
c. Short-term memory
d. Working memory
e. Intermediate-term memory

44. The first person to create an intelligence test was:

a. Alfred Binet
b. Noam Chomsky
c. William James
d. B. F. Skinner
e. Charles Spearman

45. ____________ is recognized for coining the term "g" for general intelligence.

a. Alfred Binet
b. Noam Chomsky
c. William James
d. B. F. Skinner
e. Charles Spearman

46. Motivation can be influenced by all of the following biological and social-psychological factors except:

a. Achievement
b. Affiliation
c. Hunger
d. Instinct
e. Sex

47. Factors that motivate hunger are:

a. Achievement and affiliation
b. Achievement and reproduction
c. Glucose and insulin
d. Reproduction and glucose
e. Affiliation and instinct

48. What part of the brain is said to increase hunger?

a. Amygdala
b. Hippocampus
c. Lateral hypothalamus
d. Thalamus
e. Ventromedial hypothalamus

Use the following choices to answer questions 49 – 52:

a. Cannon-Bard theory
b. Excitation transfer
c. James-Lange theory
d. The set point
e. Two-factor theory

49. Each person has a weight that the body works to maintain. This is known as:

50. __________ states that arousal and a subjective emotional experience will occur at the same time when a person thinks that a stimulus can affect his well-being.

51. A pounding heartbeat that causes a person to experience fear is an example of:

52. The belief that what we call each emotion is what makes emotions different from one another is known as __________. This concept says that the physiological arousal is the same regardless of which emotion one experiences.

53. Which type of research method lends itself to researchers making inferences about how people develop over a period of time?

a. Blind
b. Double-blind
c. Longitudinal
d. Cohort
e. Case study

54. What type of research method would be utilized to track different people at varying age levels over a long period of time?

a. Cross-sectional
b. Cross-sequential
c. Longitudinal
d. All of the above
e. None of the above

55. A researcher wants to study a group of 25-year-old participants for 10 years. What type of research method would the researcher be using?

a. Cross-sectional
b. Cross-sequential
c. Longitudinal
d. Case study
e. Double-blind

56. Which of the following is a stage in Piaget's theory of cognitive development?

a. Autonomy vs. doubt and shame
b. Identity vs. role confusion
c. Trust vs. mistrust
d. Sensorimotor
e. Proprioceptive

57. Which of these terms is not part of Piaget's theory of cognitive development?

a. Assimilation
b. Conservation
c. Object permanence
d. Proprioception
e. Reversibility

58. The sensorimotor stage in Piaget's theory of cognitive development is characterized by a lack of:

a. Assimilation
b. Conservation
c. Object permanence
d. Proprioception
e. Locomotion

59. A child between the ages of 1 and 3 years will experience this crisis in Erikson's theory of psychosocial development.

a. Autonomy vs. doubt and shame
b. Identity vs. role confusion
c. Trust vs. mistrust
d. Intimacy vs. isolation
e. Industry vs. inferiority

60. Which of these stages in Erikson's theory of psychosocial development is characterized by the tension between altruism and selfishness?

a. Autonomy vs. doubt and shame
b. Identity vs. role confusion
c. Trust vs. mistrust
d. Generativity vs. Stagnation
e. Integrity vs. despair

61. Which of the following stages is not indicative of what a child desires to accomplish versus what a child is allowed to do?

a. Intimacy vs. Isolation
b. Identity vs. role confusion
c. Trust vs. mistrust
d. Initiative vs. guilt and industry
e. Autonomy vs. doubt and shame

62. Which theorist believed that a person's actions are motivated by unconscious needs?

a. Alfred Adler
b. Karen Horney
c. Erik Erikson
d. Jean Piaget
e. Ian Pavlov

63. In his theory of psychoanalysis, __________ is known for his development of the following personality components: the id, ego, and superego.

a. Carl Jung
b. Karen Horney
c. Sigmund Freud
d. All of the above
e. None of the above

64. Which personality component operates in accordance with the pleasure principle?

a. Ego
b. Id
c. Superego
d. Superid
e. Hypoego

65. The Oedipus complex is a part of which stage in Freud's psychosexual stages?

a. Anal stage
b. Oral stage
c. Phallic stage
d. Latency stage
e. Genital stage

66. Johnny love's soccer and wants to join the soccer team. Though he does not particularly like football, his parents press him to join the football team. Johnny ends up joining the football team in order to please his parents. This is an example of:

a. Conditions of worth
b. Ideal self
c. Morality principle
d. Reality principle
e. Self-actualization

67. Reciprocal determinism is part of the ____________ approach to personality.

a. Humanistic
b. Individual-difference
c. Psychosocial
d. Social cognitive
e. Evolutionary

68. Which of the following is NOT one of the Big Five personality traits?

a. Aggression
b. Conscientiousness
c. Extroversion
d. Neuroticism
e. Openness

69. Which branch of psychology focuses on psychological disorders?

a. Abnormal psychology
b. Behavioral neuroscience
c. Developmental psychology
d. Physiological psychology
e. Social cognitive psychology

70. The child stared at Jesse because he walked to the water fountain, drank some water, walked back to the same spot he was previously in, walked back to the water fountain, and drank some more water. Jesse did this at least three times. Jesse is probably suffering from:

a. Anxiety disorder
b. Generalized anxiety disorder
c. Obsessive-compulsive disorder
d. Panic disorder
e. Phobia

71. People who have ______________ typically suffer from depression, mania, or both.

a. Conversion disorder
b. Dissociative dissonance
c. Mood disorder
d. Personality disorder
e. Somatoform disorder

72. Ralph left his job in the middle of the day without letting anyone know that he was leaving. He traveled a few hours, but he couldn't remember his past. Ralph became confused about who he was. He eventually took on a new identity. Ralph more than likely experienced:

a. Dissociative amnesia
b. Dissociative fugue
c. Dissociative identity
d. Panic disorder
e. Psychosis

73. This type of schizophrenia is characterized by delusions of grandeur or delusions of persecution. It is known as:

a. Catatonic
b. Disorganized
c. Echolalia
d. Paranoid
e. Undifferentiated

74. Jack has all the physical symptoms of a disease, but he does not have the disease. Jack has which of the following types of disorder?

a. Anxiety
b. Dissociative
c. Mood
d. Personality
e. Somatoform

75. Jane is the type of person who does not trust people. She is very suspicious of those around her. Jane is suffering from which of the following?

a. Antisocial personality
b. Borderline personality disorder
c. Narcissistic personality
d. Paranoid personality
e. Paranoid schizophrenia

76. The _____________ approach to abnormal behavior suggests that abnormal behavior is due to a person's consistently thinking in an abnormal manner.

a. Cognitive
b. Learning or behavioral
c. Medical
d. Psychoanalytic
e. Social

77. Jesse struggled with depression one summer. His mother began to bring him breakfast in bed every day to cheer him up. Jesse began sleeping in even longer. When he did get up, he kept completely to himself. The more Jesse withdrew, the more his mother showered him with attention and gifts. This explanation of abnormal behavior comes from which of the following perspectives?

a. Cognitive approach
b. Learning or behavioral approach
c. Medical approach
d. Psychoanalytic approach
e. Social approach

78. Psychological approaches deal with all of the following therapies except:

a. Behavior modification
b. Cognitive therapies
c. Humanistic therapies
d. Psychoanalysis
e. Surgical therapies

Use the following answer choices for questions 79 - 84.

a. Behavior modification
b. Biological therapies
c. Cognitive therapies
d. Humanistic therapies
e. Psychoanalysis

79. Catharsis occurs when energy that was once used to repress memories becomes available because the repressed memory has been brought to consciousness and dealt with. Which approach describes this term?

80. Free association is a therapeutic technique used in:

81. "Active learning" is a term introduced by Carl Rogers in which therapies?

82. According to_________________, the way a person thinks is the culprit for abnormal behavior.

83. Systematic desensitization is a technique used in_______________.

84. Which approach depends on drugs or surgery to change how the brain functions?

85. Which of the following is not an area in social psychology?

a. Social cognition
b. Social influence
c. Social relationships
d. Group behavior
e. Evolutionary influence

86. How information about other people is processed is known as:

a. Social cognition
b. Social influence
c. Social relationships
d. Group behavior
e. Evolutionary influence

87. Jamia does not believe in abortion. She has the attitude that abortion is murder. Jamia gets pregnant and has an abortion. She experiences a great deal of anxiety about the abortion. Jamia now spends most of her time explaining that there are times when women are forced to get an abortion even when they do not want to. She desperately wants to feel good about the decision she has made. Jamia's situation is an example of:

a. Attribution theory
b. Actor-observer difference
c. Cognitive dissonance theory
d. Fundamental attribution error
e. Situation attribution

88. ___________ was responsible for doing a phony learning study in which teachers were told to administer an electrical shock to students every time a student gave a wrong answer.

a. Solomon Asch
b. Kitty Genovese
c. Karen Horney
d. Stanley Milgram
e. Carl Rogers

89. Sarah asked her friend to babysit while her boyfriend took her on a romantic date. Her friend promised that she would babysit. Sarah then told her friend that she would be gone for a week on this romantic date. Sarah used a technique called:

a. Door-in-the-face
b. Foot-in-the-door
c. Low-balling
d. The minimax principle
e. Social-exchange theory

90. __________ was a woman who was raped and killed in 1964 while thirty-eight witnesses watched. The witnesses did not call the police until after the killer was gone.

a. Virginia E. Johnson
b. Kitty Genovese
c. Karen Horney
d. Lana Brock
e. Jane Jacobs

91. If helping someone will benefit more than it will hurt a person, that person will most likely render assistance. This is known as:

a. Door-in-the-face
b. Foot-in-the-door
c. Low-balling
d. The minimax principle
e. Social-exchange theory

92. A test that looks as though it is measuring what it is supposed to measure has:

a. Content validity
b. Construct validity
c. Cronbach's alpha
d. Internal consistency
e. Predictive validity

93. Which of the following is not referred to as a descriptive statistic?

a. Mean
b. Regression
c. Standard deviation
d. Mode
e. Range

94. The entire membership of any group or entity is called the:

a. Population
b. Sample
c. Subject
d. Subset
e. Unit of analysis

Answers and Explanations

1. E: Wilhelm Wundt. Wilhelm Wundt was a pioneer in creating the first psychology laboratory, in Leipzig, Germany. As a structuralist, Wundt wanted to study from a scientific perspective how individuals sense and perceive their surroundings. This started a controversy over what the scope of psychology should be and how the study of psychology should look.

2. D: G. Stanley Hall. was a pioneer known for developing the first psychology laboratory in the United States. Hall established his laboratory at John Hopkins in 1883. Freud was a German psychologist active between roughly 1890 and the 1930s in Europe. William James was active in Cambridge, Massachusetts in the late 1800s, but he was not known for developing a psychology laboratory. Pavlov was active between the 1890s and the 1920s in St. Petersburg, Russia. Wilhelm Wundt was known as the founder of experimental psychology and established the first experimental psychology laboratory in 1879 in Liepzig, Germany.

3. C: Structuralists. Structuralists were concerned with the examination of mental processes. They relied on a technique known as introspection to study the basic elements of mental experiences. Introspection consists of being able to consciously address one's thoughts and emotions. Because of its subjectivity, it does not lend itself to children or animals, because they would not be able to reflect introspectively. For this reason, this method of studying mental experiences quickly fell by the wayside.

4. B: Cerebral. The behavioral, psychodynamic, and humanistic, as well as the cognitive and biological, approaches to human behavior are all part of psychology today, probably because of its philosophical roots. Generally, psychologists deal with the structure and functions of human behavior. Cerebral psychology is not a school of thought.

5. C: The psychodynamic approach deals with the idea that a person's behavior, thoughts, and emotions come from society's restrictions on the manifestation of a person's innate drives. Freud believed that sexual and aggressive drives are the most significant in human beings. Since society limits both drives, Freud believed that people struggle with meeting their personal needs versus displeasing others. According to Freud, a person's personality is reliant on how these issues are solved during the first two years or so of childhood.

6. B: The humanistic approach to understanding human behavior is driven by the idea that a person has a need to reach self-actualization, which includes the proclivity to seek after the highest possible growth and development that is attainable. In this approach, each individual has his or her own distinctive needs, desires, talents, skills, etc. According to the humanistic approach, a person who is well adjusted must be free to express his or her own uniqueness.

7. C: The placebo effect. The placebo effect occurs when participants experience changes because they believe they are receiving a special treatment, even when they are not receiving the active treatment. To get an accurate measure of how much a group is affected by the placebo effect, control group participants may receive a placebo that appears identical to the treatment but does not contain the active ingredient. It is considered a blind study when participants do not know whether they are receiving the special treatment. Likewise, in a double-blind study, neither researchers nor participants know who is getting the special treatment.

8. A: Case study. A case study lends itself to studying only one person or entity, such as a school, at a time. The case study is an in-depth research effort that focuses on the person or organization, finding out as much information about the subject as possible from different sources. Freud utilized this type of research to build his theory of psychoanalysis. He did a sequence of case studies.

9. A: Behavioral neuroscience is the study of how the different parts of the body interact with one another and how this communication affects behavior. It deals mostly with the nervous system, which consists of brain structures, neurotransmitters, and neurons that are organized in a way that creates a pathway for information to move freely from one part of the body to another.

10. B: Association. Association neurons, also called interneurons, interact or communicate with other neurons or nerve cells. Data are transferred to the spinal cord and brain from body tissues and sense organs. This is done by sensory organs or afferent neurons. Motor or efferent neurons transmit information from the spinal cord and brain back to the body tissues and sense organs.

11. D: Voluntary movement. Sleep, mood, appetite, and arousal (involuntary functions) are all affected by serotonin. Serotonin is a neurotransmitter that regulates these activities in the brain depending on how much serotonin the brain is receiving. People who suffer from some forms of depression are said to have low levels of serotonin. Serotonin does not control voluntary movement (example: walking, chewing).

12. D: Somatic. The somatic nervous system does two things. One, it transfers data to the central nervous system from the sense organs, muscles, and skin. This allows a person to feel pain, pressure, and temperature. Two, it sends information to the skeletal muscles from the central nervous system. This causes voluntary physical reactions. The somatic nervous system is a division of the peripheral nervous system.

13. E: Sympathetic. The sympathetic nervous system is responsible for elevating blood sugar levels. Its job is to get a person ready to act by making him or her cognizant of something that is scary, exciting, or disturbing. The sympathetic nervous system does this by not only elevating blood sugar, but making the heart beat faster, minimizing digestion, and widening the arteries as well as stimulating sweat glands. Additionally, the sympathetic nervous system is one of the divisions of the autonomic nervous system. The other division of the autonomic nervous system is the parasympathetic nervous system.

14. A: Autonomic. The autonomic nervous system is responsible for regulating a person's internal organs and glands, including some muscles. Generally, the autonomic nervous system works involuntarily, though it can work voluntarily. It consists of two divisions which control opposite functions. The two divisions of the autonomic nervous system are the sympathetic nervous system and the parasympathetic nervous system. The sympathetic nervous system is responsible for getting a person excited or alarmed, whereas the parasympathetic nervous system is responsible for what happens to a person in a state of relaxation, such as slowing down a person's heart rate, breathing, and digestion.

15. B: Hippocampus. The hippocampus deals with the functioning of a person's memory. It is important to note that the brain is made up of a bunch of groups of neurons called neural networks. These neural networks have similar but unique jobs. Even though the networks or groups of neurons each have their own function, the groups often physically run through other parts of the brain. The hippocampus is a part of the limbic system.

16. B: Perception. Perception is the mental development of a picture of one's environment.

17. C: Sensation. Psychophysics is the part of psychology that deals with sensation. Sensation is the capacity one has to sense stimuli through the various senses.

18. D: Sensory adaptation. A person experiences sensory adaptation when her awareness of a table in the kitchen diminishes to the point where she gives almost no thought to it. When people see certain items all the time, they stop taking note of them, diminishing sensitivity to these items. In order for attention to stimulus to remain constant, the stimulus must change in some way.

19. E: Signal detection theory. Signal detection theory is dependent upon an individual's expectations, past experiences, and motivation. These psychological factors determine a person's capacity to give attention to stimulus.

20. A: Just noticeable difference (JND). Just noticeable difference is also known as the difference threshold. It is the noticeable difference that a person senses between two similar stimuli.

21. C: Linear perspective. Linear perspective is a type of depth perception in which only one eye is required. Our depth perception cues us to the distance between ourselves and visible objects. When we need only one eye to perceive distance, this is known as a monocular cue. Likewise, when two eyes are used to perceive distance, this is called a binocular cue. The monocular cue in linear perspective is that we perceive parallel lines as converging as they lie farther away.

22. D: Motion parallax is also known as relative motion. It is a monocular cue that causes stable objects to appear to be in motion when a person is in motion. Objects closer to the fixation point (the thing the person is looking at) appear to be moving backward. The closer the object is to the fixation point, the faster the object would seem to be moving. Things that are farther from the fixation point will appear to be moving with the person at a slower pace as the object gets farther away.

23. A: The brain stem prevents the transference of messages originating in the motor cortex. This prevents people from acting out their dreams. The body becomes basically paralyzed when the brain stem does not allow messages from the motor cortex to reach the brain. The brain stem is located where the spinal cord connects to the skull. It regulates the heartbeat and breathing. It has the capacity to stop messages from getting to other parts of the brain.

24. D: REM. The dream state is generally characterized by rapid eye movement (REM). This state of sleep is also referred to as paradoxical sleep because the person sleeping seems to be in a relaxed state, yet cortical activity is extensive. REM sleep is typically about ten minutes during the first cycle of sleep. REM sleep tends to get longer each time a sleeper passes through this stage in a cycle.

25. C: Narcolepsy. Narcolepsy is a sleep disorder in which a person involuntarily falls into sudden sleep modes throughout the day. Insomnia is another sleep disorder in which a person is consistently unable to fall asleep or stay asleep. Likewise, sleep apnea is a sleeping disorder in which a person intermittently stops breathing while sleeping. This can happen as many as one hundred times a night. Each episode causes the sleeper not to get enough oxygen, which wakes the person up enough to gasp for more oxygen.

26. C: Latent content. Latent content, according to Sigmund Freud, is repressed sexual or aggressive desires that manifest in dreams. The manifest content of dreams, according to Freud, consists of the actual pictures that the dreamer sees. Activation-synthesis theory suggests that dreamers make up dreams based on random pictures that were generated by the brain during sleep time. According to activation-synthesis theory, the construction of dreams is an attempt on the part of the dreamer to make sense out of the random pictures. When people miss dreaming for a length of time, they typically engage in what is known as "REM rebound," where they experience longer REM sleep periods at a later time.

27. B: Dissociation. Dissociation occurs when a hypnotized person is still aware of all activities while under hypnosis. This is often called a split in consciousness. Hypnosis is said to be a relaxed state that is characterized by the ability to accept suggestions. There is no known research that proves that a hypnotized person would do something contrary to the person's nature.

28. A: Classical conditioning. Classical conditioning and operant conditioning are techniques used to produce associative learning. Classical conditioning is a procedure whereby learning takes place by connecting two stimuli, while operant conditioning is a procedure that associates a stimulus with a response in order to stop or cause a behavior. Observational learning is where operant behavior can be learned indirectly by watching what happens to the person being conditioned.

29. A: Classical conditioning. Classical conditioning occurs when a person learns by associating a conditioned stimulus to an unconditioned stimulus. An unconditioned stimulus gets a certain response. The goal of classical conditioning is to get the same response from a neutral stimulus that an unconditioned stimulus gets. The neutral stimulus then becomes a conditioned stimulus.

30. A: Classical conditioning. A neutral stimulus is the stimulus that is paired with the unconditioned stimulus to get the same response caused by the unconditioned stimulus. When the same response is obtained, the neutral stimulus becomes the conditioned stimulus.

31. A: Classical conditioning. Prior to classical conditioning, the unconditional stimulus produces an unconditioned response. This response happens without any prompting or conditioning.

32. C: Operant conditioning. Operant conditioning is characterized by reinforcement as well as punishment. Operant conditioning is a technique used to connect the stimulus to the response in order to stop or cause a behavior. Reinforcement is the application or removal of a stimulus in order to get a desired behavior.

33. C: Operant conditioning. In operant conditioning, designations of "negative" or "positive" indicate what is going on with the stimulus. "Negative" means that a stimulus has been removed, while "positive" means that a stimulus has been added. Positive and negative reinforcements and punishments are applied and removed in order to increase or decrease behavior.

34. B: Observational learning. Observational learning occurs when a person learns the consequences of behavior by watching what happens to someone else. The person or persons being observed are referred to as model(s).

35. B: Observational learning. Classical conditioning requires the introduction of a stimulus, while operant conditioning requires the introduction or removal of a stimulus. Observational learning results from watching the consequences that happen to another person.

36. D: Non-associative learning. Non-associative learning occurs when a single stimulus is repeatedly offered or seen causing a lasting change in behavior. Habituation is an example of non-associative learning. It happens when a single stimulus being repeatedly seen or offered causes a person to respond less and less to the stimulus.

37. B: Confirmation bias. Confirmation bias describes a person's tendency to look for information that supports a bias or belief while ignoring data that would not support the bias or belief. This is considered an error in judgment that can serve as a block in resolving issues or problems because of faulty thinking. It is an error in how a person thinks and solves problems.

38. C: Functional fixedness. Functional fixedness is about a person's inability to go beyond what is known about the use of an item. In other words, a person with functional fixedness could not perceive using a shoe to kill a fly because shoes are made to be worn. He would be fixed on the traditional use of the shoe, unable to see other uses. Functional fixedness is another error in judgment which can serve as a block to resolving issues or problems because of faulty thinking. It is an error in how a person thinks and solves problems.

39. A: The availability heuristic. The availability heuristic is a shortcut to solving problems. A heuristic is basically a way to solve a problem using some type of technique. Heuristics can help or impede a person's ability to resolve problems or issues. The availability heuristic is one of these techniques that may or may not be helpful. It occurs when a person determines the likelihood of an occurrence by what is in the forefront of the person's mind.

40. E: Telegraphic speech. Telegraphic speech usually begins with a child voicing just one word and then moves on to the child articulating a word along with gestures to convey meaning. A child might say "toy" while trying to pick up a toy to indicate "give me my toy." The one-word stage generally starts at around one year of age. A two-word pattern where kids generally voice a noun and a verb together is also part of telegraphic speech. This stage typically begins at around eighteen months. Children in the two-word stage may say things like baby cry, doggie like or mommy eat. After a while, a child in the two-word stage will begin to combine an adjective with a noun such as bad boy.

41. B: Noam Chomsky. Noam Chomsky is known for his belief that children possess a language acquisition device. A language acquisition device is said to be universal, and it is a part of a child's mental system. This language acquisition device serves as a guide to interpreting and using language for specific purposes.

42. B: Attention. Attention is not a mnemonic strategy. It is the conscious sense of something in our external environment. Mnemonic strategies are used to help people learn, store, and retrieve data. This means that mnemonic devices help get information in the long-term memory as well as maintaining information in the short-term memory. Acrostics, automaticity, chunking, and rehearsal are all examples of mnemonic strategies. Acrostics such as "please excuse my dear aunt Sally" are used to help students remember important concepts. The aforementioned is utilized to remember the order of operations in mathematics. Automaticity is learning something until it becomes second nature, like driving a car. Chunking is the act of categorizing information in one unit, such as FBI, instead of each word separately. Rehearsal is simply learning something by constantly repeating it.

43. A: Long-term memory. Permanent memories are kept in long-term memory. Sensory memory is awareness for a few seconds of what the senses pick up. Short-term memory is also known as working memory. It is where memory is kept for a short period of time allowing perception of information. The data in the working memory needs to be transferred to the long-term memory in order for it to permanently retained.

44. A: Alfred Binet. Alfred Binet is credited with being the first person to create an intelligence test. This intelligence test was a group of questions about topics studied in French schools. The test scores were basically compared with other test scores of test takers the same age in order to yield a norm for each age. As such, a mental age was determined by the score the student received. A 7-year-old student, for instance, who scored the same as the average 11 year old would be said to have a mental age of 11. This form of calculating intelligence is still used in intelligence quotient (IQ) tests today. IQ tests are norm-referenced tests.

45. E: Charles Spearman. Charles Spearman coined the letter "g" to stand for general intelligence. General intelligence is essentially the belief that underlies IQ tests that render one test score. It assumes that there is only one skill that gives a person the means to solve many different problems.

46. D: Instinct. Motivation can be influenced by biological and social-psychological factors such as achievement, affiliation, sex, thirst, and hunger.

47. C: Glucose and insulin. Glucose and insulin are both biological products that motivate hunger. Glucose is a blood sugar that gives the body energy. People are likely to be hungry when the glucose level in the body is low. A low glucose level indicates that a person has not eaten in a while. When glucose is high in the blood, it causes insulin to be released. Insulin is a hormone found in the pancreas. Insulin changes glucose into fat. This removes it from the blood stream.

48. C: Lateral hypothalamus. Lateral hypothalamus, consisting of both sides of the hypothalamus, increases hunger. When it is stimulated, it can cause a person to eat even the person is full. If the lateral hypothalamus is damaged, it can cause a starving person not to eat.

49. D: The set point. The set point is the weight that the body works to maintain. Each person has a different set point. Once a person's weight gets lower than the set point, the person will experience hunger, causing the person to eat more and do less activity. The person will begin to feel lethargic. This causes the person to gain weight. When a person's weight gets higher than his set point, hunger will decrease while energy increases. This will cause a person to lose weight. There are also social-psychological factors that contribute to and regulate hunger and eating.

50. A: Cannon-Bard theory. The Cannon-Bard theory of emotion states that arousal and a subjective emotional experience will occur at the same time when a person thinks that a stimulus can affect his well-being. An example would be a person experiencing an elevated heart rate while realizing that he is angry because his neighbor let a dangerous dog run rampant in the neighborhood.

51. C: James-Lange theory. In the James-Lange theory, the stimulus causes a physiological arousal, which causes an emotion. If the physiological arousal were absent, there would be no accompanying emotion.

52. E: Two-factor theory. The belief that what we call each emotion is what makes emotions different from one another is known as the two-factor theory of emotion. This concept says that the physiological arousal is the same regardless of which emotion one experiences. The same physiological change can cause love and anger alike, depending on what the individual decides to call it or how the person responds to the physiological change.

53. C: Longitudinal. Blind and double-blind studies test the influence of a particular variable on a group without their knowledge of its presence of absence. Cross-sectional, cross-sequential, and longitudinal studies all allow researchers to make inferences about how people develop or change over time. Cross-sectional studies basically compare information or views from different age groups at a certain point in time. For instance, a researcher may compare the views of 15-year-old participants, 25-year-old participants, and 35-year-old participants. The problems with this type of research are that it tracks different people without knowing whether changes are due to age, environment, or other circumstantial factors. Researchers resolve this issue by doing longitudinal studies where the same cohort is studied for a long period of time. Cross-sequential studies have combined cross-sectional and longitudinal studies to track people of different ages over a long period of time.

54. B: Cross-sequential. Cross-sequential studies are a type of research method utilized to track different people at varying age levels over a long period of time. It is a combination of the cross-sectional and longitudinal research methods.

55. C: Longitudinal. Longitudinal studies track a group of people who are the same age for a long period of time. Research on a group of 25-year-old participants for 10 years is an example of a longitudinal study.

56. D: Sensorimotor. Piaget's four stages of cognitive development are sensorimotor (infancy); pre-operational (toddler and early childhood); concrete operational (elementary and early adolescence); formal operational (adolescence and adulthood). Autonomy vs. doubt and shame, identity vs. role confusion, and trust vs. mistrust are all stages in Erikson's theory of psychosocial development. According to Erikson's theory, some type of tension must exist in order for change to take place. Erikson's theory of psychosocial development has eight stages, in which a person struggles through crises to determine her character.

57. D: Proprioception. Proprioception is the awareness of the movement and position of the body in space, and it is not part of Piaget's theory of cognitive development. Assimilation, conservation, object permanence, and reversibility are all part of Piaget's theory of cognitive development. Assimilation is the process of joining new information with old information in order to make sense out of the new information. Conservation is the understanding that just because the form of something changes does not mean that its quantity changes. Object permanence is the ability to understand that items still exist even though the person may not see or sense them. Reversibility is the ability to mentally rearrange the steps in a process.

58. C: Object permanence. Object permanence is the ability to understand that items still exist even though the person may not see or sense them. The sensorimotor stage in Piaget's theory of cognitive development is characterized by a lack of object permanence.

59. A: Autonomy vs. doubt and shame. Autonomy vs. doubt and shame is a stage in Erikson's theory of psychosocial development. It is a crisis that occurs when a child is between the ages of 1 and 3 years.

60. D: Generativity vs. stagnation. Generativity vs. stagnation is the seventh stage in Erikson's theory of psychosocial development. It generally happens around the ages of 36–55. The crisis in this stage is whether to be altruistic or selfish, since one's children are no longer at home. Will the person share his life's knowledge, wisdom, and experience with younger people or will the person concentrate on his own physical and mental capabilities?

61. A: Intimacy vs. isolation. Autonomy vs. doubt and shame, identity vs. role confusion, industry vs. inferiority, initiative vs. guilt and industry, and trust vs. mistrust are all stages are indicative of what a child desires to accomplish versus what a child is allowed to do.

62. B: Karen Horney. Carl Jung, Karen Horney, and Sigmund Freud all agreed that a person's actions are motivated by unconscious needs to please others and still meet her own needs.

63. C: Sigmund Freud. In his theory of psychoanalysis, Sigmund Freud developed a theory of personality components known as the id, the ego, and the superego. These components describe the unique thoughts, emotions, and actions of an individual. The id is the biological portion of personality; the ego is the rational aspect of personality; and the superego is essentially the social portion of personality.

64. B: id. The id is one of three components of personality in Sigmund Freud's theory of psychoanalysis. It is the component that deals with the biological aspect of personality. The id operates in accordance with the pleasure principle. The pleasure principle basically says that a person will do what makes him feel good at any given point in time.

65. C: Phallic stage. The Oedipus complex is a part of the phallic stage in Freud's psychosexual stages. The phallic stage begins at about 4 years of age, according to Freud. What happens during this stage depends on whether the child is a boy or a girl. If the child is a boy, he will experience the Oedipus complex. This is where the boy becomes sexually attracted to his mother and fears that his father may cut off the boy's penis to get rid of the competition. The boy begins to feel castration anxiety. Girls, on the other hand, experience penis envy when they realize that they do not have a penis. Girls will then begin to desire their fathers.

66. A: Basically, conditions of worth are an imposition by parents and others put on children to do what the parents or others want in order to be valued. This causes the child to give up her true self in order to please the person imposing these conditions of worth.

67. D: Social cognitive. Reciprocal determinism is part of the social cognitive approach to personality. Reciprocal determinism is the idea that a person's thoughts, actions, and environment basically work together to determine a person's behavior.

68. A: The Big Five personality traits are agreeableness, conscientiousness, extroversion, neuroticism, and openness. This classification system is an attempt to collapse the many different traits pertaining to personality into a few foundational traits that describe consistent behavior.

69. A: Abnormal psychology. Abnormal psychology is the branch of psychology that focuses on psychological disorders. There are many psychological therapies that deal with psychological disorders, including, behavior modification, cognitive therapies, humanistic therapies, and psychoanalysis.

70. C: Obsessive-compulsive disorder (OCD). When people are compelled to repeat behaviors, it is a compulsion that they cannot control. Compulsions can manifest themselves in any form, including constantly checking doors, repeatedly washing hands, or constantly brushing the teeth. Obsessions are also a part of OCD. Obsessive behaviors can include a preoccupation with germ, impending doom, or cleanliness.

71. C: Mood disorders. People with mood disorders typically struggle with depression, mania, or both. A person with a major depressive disorder will experience sadness, hopelessness, and discouragement. Each feeling will last for at least 14 days. People with this type of disorder usually lose interest in anything enjoyable. Bipolar disorders cause people to alternate opposite mood swings, such as going from depression to excitement, which leads to taking risky chances. This excessive enthusiasm is called mania.

72. B: Dissociative fugue. Dissociative fugue occurs when a person suddenly adventures away from home or work, does not remember his past, and becomes confused about his identity. He will sometimes take on a new identity. Dissociative amnesia occurs when a person experiences a stressful event, causing him to forget information or pieces of information. It can be brought on by other factors as well. Dissociative identity disorder is another name for multiple personalities. A person with dissociative identity disorder will have at least two separate personalities. One personality is not necessarily aware of the other.

73. D: Paranoid schizophrenia. People often get schizophrenia mixed up with multiple personalities. People with schizophrenia suffer from delusions and hallucinations, while a person with multiple personalities has at least two separate personalities. Paranoid schizophrenia is characterized by delusions of grandeur or delusions of persecution. A person suffering from delusions of grandeur will believe that he is an influential or famous person. Someone struggling with delusions of persecution will think that people are out to get him and want to harm him. Typically, a person who has delusions of persecution will hear voices that perpetuate his delusions, such as "you are being watched."

74. E: Somatoform. Somatoform disorders occur when a person has all the physical symptoms of a disease, but he does not medically have the disease. Conversion disorder is a type of somatoform disorder in which the motor or sensory abilities are somehow impaired, but the impairment is due to psychological issues rather than neurological problems. Another somatoform disorder is hypochondriasis, where a person is so afraid of or preoccupied with having an illness that no one can convince him otherwise (not even a doctor). It is important to note that a person with hypochondriasis does not have any real physical problems.

75. D: Paranoid personality. Paranoid personality is characterized by distrust and suspicion. A person who has a paranoid personality does not suffer from delusions, but this person will be distrustful and suspicious. A person with paranoid schizophrenia does, however, suffer from delusions of grandeur or of persecution. Borderline personality disorder is where a person is incapable of keeping relationships and has mood swings in emotions and self-image. An antisocial personality lacks a conscience, is impulsive, and ignores the rights of others. Narcissistic personalities are incapable of showing empathy for others. They will stop at nothing to be recognized or praised, even if the notoriety is negative. These personalities are consumed with fantasies of recognition of successes or accomplishments.

76. A: Cognitive. The cognitive approach to abnormal behavior suggests that abnormal behavior is due to a person's consistently thinking in an abnormal manner. For instance, a person who is depressed may think that her success is controlled by someone or something other than herself. The same person will insist that her failures are because of her own inadequacies.

77. B: The learning or behavioral approach suggests that abnormal behavior is a learned behavior that has been classically or operantly conditioned in some way. Jesse's example shows how someone can teach a person how to behave abnormally. Jesse was operantly conditioned by his mother, who was only trying to help him. She did not understand that she was reinforcing abnormal behavior by rewarding him.

78. E: Surgical therapies. Behavior modification, cognitive therapies, psychoanalysis, and humanistic therapies are all psychological approaches to psychological disorders. The other way is through medical approaches, which use drugs or surgery to treat patients. Psychological therapies depend on some type of building of a relationship between client and therapist.

79. E: Psychoanalysis. Psychoanalysis describes catharsis as a term used in this approach. Energy that was once used to repress memories that have returned to consciousness can through catharsis be used to deal with this problem in a healthy manner.

80. E: Psychoanalysis. Free association occurs when a psychoanalyst guides a client into a deep state of relaxation with instructions to say the first thing about an incident of memory that comes to mind. This is often done to help clients retrieve painful memories or dreams.

81. D: Humanistic therapies. "Active learning" is a term introduced by humanist Carl Rogers to provide client-centered therapy. The term "client," as opposed to "patient," is generally utilized when dealing with psychological disorders. Active learning is a process by which a therapist repeats what the client says in the form of a paraphrase. The therapist asks the client to expound on her statements and make assertions clear. Additionally, the therapist engaging in active listening restates what he thinks the client has been saying about her feelings.

82. C: Cognitive therapies. Cognitive therapies deal with the way a person thinks in relation to abnormal behavior. Because actions are driven by thoughts, thinking in an abnormal manner leads to abnormal behavior. Cognitive therapies basically try to change the way a person thinks so that he can view the world in a healthy, rational manner.

83. A: Behavior modification. Behavior modification uses classical and operant conditioning in order to alter abnormal behavior. Systematic desensitization is a technique used in behavior modification. Relaxation procedures are often leaned before a systematic desensitization program begins. A client is slowly desensitized by replacing anxiety with relaxation. The therapist simulates a subtle fear-arousing scenario just to have the client relax during the scenario. Step by step, the therapist will increase the dosage of fear, each time having the client relax during the situation. The fear-arousing scenario will gradually mimic the original situation that caused the fear, until the client can relax during the same situation that originally caused the fear.

84. B: Biological therapies. Biological therapies or medical therapies depend on drugs or surgery to change how the brain functions.

85. E: Evolutionary influence. Social cognition, social influence, group behavior, and social relationships are all areas in social psychology, which deals with how a person's actions are swayed by others. Evolutionary psychology is another major research area of the study of psychology.

86. A: Social cognition. How information about other people is processed is known as social cognition. Attribution theory gives two types of explanations that people tend to use to describe how other people behave. The concepts in the theory do not denote rational or logical thinking on the part of the person doing the attributing. Dispositional or internal attributions deal with explanations that have something to do with internal factors such as maturity, intelligence, and personality. An example of dispositional attribution would be a person's attributing his neighbor's quick response to the neighbor's wisdom. When a person's behavior is attributed to external sources, this is called situational or external attribution. An example of external attribution is where a person notices that a neighbor has arrived home at the precise time a UPS driver is delivering a package. The person attributes luck to the neighbor's getting home just in time to receive the package.

87. C: Cognitive dissonance theory. Cognitive dissonance theory says that a person may do that which is the opposite of her belief or attitudes in order to explain away her behavior and thus feel better about it. For instance, Jamia got an abortion despite a strong belief/attitude against it.

88. D: Stanley Milgram. Stanley Milgram was responsible for doing a phony learning study in which teachers were told to shock students ever time a wrong answer was given. The teachers were told that each shock would be progressively worse. If a teacher tried to decline participation, the authority would insist that the teacher continue. Even though no electrical shocks were actually given, the students and teachers believed that the shocks were being given. Students began to complain of physical symptoms as the supposed shocks increased. Sixty-three percent of the teachers delivered shocks until the end. This experiment was done to show the level of obedience to authority.

89. C: Low-balling. Low-balling occurs when someone gets a person to agree to or commit to something before all the information is given about what will be required to fulfill the agreement or commitment. Sarah asked her friend to babysit while she went out on a date with her boyfriend, and Sarah's friend agreed; of course, Sarah didn't tell her at the time that the date would last a week.

90. B: The Kitty Genovese incident actually happened in Queens, New York. The more witnesses there are, the less likely it is that someone will call for help in situations like this one, due to diffusion of responsibility. This diffusion leads to what is called the bystander effect.

91. E: Social-exchange theory. According to this theory, a person's goal in life is to get as many rewards as possible while not having to pay the costs. This is called the minimax principle.

92. A: Content validity. Content or face validity refers to the ability of a test to look like it is measuring what it is supposed to measure. For instance, face validity is usually used for driver's tests. This test of validity would not be used in psychological tests.

93. B: Regression. Mean, mode, range, and standard deviation are descriptive statistics. The mean is the average, the mode is the score that is obtained the most, and standard deviation is how the scores are dispersed in relation to the mean in a set of data. Regression is a statistical procedure that allows for outcome prediction, not data description.

94. A: Population. In research, a population is the entire membership of any group or entity. An example might be Black Americans. The population in this case would have to include every single Black American. None could be left out in order for it to be a population.

How to Overcome Test Anxiety

Just the thought of taking a test is enough to make most people a little nervous. A test is an important event that can have a long-term impact on your future, so it's important to take it seriously and it's natural to feel anxious about performing well. But just because anxiety is normal, that doesn't mean that it's helpful in test taking, or that you should simply accept it as part of your life. Anxiety can have a variety of effects. These effects can be mild, like making you feel slightly nervous, or severe, like blocking your ability to focus or remember even a simple detail.

If you experience test anxiety—whether severe or mild—it's important to know how to beat it. To discover this, first you need to understand what causes test anxiety.

Causes of Test Anxiety

While we often think of anxiety as an uncontrollable emotional state, it can actually be caused by simple, practical things. One of the most common causes of test anxiety is that a person does not feel adequately prepared for their test. This feeling can be the result of many different issues such as poor study habits or lack of organization, but the most common culprit is time management. Starting to study too late, failing to organize your study time to cover all of the material, or being distracted while you study will mean that you're not well prepared for the test. This may lead to cramming the night before, which will cause you to be physically and mentally exhausted for the test. Poor time management also contributes to feelings of stress, fear, and hopelessness as you realize you are not well prepared but don't know what to do about it.

Other times, test anxiety is not related to your preparation for the test but comes from unresolved fear. This may be a past failure on a test, or poor performance on tests in general. It may come from comparing yourself to others who seem to be performing better or from the stress of living up to expectations. Anxiety may be driven by fears of the future—how failure on this test would affect your educational and career goals. These fears are often completely irrational, but they can still negatively impact your test performance.

Elements of Test Anxiety

As mentioned earlier, test anxiety is considered to be an emotional state, but it has physical and mental components as well. Sometimes you may not even realize that you are suffering from test anxiety until you notice the physical symptoms. These can include trembling hands, rapid heartbeat, sweating, nausea, and tense muscles. Extreme anxiety may lead to fainting or vomiting. Obviously, any of these symptoms can have a negative impact on testing. It is important to recognize them as soon as they begin to occur so that you can address the problem before it damages your performance.

The mental components of test anxiety include trouble focusing and inability to remember learned information. During a test, your mind is on high alert, which can help you recall information and stay focused for an extended period of time. However, anxiety interferes with your mind's natural processes, causing you to blank out, even on the questions you know well. The strain of testing during anxiety makes it difficult to stay focused, especially on a test that may take several hours. Extreme anxiety can take a huge mental toll, making it difficult not only to recall test information but even to understand the test questions or pull your thoughts together.

Effects of Test Anxiety

Test anxiety is like a disease—if left untreated, it will get progressively worse. Anxiety leads to poor performance, and this reinforces the feelings of fear and failure, which in turn lead to poor performances on subsequent tests. It can grow from a mild nervousness to a crippling condition. If allowed to progress, test anxiety can have a big impact on your schooling, and consequently on your future.

Test anxiety can spread to other parts of your life. Anxiety on tests can become anxiety in any stressful situation, and blanking on a test can turn into panicking in a job situation. But fortunately, you don't have to let anxiety rule your testing and determine your grades. There are a number of relatively simple steps you can take to move past anxiety and function normally on a test and in the rest of life.

Physical Steps for Beating Test Anxiety

While test anxiety is a serious problem, the good news is that it can be overcome. It doesn't have to control your ability to think and remember information. While it may take time, you can begin taking steps today to beat anxiety.

Just as your first hint that you may be struggling with anxiety comes from the physical symptoms, the first step to treating it is also physical. Rest is crucial for having a clear, strong mind. If you are tired, it is much easier to give in to anxiety. But if you establish good sleep habits, your body and mind will be ready to perform optimally, without the strain of exhaustion. Additionally, sleeping well helps you to retain information better, so you're more likely to recall the answers when you see the test questions.

Getting good sleep means more than going to bed on time. It's important to allow your brain time to relax. Take study breaks from time to time so it doesn't get overworked, and don't study right before bed. Take time to rest your mind before trying to rest your body, or you may find it difficult to fall asleep.

Along with sleep, other aspects of physical health are important in preparing for a test. Good nutrition is vital for good brain function. Sugary foods and drinks may give a burst of energy but this burst is followed by a crash, both physically and emotionally. Instead, fuel your body with protein and vitamin-rich foods.

Also, drink plenty of water. Dehydration can lead to headaches and exhaustion, especially if your brain is already under stress from the rigors of the test. Particularly if your test is a long one, drink water during the breaks. And if possible, take an energy-boosting snack to eat between sections.

Along with sleep and diet, a third important part of physical health is exercise. Maintaining a steady workout schedule is helpful, but even taking 5-minute study breaks to walk can help get your blood pumping faster and clear your head. Exercise also releases endorphins, which contribute to a positive feeling and can help combat test anxiety.

When you nurture your physical health, you are also contributing to your mental health. If your body is healthy, your mind is much more likely to be healthy as well. So take time to rest, nourish your body with healthy food and water, and get moving as much as possible. Taking these physical steps will make you stronger and more able to take the mental steps necessary to overcome test anxiety.

Mental Steps for Beating Test Anxiety

Working on the mental side of test anxiety can be more challenging, but as with the physical side, there are clear steps you can take to overcome it. As mentioned earlier, test anxiety often stems from lack of preparation, so the obvious solution is to prepare for the test. Effective studying may be the most important weapon you have for beating test anxiety, but you can and should employ several other mental tools to combat fear.

First, boost your confidence by reminding yourself of past success—tests or projects that you aced. If you're putting as much effort into preparing for this test as you did for those, there's no reason you should expect to fail here. Work hard to prepare; then trust your preparation.

Second, surround yourself with encouraging people. It can be helpful to find a study group, but be sure that the people you're around will encourage a positive attitude. If you spend time with others who are anxious or cynical, this will only contribute to your own anxiety. Look for others who are motivated to study hard from a desire to succeed, not from a fear of failure.

Third, reward yourself. A test is physically and mentally tiring, even without anxiety, and it can be helpful to have something to look forward to. Plan an activity following the test, regardless of the outcome, such as going to a movie or getting ice cream.

When you are taking the test, if you find yourself beginning to feel anxious, remind yourself that you know the material. Visualize successfully completing the test. Then take a few deep, relaxing breaths and return to it. Work through the questions carefully but with confidence, knowing that you are capable of succeeding.

Developing a healthy mental approach to test taking will also aid in other areas of life. Test anxiety affects more than just the actual test—it can be damaging to your mental health and even contribute to depression. It's important to beat test anxiety before it becomes a problem for more than testing.

Study Strategy

Being prepared for the test is necessary to combat anxiety, but what does being prepared look like? You may study for hours on end and still not feel prepared. What you need is a strategy for test prep. The next few pages outline our recommended steps to help you plan out and conquer the challenge of preparation.

Step 1: Scope Out the Test

Learn everything you can about the format (multiple choice, essay, etc.) and what will be on the test. Gather any study materials, course outlines, or sample exams that may be available. Not only will this help you to prepare, but knowing what to expect can help to alleviate test anxiety.

Step 2: Map Out the Material

Look through the textbook or study guide and make note of how many chapters or sections it has. Then divide these over the time you have. For example, if a book has 15 chapters and you have five days to study, you need to cover three chapters each day. Even better, if you have the time, leave an extra day at the end for overall review after you have gone through the material in depth.

If time is limited, you may need to prioritize the material. Look through it and make note of which sections you think you already have a good grasp on, and which need review. While you are studying, skim quickly through the familiar sections and take more time on the challenging parts.

Write out your plan so you don't get lost as you go. Having a written plan also helps you feel more in control of the study, so anxiety is less likely to arise from feeling overwhelmed at the amount to cover.

Step 3: Gather Your Tools

Decide what study method works best for you. Do you prefer to highlight in the book as you study and then go back over the highlighted portions? Or do you type out notes of the important information? Or is it helpful to make flashcards that you can carry with you? Assemble the pens, index cards, highlighters, post-it notes, and any other materials you may need so you won't be distracted by getting up to find things while you study.

If you're having a hard time retaining the information or organizing your notes, experiment with different methods. For example, try color-coding by subject with colored pens, highlighters, or post-it notes. If you learn better by hearing, try recording yourself reading your notes so you can listen while in the car, working out, or simply sitting at your desk. Ask a friend to quiz you from your flashcards, or try teaching someone the material to solidify it in your mind.

Step 4: Create Your Environment

It's important to avoid distractions while you study. This includes both the obvious distractions like visitors and the subtle distractions like an uncomfortable chair (or a too-comfortable couch that makes you want to fall asleep). Set up the best study environment possible: good lighting and a comfortable work area. If background music helps you focus, you may want to turn it on, but otherwise keep the room quiet. If you are using a computer to take notes, be sure you don't have any other windows open, especially applications like social media, games, or anything else that could distract you. Silence your phone and turn off notifications. Be sure to keep water close by so you stay hydrated while you study (but avoid unhealthy drinks and snacks).

Also, take into account the best time of day to study. Are you freshest first thing in the morning? Try to set aside some time then to work through the material. Is your mind clearer in the afternoon or evening? Schedule your study session then. Another method is to study at the same time of day that you will take the test, so that your brain gets used to working on the material at that time and will be ready to focus at test time.

Step 5: Study!

Once you have done all the study preparation, it's time to settle into the actual studying. Sit down, take a few moments to settle your mind so you can focus, and begin to follow your study plan. Don't give in to distractions or let yourself procrastinate. This is your time to prepare so you'll be ready to fearlessly approach the test. Make the most of the time and stay focused.

Of course, you don't want to burn out. If you study too long you may find that you're not retaining the information very well. Take regular study breaks. For example, taking five minutes out of every hour to walk briskly, breathing deeply and swinging your arms, can help your mind stay fresh.

As you get to the end of each chapter or section, it's a good idea to do a quick review. Remind yourself of what you learned and work on any difficult parts. When you feel that you've mastered the material, move on to the next part. At the end of your study session, briefly skim through your notes again.

But while review is helpful, cramming last minute is NOT. If at all possible, work ahead so that you won't need to fit all your study into the last day. Cramming overloads your brain with more information than it can process and retain, and your tired mind may struggle to recall even previously learned information when it is overwhelmed with last-minute study. Also, the urgent nature of cramming and the stress placed on your brain contribute to anxiety. You'll be more likely to go to the test feeling unprepared and having trouble thinking clearly.

So don't cram, and don't stay up late before the test, even just to review your notes at a leisurely pace. Your brain needs rest more than it needs to go over the information again. In fact, plan to finish your studies by noon or early afternoon the day before the test. Give your brain the rest of the day to relax or focus on other things, and get a good night's sleep. Then you will be fresh for the test and better able to recall what you've studied.

Step 6: Take a Practice Test

Many courses offer sample tests, either online or in the study materials. This is an excellent resource to check whether you have mastered the material, as well as to prepare for the test format and environment.

Check the test format ahead of time: the number of questions, the type (multiple choice, free response, etc.), and the time limit. Then create a plan for working through them. For example, if you have 30 minutes to take a 60-question test, your limit is 30 seconds per question. Spend less time on the questions you know well so that you can take more time on the difficult ones.

If you have time to take several practice tests, take the first one open book, with no time limit. Work through the questions at your own pace and make sure you fully understand them. Gradually work up to taking a test under test conditions: sit at a desk with all study materials put away and set a timer. Pace yourself to make sure you finish the test with time to spare and go back to check your answers if you have time.

After each test, check your answers. On the questions you missed, be sure you understand why you missed them. Did you misread the question (tests can use tricky wording)? Did you forget the information? Or was it something you hadn't learned? Go back and study any shaky areas that the practice tests reveal.

Taking these tests not only helps with your grade, but also aids in combating test anxiety. If you're already used to the test conditions, you're less likely to worry about it, and working through tests until you're scoring well gives you a confidence boost. Go through the practice tests until you feel comfortable, and then you can go into the test knowing that you're ready for it.

Test Tips

On test day, you should be confident, knowing that you've prepared well and are ready to answer the questions. But aside from preparation, there are several test day strategies you can employ to maximize your performance.

First, as stated before, get a good night's sleep the night before the test (and for several nights before that, if possible). Go into the test with a fresh, alert mind rather than staying up late to study.

Try not to change too much about your normal routine on the day of the test. It's important to eat a nutritious breakfast, but if you normally don't eat breakfast at all, consider eating just a protein bar. If you're a coffee drinker, go ahead and have your normal coffee. Just make sure you time it so that the caffeine doesn't wear off right in the middle of your test. Avoid sugary beverages, and drink enough water to stay hydrated but not so much that you need a restroom break 10 minutes into the test. If your test isn't first thing in the morning, consider going for a walk or doing a light workout before the test to get your blood flowing.

Allow yourself enough time to get ready, and leave for the test with plenty of time to spare so you won't have the anxiety of scrambling to arrive in time. Another reason to be early is to select a good seat. It's helpful to sit away from doors and windows, which can be distracting. Find a good seat, get out your supplies, and settle your mind before the test begins.

When the test begins, start by going over the instructions carefully, even if you already know what to expect. Make sure you avoid any careless mistakes by following the directions.

Then begin working through the questions, pacing yourself as you've practiced. If you're not sure on an answer, don't spend too much time on it, and don't let it shake your confidence. Either skip it and come back later, or eliminate as many wrong answers as possible and guess among the remaining ones. Don't dwell on these questions as you continue—put them out of your mind and focus on what lies ahead.

Be sure to read all of the answer choices, even if you're sure the first one is the right answer. Sometimes you'll find a better one if you keep reading. But don't second-guess yourself if you do immediately know the answer. Your gut instinct is usually right. Don't let test anxiety rob you of the information you know.

If you have time at the end of the test (and if the test format allows), go back and review your answers. Be cautious about changing any, since your first instinct tends to be correct, but make sure you didn't misread any of the questions or accidentally mark the wrong answer choice. Look over any you skipped and make an educated guess.

At the end, leave the test feeling confident. You've done your best, so don't waste time worrying about your performance or wishing you could change anything. Instead, celebrate the successful completion of this test. And finally, use this test to learn how to deal with anxiety even better next time.

Review Video: Test Anxiety
Visit mometrix.com/academy and enter code: 100340

Important Qualification

Not all anxiety is created equal. If your test anxiety is causing major issues in your life beyond the classroom or testing center, or if you are experiencing troubling physical symptoms related to your anxiety, it may be a sign of a serious physiological or psychological condition. If this sounds like your situation, we strongly encourage you to seek professional help.

Online Resources

Due to our efforts to try to keep this book to a manageable length, we've created a link that will give you access to all of your online resources:

mometrix.com/resources719/ibpsychology

It's Your Moment, Let's Celebrate It!

Share your story @mometrixtestpreparation